Breadmaking: The Modern Revolution

BREADMAKING
The Modern Revolution

Edited by A. Williams

CENTURY
London Sydney Auckland Johannesburg

First published in Great Britain in 1975 by Hutchinson Benham Ltd
An imprint of the Hutchinson Group

Reissued in 1989 by Century Benham Ltd

A division of Century Hutchinson Ltd
Brookmount House, 62-65 Chandos Place, Covent Garden, London WC2N 4NW

Century Hutchinson Australia (Pty) Ltd
89-91 Albion Street, Surry Hills, New South Wales 2010, Australia.

Century Hutchinson New Zealand Ltd
PO Box 40-086, 32-34 View Road, Glenfield, Auckland 10, New Zealand

Century Hutchinson South Africa (Pty) Ltd
PO Box 337, Bergvlei 2012, South Africa

Set in Monotype Times

Printed and bound in Great Britain by
Anchor Press Limited, Tiptree, Essex.

ISBN 0 09 120890 4

Contents

Editor's Acknowledgement

The composition of this book is a true reflection of Arkady's recipe for success; a real team effort. As Editor I have endeavoured, firstly to combine the collective knowledge and experience of our own company's bakers and technologists, secondly to glean further specialist information and assistance from some of our many friends in the baking industry, and thirdly to attempt to put this wealth of information into book form; a book intended as a practical manual for the Chorleywood Bread Process. It is hoped that it will in some measure assist those engaged in the industry to a better understanding of what has become over the last decade the accepted method of plant bread production in the United Kingdom.

Where there are defects they should not be attributed to the sources of information, rather they are errors in 'translation' where I have not exercised sufficient care in transposing conversations and written communications onto the printed page.

In particular I wish to thank the following people for their help, both in providing much of the raw material of the book and for their constructive criticism during its production:

From the FMBRA, Dr N. Chamberlain and Mr T. H. Collins, from RHM Bakeries, Mr W. Anderson, from Associated British Foods, Dr W. Elstow and Mr D. Wallington, and from Distillers Ltd., Mr H. Sykes. Kind acknowledgement is also made to Mr F. Aitchison, Director of William Jackson and Sons Ltd, for his co-operation in providing bakery plant photographs.

Within my own organisation almost everyone has been involved to some degree. Mr M. Ball and Mr N. Clyde of Tweedy of Burnley provided much of the detail of the sections devoted to machinery.

The British Arkady Co. Ltd, bakery staff – Mr G. Brown, Mr C. Parr and Mrs E. Grindrod – produced bread other than that purchased from commercial plant bakeries, which was then photographed by Mr P. G.

Banks. They were asked for, and provided, commercial loaves not exhibition bread. Mr W. P. Ford and Mr W. Pringle, the British Arkady Co. Ltd, past and present technical directors respectively, were both pressed into service and whatever semblance of order and correct English finally emerged is in no small measure due to the efforts of Mr A. E. Stott.

Mr David Tomlinson did so much of the work that rather than thank him I feel that he should be called in to share the blame! I am indeed extremely grateful to everyone who has contributed, whether in large or small measure. Such help is invaluable.

Lastly I must thank Mr F. S. C. Freeman and the directors of the British Arkady Co. Ltd, for providing the facilities, encouragement and the continued practical support, without which the book would have remained a pipe dream.

Foreword

It was with pleasure that I accepted the invitation to write a Foreword to this book. My ready willingness to do so stems from my esteem for the contributions that the British Arkady Co. has made to the advancement of bakery technology, my first-hand experience of the almost dedicated practical and advisory service it has provided for the industry for half a century and my awareness of the need for a comprehensive and authoritative book on the new technology that has come to fruition over the past ten years and which represents a revolutionary advancement.

The Company introduced its bread improver 'Arkady' – for long now a household word in the bakery industry – to the United Kingdom market in 1921. Its scientifically based formulation and the quality control screening to which it was subjected guaranteed its success and before many years had passed it had almost become a standard dough ingredient.

Within three years, the Company provided concrete evidence that its interest in the industry it served went beyond the selling of 'Arkady'; it produced *The Arkady Review*, a publication planned to provide articles by experts on scientific and technological subjects of concern to bakers and confectioners. This attitude has strengthened over the years and there must be very few authorities in the cereal field who have not contributed, and gladly, to *The Arkady Review*.

Research work on the potentialities of enzyme-active soya flour led the Company to build a soya mill in 1935 and to produce additional technological aids for the baking industry. It was able also to develop other soya-based products that were useful adjuncts in other industries.

Some years later this diversification was expanded. Firstly there came a range of complete mixes for cakes, scones, pastry, etc., particularly for use in institutions and industrial canteens, and this was followed in recent years by various texturised vegetable protein products.

These diversifications in no degree weaned the Company's interests away from its first concern, the baking industry. Concomitantly with the various soya researches, the Company carried on investigations into specialised fatty compounds, which eventuated in patents and new processing aids for the baking industry. Also during this period the Company once again displayed its characteristic forward-looking attitude by developing cysteine-based products in anticipation of the addition of this substance to the list of permitted bread additives.

It was not my intention to write a eulogy of the Company and I hope readers will accept the foregoing text for what it is intended to be and that is an attempt to show that the production of this book is a characteristic effort by the Company to provide helpful service to the baking industry and to show also that the writing of the book could not be in better hands.

I have read the first draft and it leaves me in no doubt that in its final form this book will be welcomed and used to advantage by bakers and by others who are associated with the activities of the industry. Certainly it will also be a valuable text for students.

I wish it well and hope – and I am sure this is a hope that will be echoed by bakers throughout the land – that during the next fifty years the British Arkady Co. may make as many valuable contributions to technological progress in and provide as much guidance to the baking industry as it has done during the fifty years that this book celebrates.

A. J. Amos

PART I

The historical background

1. Earlier dough development processes

For centuries bread has been made by some process of fermentation which results in the aeration of the dough. This has generally been a lengthy process lasting anything from five to twenty-four hours.

While the aeration builds up there has been time for a modification to occur in the gluten structure of the dough which makes the dough capable of stretching. This has been known as dough development, and it has always been associated with, and thought to be brought about by, fermentation.

Only in the last fifty to sixty years has there been available a fast fermenting agent (compressed yeast) which would bring about sufficient aeration in a matter of an hour or two before baking. So it has only recently been possible to ask, if the *aeration* of the dough is rapid, can the *development* of the dough be brought about by rapid mechanical means?

We have heard much of this subject of mechanical development of dough since 1950, but think for a moment of the way the bread was made which was winning all the main prizes at the Bakers' Exhibitions in London and other centres from about 1910 to 1930.

The dough was well mixed but the fermentation process before scaling off was no more than a half hour. Yet the volume of the bread was nearly double that of ordinary bread of the same weight and the texture was fine and even. Famous names of prize-winners in this era were John Mackman and Jack Irons.

How was this remarkably rapid dough development achieved? The dough was mechanically worked through brake rolls, folding, re-braking, folding again and so on up to 15–20 times. In this way every particle of dough was mechanically stretched and re-stretched in different directions and in rapid succession. It was brought to a state where it would stretch and not tear when the dough was proved in the tin and then baked. Was this mechanical dough development in its infancy? This kind of mechanical development of dough was only made possible because small quantities of dough were involved. It was not a process that could be applied to ordinary bread production.

Then in 1926 a most prophetic paper was published in *Cereal Chemistry,* Volume 3, with the title 'Mechanical Modification of Dough to make it possible to bake bread with only the fermentation in the pan' by C. O. Swanson and E. B. Working of the Kansas State Agricultural College. It was reported that small doughs mixed for fifteen minutes at 60 rpm, or for seven minutes at 120 rpm, and tinned immediately, produced bread better in every way than bread mixed for three minutes and then fermented for 100 minutes before being tinned.

The question was asked, 'Will it be possible to use this method of mechanical modification of dough in the commercial bakery?' It was foreseen that there would be big savings in time, dough room space and materials, but the problems to be solved would be (1) the amount of power required for mixing large doughs at high speed and (2) to control the rise in dough temperature.

The dough mixer used had four moving pins describing a planetary motion around three pins fixed to the bottom of the bowl.

The dough recipe was as follows:

	Actual	*Based on 100 lb flour*	*Based on 280 lb flour*
Flour	340 gm	100	280 lb
Water	210 gm	61·7	173 lb
Yeast	10 gm	2·94	8 lb 4 oz
Salt	5 gm	1·47	4 lb 2 oz
Lard	5 gm	1·47	4 lb 2 oz
Sugar	15 gm	4·41	12 lb 6 oz

All ingredients were brought to a temperature of 32°C (90°F) but the dough temperature was not stated.

These experiments were real pioneering work, but were largely overlooked for many years. The conclusions drawn form a very accurate forecast of the developments which were to come twenty-five to thirty years later.

After 1926 it seemed that the work of Swanson and Working was largely ignored. But at least one eminent American cereal chemist, Dr J. C. Baker, had studied their paper and it became apparent later that it formed part of the background to his own thoughts on the problem of dough development. His first important publication, of which this subject formed a part, appeared in *Cereal Chemistry*, May 1937.

Initially, Baker was concerned with the formation of gas bubbles in dough and their influence on bread texture. He postulated that individual dough bubbles were initiated by the air 'emulsed' into the dough during mixing. He experimented with doughs given prolonged mixing in air, in high vacuum, in gases other than air, and in the presence of an oxidising agent such as potassium bromate. His conclusions showed that his thinking had now become clearly directed towards the effect on dough of the mixing action *and* of both oxygen and chemical oxidants.

He claimed that mixing had the effect of arranging the molecules in reactive relationship to one another and that subsequently the oxidant (potassium bromate) caused these 'arranged' molecules to react with one another. He speculated that there might be an optimum combination of mixing time and oxidant level, but was not able at that time to arrive at any definite figures.

In May 1940 Baker gave two papers at the annual meeting of the American Society of Cereal Chemists (*Cereal Chem.,* Vol. 18, 1941) concerned with gas-cell production and retention. In order to examine the action of mixing in isolation, he devised a 'no-time' breadmaking process in which mixing could be followed by the application of vacuum or gas at high pressure which was immediately followed by gentle extrusion of the dough into a pan with no other mechanical work applied to the dough. He demonstrated that a no-time dough containing oxidant required much less mixing action than a dough without oxidant and that there was an optimum oxidant level and mixing time for no-time doughs mixed in air. He showed that the effect of oxidant was in fact to stabilise the gas cells so that they were able to withstand the pressures generated during proving and baking without coalescing into larger, coarse gas cells as they did in unoxidised no-time doughs.

The second paper gives some insight into Baker's increasing interest in the role of mixing as a gluten modifier. He concludes that the *type* of mixing applied is of importance to gluten structure and subsequent gas-cell type and distribution. Mixing devices which tear, rub, or cut are to be avoided, but there is particular virtue in stretching dough during mixing.

In retrospect one can see that these experiments contain all the steps subsequently to be used in the commercial Do-Maker process which

Baker developed for the Wallace & Tiernan Company. One suspects that from 1940 onwards the work of Baker's research team must have been increasingly directed towards the production of a new commercial process based on the novel concept of continuous dough development, followed by direct panning of the dough.

A continuous dough-mixing process was one solution to the difficulties foreseen by Swanson and Working in 1926 in mixing large batches of dough at high speed. A continuous plant could mix small quantities of dough at any one time, but by mixing quickly and continuously the necessary output of dough for normal plant bakery production could be secured.

The work culminated in the remarkable American patent by Dr J. C. Baker which was applied for in August 1950 and a corresponding application for a British patent was made in August 1951. The patent itself, US Patent 2,953,460, still merits close examination by anyone who wishes to have a full understanding of the theory and practice of mechanical dough development. One is tempted to quote the entire document, but the following passages serve to illustrate its general quality:

> It has been explained above that the term development refers to a change occurring with continuing mixing in the physical properties of the plastic (non-gaseous) material constituting the dough mixture and that full development can be measured as an optimum ability of the dough to retain gas cells in subsequent processing and baking.
>
> Improving (oxidising) agents are not only useful but seem unusually significant in my process . . . they appear to be critically important for best realisation of the described advantageous results.

This patented equipment was referred to as the Wallace & Tiernan's Do-Maker plant.

A fermentation period over several hours was considered necessary to provide the right bread flavour and taste. This was carried out in a liquid broth containing sugars, malt, yeast, and yeast food. The fermented broth was continuously made into a dough with flour and the other dough ingredients in a pre-mixer and then pumped into the high-speed developer chamber. After only 1–2 minutes of this intensive mechanical kneading under pressure, the dough was extruded directly into the pans and so the divider, hander-up, first prover and moulder were all dispensed with, and only final proof was needed before baking.

Top, Do-Maker Developer Head – external view.
Above, Do-Maker Developer Head – internal view.

Such a continuous process necessitated accurate metering of:

(1) dry ingredients such as flour, salt, sugar and milk powder
(2) fermented broth and water
(3) solutions of oxidant salts such as bromate and iodate
(4) melted shortening

All the metering devices had to be accurate and reliable before a consistent dough could be made hour after hour in the pre-mixer. [A further aid to dough consistency was thought to be that the Wallace & Tiernan pre-mixer design provided for a certain amount of back tracking of the dough, thus reducing variations stemming from minor variations in ingredient metering.] This in itself must have been a mammoth task. So, it is not surprising that the evaluation and development time needed for such a plant extended over years, and the amount of research work involved was enormous.

After the dough was made it was continuously pumped into the high-speed developer chamber which contained about 120 lb of dough. This was pulled and stretched and sheared for 1–2 minutes by impellers moving at 75–115 rpm and under a pressure of 10–40 lb/square inch in excess of atmospheric pressure. As already stated this dough was extruded into pans and only needed a final proof prior to baking.

The first plant was tried out in Great Britain in Chibnall's Bakery in London in the late 1950s.

The type of bread and crumb structure produced could be regulated by controlling:

(1) the amount of pre-mixing
(2) the rate of dough travelling through the developer
(3) the temperature of the dough (about 98°F)
(4) the pressure in the developer
(5) the speed of the mixing elements in the developer
(6) the injection of gas into the developer.

One has to bear in mind that the plant was designed in America for the American type of bread, which is larger, softer and of finer texture than British bread. It was so fine and uniform in texture that it was hardly acceptable in Britain as normal bread – being sometimes referred to as 'sponge-cake' bread. Other complaints were made about its keeping qualities and woollen appearance, so a good deal of experimentation in bakeries was undertaken to make the bread look to the consumer more like normal English bread. Ultimately this was partly achieved by giving the dough pieces a first proof and a mould before panning, but to do this the amount of water in the dough had to be reduced, because the extruded dough was so sticky it was really only suitable for direct panning. This modified process came much later when both the Chorleywood Bread Process as a batch development process and a number of continuous processes largely developed in Britain were already well established in the industry.

Having blazed a new trail in both America and Britain, the Do-Maker plant was not successful in Britain because it made a loaf of bread that was too different from the usual types of bread available at that time and because the industry was not then prepared to accept such a radical change in its thinking.

The interest aroused by the Wallace & Tiernan process had profound effects on British bakers, bakery engineers and cereal technologists. There was by 1959 a commercial Wallace and Tiernan bakery plant in operation. As we will see, it also was partly responsible for the work at Chorleywood in the period 1960–2, which resulted in the evolution of the Chorleywood Bread Process as a commercial bread-making process based on the Tweedy batch mixer which will be discussed in Chapter 2.

Baker Perkins' continuous sponge and dough plant

At about the same time a number of continuous processes made their appearance, no doubt also to some extent inspired by the Do-Maker process. Baker Perkins decided the best line to pursue was a fermented sponge containing 50% of the total flour, followed by a dough which, because so much of the flour had been fermented in the sponge for 4–8 hours, did not need such an intense mechanical development in the dough. Nor was an abnormally high dough temperature involved, for example, 80°F instead of the high nineties in the Do-Maker process. However, as the sponge was fermented at 80°F a refrigeration plant was necessary to cool the sponge before mixing took place.

They therefore developed a plant in which all the ingredients for the sponge and dough were fed automatically, and they modified the Swedish Iverson mixer for dough development. Commercial plant trials began in 1962 using this system. (British Patents Nos. 934,255 and 934,256 published in 1963.) The dough from this mixer was discharged

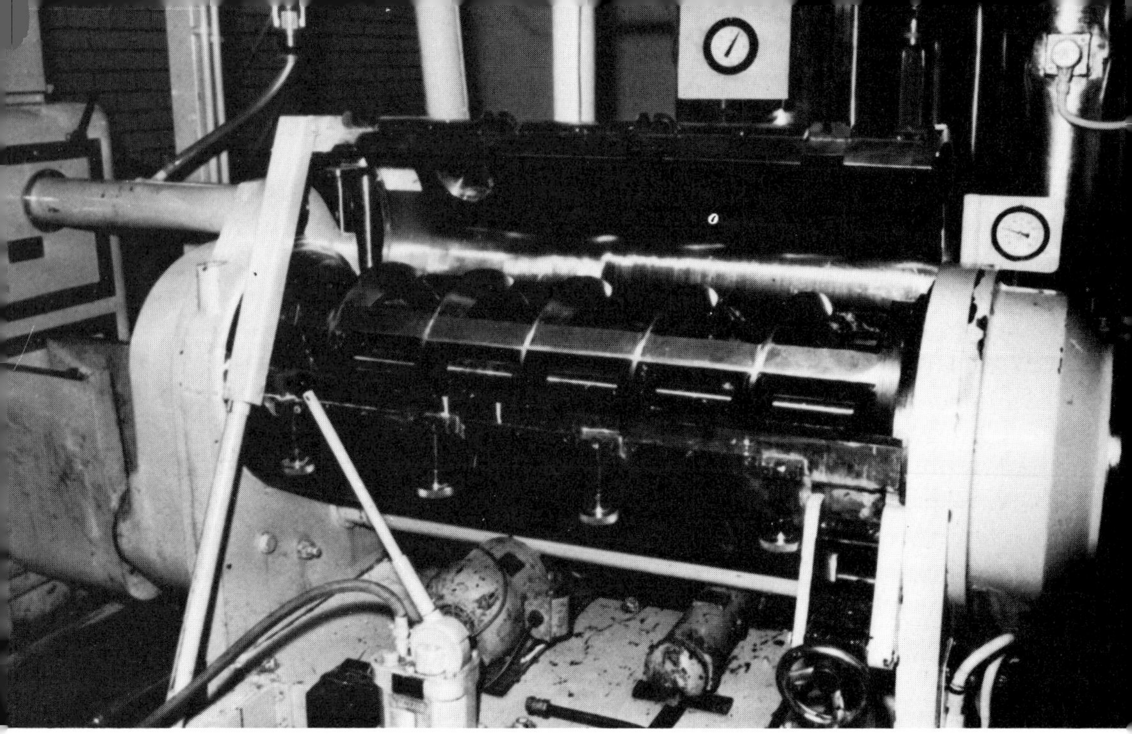

Top, the mixing/developing chamber of the Baker-Iverson plant.
Above, automatic panning unit of the Baker-Iverson plant.

into a new patented divider or divider-panner (British Patent No. 934,257 published in 1963) from which the dough pieces were delivered straight into the tins without any moulding or first proof.

It was not until 1965 that a full-scale commercial plant totally committed to the process, including direct panning, was in full production. This plant ran in several bakeries for a year or two, and some excellent bread was produced. This bread did not have the ultra-fine cellular crumb structure produced by the Do-Maker plant and was therefore similar to good-textured conventional bread. It had excellent keeping qualities and a good flavour. Unfortunately, there were several disadvantages:

(1) the sponge process reduced the yield per sack as against straight no-time dough processes

(2) the process necessitated a complicated and expensive plant, which proved difficult to engineer

(3) it required more men to operate it than did the traditional bulk fermentation processes

This was a gallant attempt to combine the best of the older principles of breadmaking with continuous mechanical development, but it could not compete with less expensive ways of producing bread continuously.

Henry Simon-Strahmann plant

This process is described in British Patents No. 909,765 published in 1962 and No. 977,973 published in 1964.

This was another interesting plant which at the time seemed likely to be successful. Several commercial bakery installations were completed and became operational for various periods of time. In all cases the Strahmann system was eventually replaced with what the baking industry regarded as more capable plant.

This Simon-Strahmann plant operated continuous doughmaking with the dough mechanically developed through a modified German type of mixer (British Patent No. 777,251 published in 1957). It passed on to a special divider (British Patent No. 1,004,885 published in 1965) which had a gentler action on the dough pieces and after a short rest these were moulded in a conventional manner.

The design of the Simon-Strahmann mixer appalled craftsmen bakers when it was first introduced, for it was like a series of glorified meat mincing machines. On a central shaft running at 120–300 rpm were mounted a series of twenty impellers and in front of each impeller was a static plate with a number of holes which varied in size from one and one quarter inches down to a half inch diameter, according to the position of the plate along the mixing cylinder. The dough was forced through the holes in these plates by the impeller behind it. One could hardly believe that presentable bread could be produced by such a ruthless tearing action on the dough, but the results were better than anticipated.

It is difficult to say to what extent factors such as plant design, efficiency, cost and other commercial considerations combined to cause the disappearance of this plant from British bakeries.

The Oakes continuous mixer/modifier

A third continuous breadmaking plant was designed in Great Britain by E. T. Oakes Limited, who had already established a great reputation for their continuous cake-making plants. This process appeared rather later than those previously described. It was not introduced commercially until 1964. Its design was patented in British Patent No. 867,428 published in 1961 and is more fully described later in this book on pages 93 and 94.

The Oakes mixer/modifier is compact in size and yet flexible with respect to the type of bread it can produce. It is specially designed for easy dismantling and cleaning.

The dough is extruded as a continuous ribbon and can be put through a conventional divider or an Oakes Continuous Automatic divider which has been designed to give greater uniformity and also increased accuracy in dough weight. The dough pieces then go through the conventional hander-up, first prover, moulder and final prover before baking. This machine is the only continuous mixer which can be counted as a commercial success in the British baking industry.

Batch mixers

In the late 1950s most forward-looking men in the British baking industry would probably have predicted that the future must be in some form of continuous dough development system. It is ironic that the Chorleywood Bread Process, a no-time batch process which was to

Top, the Strahmann continuous dough developer – expanded view.
Above, the Oakes continuous mixer/modifier.

largely supplant them, was evolved from an attempt by the BBIRA* to determine the critical factors involved in the commercial application of continuous systems.

Although each continuous process had its own pitfalls as has been outlined, it is undoubtedly true that, with the exception of the Oakes, a major reason why they were largely abandoned by the late 1960s was the remarkable success of the Chorleywood process commercially based on the Tweedy mixer. Its rapid growth from the initial idea to test bakery experimentation and then to its commercial exploitation on the plant scale forms the subject of the next chapter.

Note

The March 1965 issue of *The Arkady Review* describes the batch mixers available at that time for the Chorleywood Bread Process. A number of continuous processes are also described, but, by then, batch mixing was in the ascendency, and the only continuous mixer in general use was the Oakes.

*The British Baking Industries Research Association – now part of the Flour Milling and Baking Research Association.

2. The history of the Chorleywood Bread Process

As we have seen in the first chapter, the work of Baker in the United States culminated in the Do-Maker process, a continuous dough developer utilising a brew stage prior to development. A full-scale plant Do-Maker was installed in Chibnall's Associated British Foods bakery as early as 1956. It took the bakery staff two years to iron out all the problems of modifying what was a quite successful plant in the USA to suit the production of the type of bread favoured in Britain. The principal problems involved were that the process had to be adjusted to suit the very lean recipe, the lower specific volume with a less even-textured crumb, and the different flour types and strengths in Britain. Also there was a lack of a fast-acting oxidant such as potassium iodate which was permitted in the USA but not in Britain. Even so, by 1959 most of the plant problems had been dealt with. But there remained one fundamental disadvantage, the bread quality was not acceptable to the British market. The crumb texture was too fine and uniform, and the bread itself had a weak structure; this was particularly critical in sliced bread which had very poor 'butterability', tearing very easily when one attempted to spread butter or margarine.

The BBIRA at Chorleywood was aware of the developments in both American and British bakeries and, initially under Dr Coppock, had begun its own investigations into the possibilities of mechanical dough development using a brew system and continuous development to replace bulk fermentation (see BBIRA No. 42). In 1958, when Dr Elton took over the directorship of the Association, he made a complete review of the various research topics under investigation. He concluded that in view of its importance to the industry, the work on dough development should be given high priority.

Report 59, published after Dr Elton's arrival, shows that even at this stage the research association staff, along with the majority of UK bakery technologists, were still obsessed with the notion of brews and continuous mixing.

At this time doughs were being produced experimentally on a tiny Buss Ko Kneader with a maximum dough output of only 5–10 lb per hour. This caused considerable difficulties in maintaining very low feeding rates of flour and other ingredients with sufficient accuracy to maintain standard conditions, whilst running test series to examine the effect of variations in brew ingredients or similar parameters. One of the early findings was that if the dough was taken as it emerged from the Buss Ko Kneader and was further mixed in a high-speed batch machine (a small double Z blade Morton was the most suitable machine available) then the bread quality was greatly improved, particularly in volume and crumb texture. It became apparent that even under optimum conditions a brew system followed by development in the continuous Buss Ko Kneader was not producing optimum bread and that further mixing/development in a batch mixer was always necessary.

Dr Elton then made the crucial suggestion that what one should really do was measure the total mechanical work input to the dough. An optimum residence time had been established for the dough within the Buss Ko Kneader, and further work strongly indicated that the best bread was obtained when the dough was given a set specific amount of extra mixing in the Z blade Morton. His theory was that the critical factor producing optimum development might be the total amount of work imparted to the dough rather than the manner in which it was introduced.

Accordingly, the BBIRA staff set about devising equipment capable of testing out this novel concept. Nothing suitable was available on the market, so the physics department, under Mr Cornford, devised their own, to be suitable for use with the small Z blade Morton mixer. It was similar to the domestic electricity kilowatt-hour meter but was more sensitive, being a watt-hour meter, and also included a backing-off circuit which allowed one to discount the work input under no-load conditions, so that a true reading of the work imparted to the dough could be obtained. Dr Elton considered the project to be of such special importance that Mr T. W. Collins, who was already doing practical work under Mr J. Devlin, should devote his time exclusively to it. The subsequent investigation clearly showed that there was an optimum work input range centred on 0·4 horsepower minutes per pound. (These were the units first chosen by the research team, although they subsequently switched to electrical units.) As 0·4 horsepower minutes per pound was almost equivalent to five watt hours per pound this level of mechanical work input became the basic characteristic feature of the process, and was found to be appropriate for a very wide range of flours. At the same time investigations began, on both types and amount of oxidants required, while interest in brews continued to decline. Brew conditions did not seem to have any overriding effect on the quality of bread produced which was, however, greatly affected by both variations in the mechanical work input level and also the type and level of oxidant incorporated into the dough.

The initial oxidant system used experimentally was that favoured in the USA for no-time doughs with continuous high-speed development – a combination of potassium bromate and potassium iodate roughly in the ratio of four parts bromate to one part iodate. Other fast-acting oxidants, such as azodicarbonamide and sodium chlorite, were also examined although they, like potassium iodate, were not permitted by British food regulations. It was concluded that a fast-acting oxidant was necessary, but that a mixture of bromate and iodate had no marked advantage over using a single level of iodate alone. For a wide range of flours, the two best systems were shown to be either a combination of 40 ppm on flour weight of potassium bromate together with 10 ppm potassium iodate, or a single addition of just 11–12 ppm of iodate alone with no slower-acting oxidant. These and similar systems were used for many years.

The state of the investigation when Dr Chamberlain joined the research association as a liaison officer in September 1959 was that the following important breakthroughs had already been made:

(1) The optimum work input level for mechanical dough development was known to be five watt hours per pound, for a batch mixer for a wide range of flours.

(2) Roughly optimum oxidant systems had been established (40 ppm potassium bromate plus 10 ppm iodate).

(3) Brews had been shown to be of relatively much less importance, in terms of bread quality, than had previously been thought.

(4) When bulk fermentation was replaced by mechanical action the critical factor appeared to be the amount and rate of work input into the dough, rather than the fact that it was imparted by means of a continuous mixing action.

(5) High-speed batch mixers were found to be capable of producing bread of quality equal to that of continuous mixers providing that the rate and level of mechanical work input was correct.

In 1959, as we have seen, the baking industry was examining several brew and continuous mixing systems on a plant trial basis. Dr Elton considered that the results obtained at the research institute could be of great importance in what was then seen as the most important current development in British baking technology. It was decided that Dr Chamberlain should concentrate single-mindedly on this one topic. In fact he and Mr Collins were both closely involved from this point onwards.

Their first joint venture was to compare the optimum work level for the Morton batch mixer with that required for a continuous system. In this they were lucky enough to secure the co-operation of Wallace and Tiernan who allowed them to use a pilot scale Do-Maker situated at Tonbridge. They were delighted to find that once again the optimum work input centred on five watt hours per pound of dough. Another big step forward had been made. It was now clearly demonstrable that two widely different systems of mixing, or, more correctly, dough developing, had one critical factor in common – they required the same optimum level of mechanical work to be imparted to the dough. (The work was summarised in the B B I R A Report No. 48.) A further useful observation was that for each system the oxidant requirements were similar, although the continuous system needed a little less. This was attributed to the fact that in the Do-Maker the dough was mixed with air under pressure, thus increasing the partial pressure of oxygen in the dough. An increased oxidising effect would result and so reduce the requirement for added chemical oxidant.

The team was again fortunate in obtaining a new version of their laboratory scale continuous mixer on permanent loan from Wallace and Tiernan. They were able to work both with this and Wallace and Tiernan's only pilot scale plant and make detailed investigation of factors such as the effect on bread quality of pressure in the mixing chamber, the water content of the dough, etc. The range of work input under various conditions was re-examined and further confirmed the figure of five watt hours per pound of dough as being the optimum. Brews were used throughout – not because they were thought to be greatly beneficial, but partly for the convenience of adding small ingredients, to some extent for historical reasons, and also due to the fact that the industry was using brews in the few continuous commercial plants operating at that time.

During the early part of 1960, when the baking industry was increasing its attempts to produce bread on the plant scale (using such continuous mixers as the Do-Maker), the research team concentrated on attempting to pin-point the important factors to control in commercial, continuous mixing systems. Ironically, as the year progressed, this work led them to the realisation that if a batch machine with the right power and capacity were available there was the possibility of producing a mechanical dough development system. This would be available to all bakers, particularly those who could not afford enormous continuous plants like the Do-Maker. The problem was that there was no batch machine in use in the baking industry capable of doing this job. A number of experiments were carried out using the then so-called 'high-speed mixers', but these were usually two sack mixers and took at least twelve minutes to impart the necessary work to the dough. Experimental work with the Morton had already shown that the work must be imparted into the dough within five minutes. Plant trials confirmed the result obtained from the Morton. Although the bread produced from the conventional high-speed mixers using the extra oxidant and mixing to five watt hours per pound was better than the normal no-time dough, it was still far inferior to the conventional bulk fermentation loaf.

There followed some months of frustration for the research team. They were only able to produce doughs of about three pounds per mix from the Morton and could not persuade any of the manufacturers of bakery machinery to develop a batch mixer of a suitable capacity for pilot plant production or to devise a modified machine for commercial scale production. To be fair, most of the manufacturers at this time were heavily committed to production of the expensive and complex continuous development systems. However, during this time the now familiar parameters of oxidant level, work input level, extra water addition, increased yeast level and fat were worked out in detail.

This period ended in a dramatic fashion. During a chance conversation Dr Chamberlain was asked if he had heard of the Tweedy mixer. He was told that there existed a high-speed batch mixer with a curious sort of shape, a hexagonal plate at the base of a cylindrical mixing chamber, which was mixing pie pastry to a smooth paste in seven seconds flat.

Dr Chamberlain saw at once that here was a possible answer to his problem. He immediately contacted Mr Brooks, the sales manager of Tweedy of Burnley, and told him of his interest in the machine. During the conversation it became clear that with some modifications this mixer might well be the right machine. It was basically a general purpose, high-speed mixer available in several forms for various diverse mixing processes, including foundry cores, paints, animal feeds and Cornish-pasty fillings. Mr Brooks was even able to claim that it had, on occasion, been used to mix bread doughs which had been baked off in the company's Chipping factory and eaten with great relish by the workers!

In February 1961 Dr Chamberlain travelled to Chipping where he met and discussed the problems and possibilities of the process with Mr Brooks and Mr Pickles, the managing director of Tweedy, a fateful meeting for the future of the baking industry. It was finally agreed that the BBIRA should take on loan a 56 lb general purpose mixer. It was zinc lined and had a painted lid, not at all suitable for use in a commercial food factory! The mixing plate was a simple hexagonal one relying on two vertical pegs, in conjunction with the standard three baffles on the walls of the mixing chamber, for its mixing action.

The machine was duly installed at the research association and baking trials began. The necessary modifications to the dough recipe compared to a bulk fermented dough had already been worked out from the 3 lb doughs mixed in the Morton, ie the desired oxidant (40 ppm potassium bromate plus 10 ppm iodate) was added, the extra water (approximately one gallon per sack) and yeast (double the normal level) and fat (2 lb per sack). The research team was also able to measure accurately the work-input level by another of their self-designed watt-hour meters which they set to the desired five watt hours per pound level.

From the first, the machine gave the desired mixing action, imparting the required work to the dough in a period of 3–4 minutes and producing batches of 50–60 lb of dough which was developed to the correct state to produce excellent bread without bulk fermentation. Once again a totally new and different mixing action fully confirmed the results from the Do-Maker and the Morton. The critical factor was once again the total amount of mechanical work incorporated into the dough.

It was now clear that the team had evolved a commercially viable process, and from this point events moved rapidly and dramatically. Mr Pickles was as enthusiastic about the process as anybody and at once made the development of a more suitable mixer the prime task of his own development team. (This will be described in due course.) In the meantime, Mr Collins and his bakery team had begun to exploit the process to the full using the crude general mixer. During the months that followed, they turned out a whole range of bread (milk bread, oven bottoms, Viennas, etc.) whilst polishing up the process and widening their knowledge of its practical details of bread production.

Dr Chamberlain and his colleagues were now convinced that they had a viable commercial breadmaking system. Their only reservation concerned the oxidising system. Low levels of oxidant, say 7 ppm of potassium bromate, were accepted without question as bread additives. But the bromate iodate combinations, or alternatively even higher additions of bromate alone, say 100–150 ppm on flour weight, although not at that time legally prohibited, were thought to be undesirable on toxicological grounds. Moreover they could well be prohibited in the expected 1963 new Bread and Flour Regulations. There was an alternative. In 1938 Melville and Shattock had demonstrated that ascorbic acid (Vitamin C) had the functional properties of a chemical oxidant in bread-dough systems. It was tried at the same level as had been used for potassium bromate, 150 ppm on flour weight, and once again the process worked first time. The final link in the chain appeared to have been made.

It was subsequently shown that the level of ascorbic acid could be cut to 75 ppm for almost all flours. At this level, notwithstanding the high cost of this ingredient, the need for extra yeast and the high power requirements of the intensive mixing action, it was possible to show a considerable real economic advantage due to the increased water in the dough and the elimination of fermentation losses. As the Food Standards Committee had recognised 80 ppm of ascorbic acid on flour weight as a normal level of usage in bread doughs, a complete and totally commercially feasible process was now at hand. All it lacked was a name. At this point the BBIRA issued report No. 59 and, in the words of Dr Chamberlain, 'We took the plunge and said, right we'll stick our name on it and come hell and high water, we'll call it the "Chorleywood Bread Process" and it can stand or fall'.

A few weeks later the modified Tweedy mixer, the original Tweedy 35 bread mixer (one of a batch of six produced at the Tweedy works in Burnley), was permanently installed at the BBIRA bakery in Chorleywood, together with a research association designed work input meter, and the work of Mr Collins and Dr Chamberlain changed somewhat in character to that of demonstrating and spreading the gospel of the new

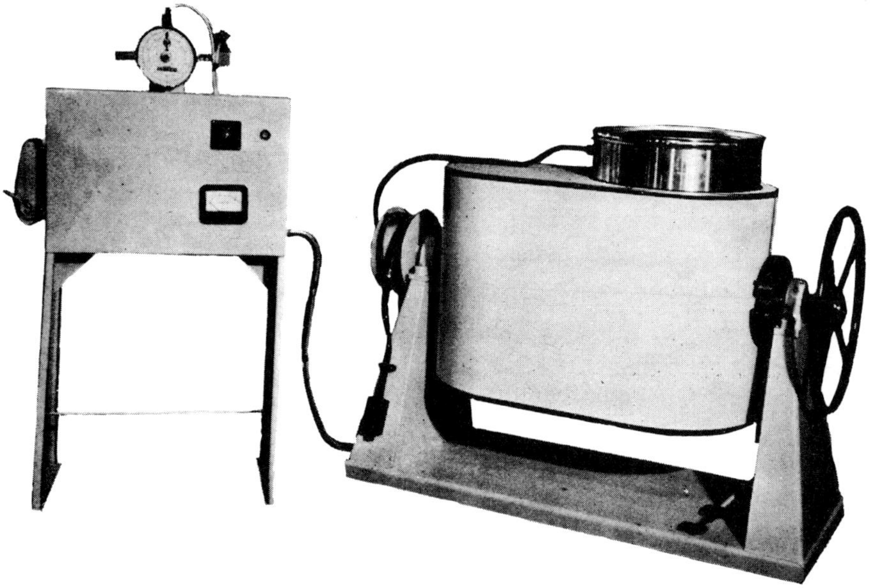

The original Tweedy 35 as supplied to the Research Association in 1961.

process. A further remarkable outcome of this will be recounted in its proper time. First it is necessary to examine more closely the history of the Tweedy mixing machine itself which is inevitably linked with the name of an outstanding mechanical engineer and servant to the baking industry, Mr Pickles.

Mr Pickles was essentially a practical engineer, having begun his working life as an apprentice in a car-repairing business in Burnley. During the 1930s his engineering ability and capacity for hard work took him to the position of foreman mechanic in one of the town's largest garages. After the war, during which time he served in the Merchant Navy, he had started a small company of his own producing wall-paper-trimming machines and then later aircraft parts.

He had obtained control of a second company, Tweedy Chipping, which produced the Peck mixer, a short time before its possibilities in bread-dough development were realised by Dr Chamberlain.

The basic Peck mixer had already incorporated into its design many of the features necessary for a mechanical dough development machine. It was essentially a tub on the inside walls of which were three baffles. Below the tub a motor was mounted which rotated a shaft projecting through the tub's base. On this shaft was a plate, the rotation of which was responsible for the mixing action.

The plate design was central to the mixing action. As it rotated at high speed (400 rpm) the plate projections threw the material in the mixer to the sides of the tub where the baffles and tub walls impeded its rotation, and an intense mixing action occurred.

The Peck was already in use in a diverse range of mixing applications, including vegetable shredding and foundry core mixing. Credit for the plate design must be accorded to Mr Brooks, senior, of Tweedy Chipping, whose design modifications were responsible for the efficient mixing action.

After the meeting in February 1961 Mr Pickles waited for the results of Dr Chamberlain's tests. As soon as it became evident that the crude general-purpose mixer was able to do the job asked of it, he started work on a prototype specifically intended for the baking industry. He is quoted as saying, 'The project had a lot of potential, but many difficulties too. Not being in the baking industry we could see the potential but didn't realise just how big the difficulties might be.'

The design team of the small company, led personally by Mr Pickles, pushed ahead rapidly. Design modifications appeared daily, if need be on the backs of cigarette packets and beer mats, so legend has it.

At the outset it was decided to produce fairly small mixer units, so as not to over tax the financial resources of the company. Also it suited what was then thought to be the best potential market, the small baker who lacked the financial resources to invest in a Do-Maker or similar machine, but who desired the advantages which might be gained from the elimination of bulk fermentation.

The first and rather unexpected problem was that of removing the dough from the mixer. The prototype stood four feet high with the motor below the mixing chamber and did not tilt. After some weeks of frustrating attempts to build doors, hinged panels, etc., into the side of the machine, the design team had the idea of mounting the motor to one side of the mixing chamber, thus giving a lower machine which could be tilted to remove the dough. The materials and design were modified to render the machine suitable for the production of food for human consumption. Six identical machines of this type were then built. There was originally no method of measuring work input, and five of the machines relied on timers, dough development being assessed by measuring dough temperature rise, as directed by Dr Chamberlain.

During this time baking tests were carried out in Burnley by the engineering team, none of whom was a baker. The tests were in stark contrast to those at Chorleywood, the only bakery apparatus in use being a converted tool furnace used to bake off the bread.

The six mixers were then dispersed throughout the industry with the help and advice of the BBIRA, so that baking trials could be instigated by anyone who might be interested in this baking novelty. One of the six was sent back to Chorleywood in August 1961, as already related, so that Dr Chamberlain and the scientific and baking staff could continue with a more careful and detailed study of the advantages and foibles of the new process.

Once again drama enters the story. In September of that year, no less a person than the late Lord Rank, on a visit to the research institute, was shown the new process. He immediately set enquiries in motion which led to Tweedy being asked if they could produce a mixer capable of handling one sack of flour (280 lb) per mix. Mr Pickles' reply was, 'Yes'. It is perhaps fortunate that at that time even he did not fully appreciate the problems which would be involved.

The first immediate step was to scale up the basic Tweedy 35 mixer tub and motor. Even the estimation of the required horsepower had to be revised.

A critical decision also faced the team. Mr Pickles was convinced that if the machine was to be a viable proposition it must be fully automatic. He wanted, therefore, an automatic feed of the major ingredients, flour and water, to the mixer and a control system which would allow the machine to virtually complete its whole filling, mixing and discharge sequence at the touch of a button.

The control system finally selected was a pneumatic one. It was cheap, simple in operation, robust and, it was hoped once the design features were correct, it would be reliable under baking conditions.

The 'Tweedy 280 Automatic' presented for the inspection of British Bakeries'* management and engineers some three months later was the result of continuous effort, sometimes up to fifteen hours a day.

The tub and mixing plate were scaled up exactly from the Tweedy 35, the motor being mounted to one side of the mixing chamber in what has become the familiar Tweedy shape. It was designed so that the plate periferal speed would exactly match that of the Tweedy 35. A recording watt-hour meter was incorporated with help and advice from English

*Later to become RHM Bakeries.

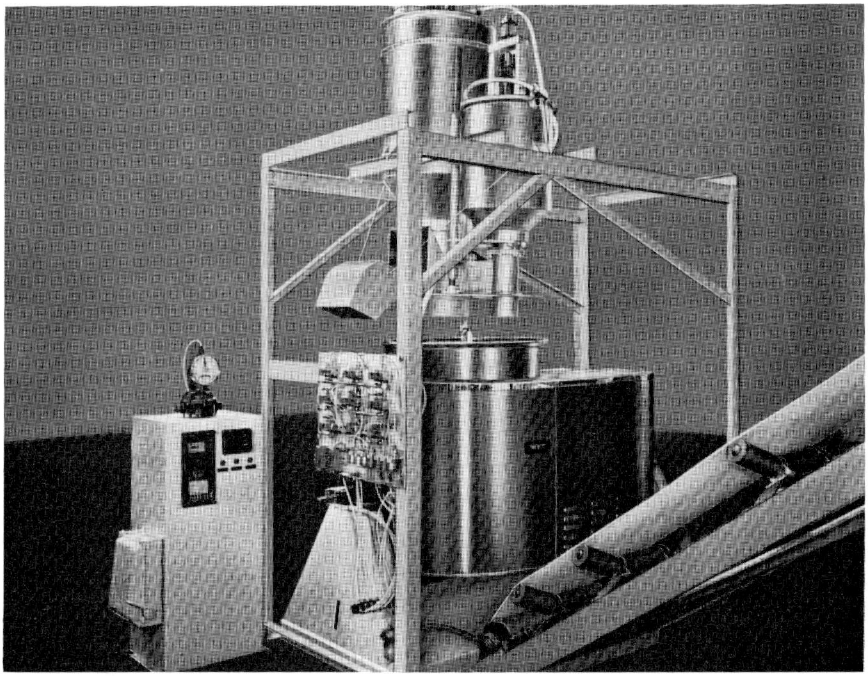

The first automatic Tweedy mixer – 1961.

Electric to measure accurately the work input, although some of the resistances were hand wound at Burnley. Two tanks were mounted side by side, over the machine – one for flour, one for water. The water was metered into the mixing bowl and the flour hopper was filled with a sack of flour before each mix, but was not weighed before discharge into the mixer.

The mixing cycle to be pneumatically controlled was as follows: machine half-tilt (for addition of small ingredients), machine vertical, lock canopy down, water in, flour in, canopy up, lid in lid clamp, mix, lid up, lid off, lock out, full tilt.

As the completed pneumatic control panel arrived on the afternoon prior to the demonstration, the design and construction team struggled until 4 am the following morning to perfect the sequence. In the event the machine functioned perfectly during the demonstration, going through its cycle according to plan (apart from a slight sticking of the flour feed corrected by a judicious and unnoticed tap from an anonymous member of the Tweedy staff).

The British Bakeries technologist assigned to the task of evaluating the new process, Mr Anderson, had done a little preliminary work on a specially constructed half sack mixer together with Mr Collins from the research association and the Tweedy staff early in December 1961 at Hales Bakery, but it was then decided to wait for the almost completed full sack mixer.

The British Bakeries organisation was satisfied with the outcome and it was agreed in March 1962 that the prototype 280 automatic mixer would be installed in one of their bakeries, Hales of Drayton, with the provision that it could be used to make two or three doughs each day, but that it must not interfere with normal production.

The proviso added to the already difficult job of the Tweedy engineers, the bakery divider hopper being some fifteen feet above ground level. The temporary, and not altogether successful, solution to this further snag was a conveyor running at an angle of forty degrees from the base of the mixer to the top of the hopper. Unfortunately doughs had a habit of reaching a height of 7–8 feet and then slowly rolling back to the mixer!

It is said that one Sunday morning a policeman who entered the bakery to book the entire design team for parking their cars in the road outside spent an hour helping solve the problem, and became so engrossed that he left still puzzling – minus his helmet!

Three weeks of work, including plate modifications and variations of mixing procedure, followed. Although the bread produced was salable, it was not of a standard acceptable to the British Bakeries production staff.

Mr Pickles and his fellow engineers realised that the scaling up of the process was in some way responsible for a loss in bread quality. At the same time they were being shown by the commercial bakery staff what was expected of a commercial loaf and what were the shortcomings of the bread produced from their mixer.

The main fault was that of crumb texture compared to a bulk fermented loaf. They were producing a crumb structure containing large gas cells visible as a coarse open structure lacking in colour, softness and resilience. Some improvement could be effected by machine modification, particularly plate design, but the basic deficiency remained.

At the end of March, Mr Anderson and Mr Collins had a meeting in Burnley with Mr Pickles to discuss the problem of the variations in texture which were bedevilling the process. Here they emphasised again that a vital factor in bread texture was that which had been examined by Baker in 1937, the influence of air occlusion on the flour particles and the capability of the mixer to subdivide residual air into small cells.

Mr Pickles was left to ponder, amongst other things, Baker's 1953 Do-Maker patent. It is said that he sat up all night, no doubt especially considering such passages as:

> The mixing operation is arranged to produce uniform results in the passing material, but is preferably limited to such mixture as will fully wet and combine all of the components and form a substantially homogeneous, lump free dough which is as yet essentially undeveloped. In this step any releasably trapped gas is allowed to escape freely, for example air or other gas that might be trapped in the dry flour. A feature of particular importance for the subsequent treatment of the dough mass is that (as continuously delivered by the first stage) it has a uniform density especially a uniform and preferably a uniformly low gas content.
>
> I have found that the character of grain or cell structure in the finished bread not only depends on the development of the dough material itself, but is also determinable and, in fact, very accurately controllable by the extent to which free gas in the dough is minutely and uniformly subdivided prior to the time when the dough experiences its final and significant expansion (as in final proofing).
>
> The nature of the ultimate cell structure is governed by the amount of free gas in the mixture as it is worked for development.

In pondering this document to the point almost of nervous exhaustion, the moment of genius conceived the application of the principle to the Tweedy mixer. Thus vacuum on a dough mixer was born.

In mid-April the new idea was revealed to the British Bakeries staff and after some preliminary work at Burnley the principle was applied to the 280 automatic mixer at Hales Bakery, West Drayton. The critical commercial tests occurred on 2 May 1962. At a vacuum level of 15 in. Hg, to quote Mr Anderson's notes of that date, 'The texture from the vacuum mixers was very fine and even – up to the highest standard'.

On 13 August 1962 the first fully automated 280 mixer with vacuum was run on a commercial plant at Hales Bakery. Two batches were mixed in the morning and six batches were scheduled for the afternoon However, the mixer failed to empty and after the 'emergency' and 'reset' buttons had been pressed, instead of completing the cycle and permitting the dough to be discharged, it went straight into the cycle for the second batch and dropped flour and water on top of the first dough still in the tub. This began a series of many incidents before the automation became reliable.

In fact, once the basics had been absorbed by the Tweedy staff, the vacuum being the final link in the chain, there followed a full year of hard continuous machine design and construction modification. Detailed rethinking of mixing plate design, selection of vacuum systems,

The Tweedy 6600 – first produced in 1973.

improvement of lid vacuum seals, flour and water feeding arrangements – including a method for batch weighing of both flour and water – apparently endless refinements of electrical circuits, pneumatic systems and work input measurement devices. The machine sold slowly at first, only six 280 Automatics were ordered in the first eighteen months. Since the entire available capital and research and development staff of the Tweedy Company was tied up in the bread mixer, it was a difficult time for the Company. The turning point was the London Bakery Exhibition of 1963. The machine was demonstrated and at once caught the imagination of the baking industry. During the next year over 100 machines were sold. The new process was accepted and the baking revolution had begun.

During the next three years the process became, and still remains, the standard method of plant bread production. It is estimated that at least 85% of plant bread dough is currently mixed in Tweedy machines.

Ironically it was only later that the small baker realised the benefits of the process originally conceived for his salvation. Now a whole range of mixer capacities, produced by several mixer manufacturers, caters for the entire range of baking establishments. The Tweedy is now available from a Tweedy 10, designed as a test bakery or demonstration model, to the Tweedy 6600 capable of feeding a fifteen sack plant.

PART II

Theory

3. A theory of mechanical dough development

Section 1 – Introduction

Prior to the introduction of mechanical dough development, the great majority of bread produced in commercial plant bakeries in England was made by a (three-hour) bulk fermentation process. Although it has been claimed, with some justice, that the advent of the new process has revolutionised breadmaking in Great Britain, it might appear in practice that in most bakeries changing to the new system only few alterations have been made in dough processing techniques and dough handling equipment. Dividing, intermediate proof, moulding, final proof and baking stages often utilise the same machinery and follow the same flow pattern, with relatively small changes, from the bulk fermentation process which it claims to replace. The essential new feature is that the conventional mixing and bulk fermentation stages have been replaced by a short period of intensive mixing in a high energy input machine followed almost immediately by dividing. A mechanical dough development process is essentially a no-time dough process by which bread, of quality equal in every respect to the best available from a bulk fermentation process, is produced. Bread production by a no-time process using conventional mixers is not unknown in the baking industry. However, this method is only employed as a stop-gap in cases of emergency and the bread produced is of inferior quality. In particular, the crumb quality of the loaf suffers, together with a loss of colour and a cell structure which lacks both the softness and resilience characteristic of the best quality bread. It is necessary, therefore, to consider in detail the changes occurring in the dough structure during mechanical dough development which confer the same benefits on the final bread structure as does mixing followed by bulk fermentation in older processes. The three breadmaking processes (up to the dividing stage) are outlined in greater detail as follows:

Recipes (for a 1 sack mix)

	3 hour fermentation		*No-time dough*		*Mechanical dough development*	
	lb	oz	lb	oz	lb	oz
Flour	280	—	280	—	280	—
Salt	5	—	5	—	5	—
Yeast	3	—	7	—	5	8
Water	160	—	162	—	167	—
Fat	2	—	2	—	2	—
Ascorbic acid	—		—		75 ppm (on flour weight)	
Dough temperature	78°F		82–84°F		86°F	

Mixing method

Bulk fermentation

Conventional slow-speed mixer – 20 minutes approx. Rest in mixing bowl for three hours in a controlled atmosphere, temperature 80°F, relative humidity 70–75% with a knock back after two hours. Divide.

Conventional No-time dough

Conventional slow-speed mixer – 25–30 minutes. No bulk fermentation. Divide immediately.

Mechanical development

High-energy impact mixer – To a work level of 5 watt hours per pound of dough in a time period of 3–5 minutes. No bulk fermentation. Divide immediately.

It must be stressed that these are basic recipes and it is assumed that the flour used is a standard commercially milled breadmaking flour, typical of those used in English bakeries.

In each case improvements in the loaf quality would be effected by alterations to the recipe. With bulk fermented doughs in commercial practice yeast foods such as calcium and ammonium salts, sophisticated fat blends and enzyme-active soya flour are usually added to produce a commercially aceptable loaf. In the case of the conventional no-time dough, the basic formula will give a poor loaf no matter how skilfull the baker, though fat and yeast foods will give some degree of improvement.

The basic mechanically developed dough formula, as stated in the text, will produce a bread quality equal to, or better than, the basic fermented dough. The recipe and mixing techniques are in fact those arrived at by the FMBRA as a result of their early researches into the process. Although there have been subsequent modifications to the process due to a greater understanding of the underlying principles which have resulted in excellent bread, the three basic points vital to its success are as follows:

There are two extra additions to the basic flour, salt, yeast, water recipe which the baker cannot do without to produce a satisfactory loaf.

(1) A critical minimum level of a specified type of fat.

(2) A high and specified level of a particular oxidising agent or combination of oxidising agents.

A third factor is also of critical importance – a specific amount of mechanical work. 5 watt hours/lb of dough must be introduced into the dough during a total mixing time of three to five minutes. The contribution of each of these three must be considered in detail, but before examining in detail any method for the production of the particular aerated structure known as bread, we need to know more about the main constituent – wheat flour – and the structure formed when it is mixed with water in the proportions which will form a dough. A typical analysis of wheat flour would be:

Moisture	13–15·5%
Starch	65–70·0%
Protein	8–13%
Cellulose (fibre) Trace	0·2%
Fat	0·8–2%
Sugar	1·5–2%
Mineral matter	0·3–0·6%

The protein fraction deserves the greatest attention. It is the unique visco-elastic property of wheat protein which enables the carbon dioxide produced during dough fermentation to be retained in the structure, so giving the characteristic porous, cellular texture which is characteristic of bread. This protein known in its hydrated form as gluten can be readily extracted from flour by hand kneading a small sample under a stream of running water. The starch is washed away leaving behind a coherent extensible rubbery mass described as 'crude gluten'. As isolated by this procedure, gluten has an average water content of about 65%, its dry components being approximately 75–80% protein, 5–15% residual carbohydrates, and a small quantity of mineral salts and same bound lipid.

Wheat flour owes its breadmaking potential to this unique protein. Of other cereals only rye possesses a protein with structural properties resembling those of gluten.

The structural network which gives bread its character is due to a film or sheet of gluten which surrounds the starch granules. There is a whole network of extensible envelopes formed which contain the carbon dioxide produced during the fermentation period and which retain the gas as it expands during the baking process.

Early work, notably by Osborne, indicated that gluten was an intimate mixture of two distinct individual proteins, glutenin and gliadin, present in nearly equal amounts. The glutenin was thought to form a nucleus to which the gliadin adhered, binding the gluten proteins into one coherent elastic mass. This division was completely arbitrary – gliadin being the fraction soluble in dilute acids and dilute alcohol. It became clear that this division was not sufficiently precise and the next steps, in which people like Baily and Blish were prominent, was the realisation that there were in fact a series of proteins apparently similar in nature but of differing molecular weights. Much work was done on the solubility of various fractions of the protein, with conflicting results, but important observations concerning the effect of dilute acids and alkali were obtained. For instance, wet gluten exposed to the action of dilute acetic acid becomes progressively and increasingly hydrated, until it eventually disintegrates into a uniform 'dispersion'. By the addition of a neutral salt to such a dispersion, or by neutralisation with alkali, it can be rapidly coagulated and recovered without apparent change in original properties. The state of knowledge in 1945 can be summarised by a series of points made by M. J. Blish in *Advances in Protein Chemistry*:

(1) Gluten protein is definitely inhomogeneous and probably consists of several components.

(2) Non homogeneity appears to increase with a decrease in solubility of the various protein fractions.

(3) Evidence of non-homogeneity may, however, be due in considerable measure to aggregation and to component interaction with 'complex formation' rather than to the actual existence of numerous individual components.

(4) The solubility characteristics of gluten present unique difficulties and complexities when attempts are made to apply and interpret modern physical methods for studying protein individuality and molecular properties.

(5) Convincing solutions of the problem of gluten structural composition and homogeneity apparently must await discovery and application of appropriate solvents, or new methods and criteria, or a combination of these developments.

New methods and criteria have indeed become available. In the first place, there is now a great deal of information about the chemical structure of proteins in general and the nature and relative strengths of the bonds which cause the individual protein molecules to have a particular physical form and a particular set of chemical properties. The macro molecular structure of many proteins has also been studied in detail by means of new techniques such as X-ray crystallography and the ultracentrifuge. By combining the results of the two fields of study, it is now possible to postulate probable structures for the gluten network.

The examination of protein structure at the molecular level follows well established principles and experience derived from studies of other proteins can be applied directly. Proteins as a class are long chain, high molecular weight substances built up from a related series of building blocks of small molecular weights known as amino acids. All but two have the same general formula: i.e. α amino acids.

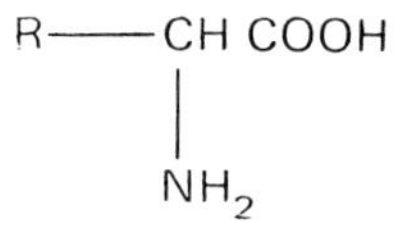

R denotes variable molecular components.

The chain is built up by linkages known as peptide bonds which are formed as follows:

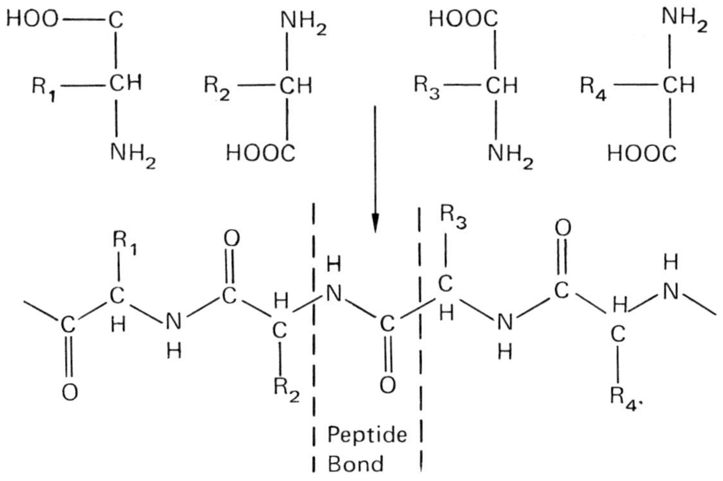

The amino acids of a typical gluten protein are listed below:

	per cent
Arginine	4·3
Lysine	2·1
Histidine	2·4
Tyrosine	4·2
Tryptophan	1·1
Phenylalanine	2·0
Cystine	1·9
Methionine	3·3
Threonine	2·5
Leucine and IsoLeucine	6·0
Valine	3·0
Glutamic Acid	36·0
Alanine	5·5
Proline	11·0

Those not present are serine, aspartic acid, glycine and hydroxyproline. The molecular structure of two of these are shown in detail because of their particular importance although the structure of all are equally well known.

(1) Glutamic Acid present to the greatest extent at 36%.

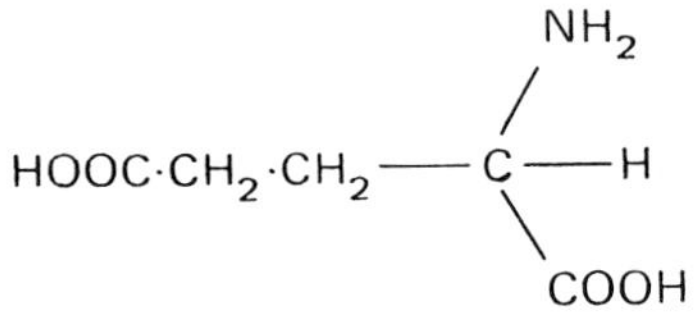

(2) Cystine – which is of particular importance in modern theories of gluten structure.

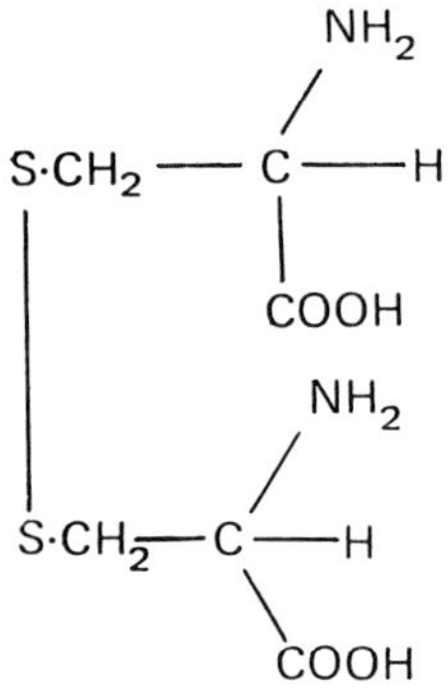

This amino-acid chain – known as a polypeptide chain – can be allied to a backbone, or skeleton, common for all proteins. For both glutenin and gliadin the average length of the polypeptide chain is in the region of 180 amino acid units per chain, but the two types differ to some extent in amino-acid composition and more important, in molecular weight. Glutenin has a molecular weight in the region of one million whilst the gliadin is much lower at about 20,000–40,000. The amino-acid sequence is described as the primary structure of the protein. Of equal importance in a consideration of gluten structure is the spacial configuration of each individual polypeptide chain and the manner in which larger protein molecules are built up from a number of polypeptide chain units. To do this we must know a little about the types of bonds occurring in protein structures.

These fall into the following groups:

(1) Disulphide linkages (covalent links).

(2) Salt links.

(3) Hydrogen bonding.
(4) Van der Waals forces.

and each will be considered in turn.

Disulphide linkages are dependant on the amino-acid cystine. As can be seen from the diagram, cystine has the ability unique amongst amino acids to provide a co-valent link bonding together two portions of protein chain, thus:

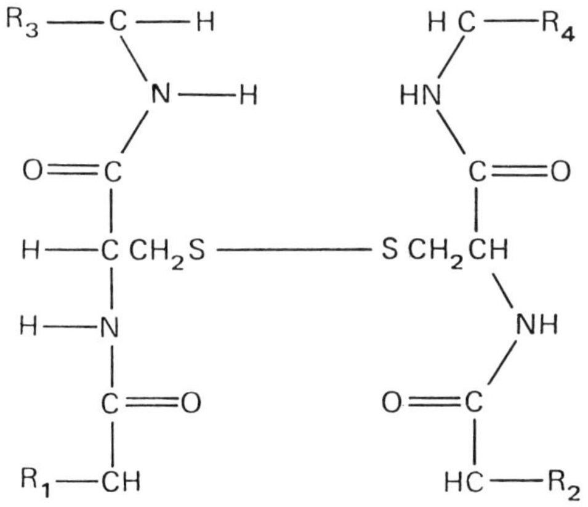

There are two ways in which such cross links can occur – inter-molecular cross links and intra-molecular cross links. Inter-molecular cross linkages are those in which two polypeptide chains are linked to each other by the -S-S- or disulphide link, thus:

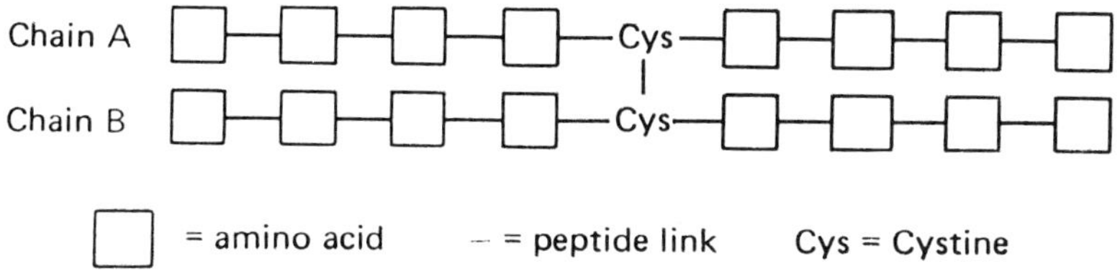

Intra-molecular links concern one chain only, doubled back upon itself, thus:

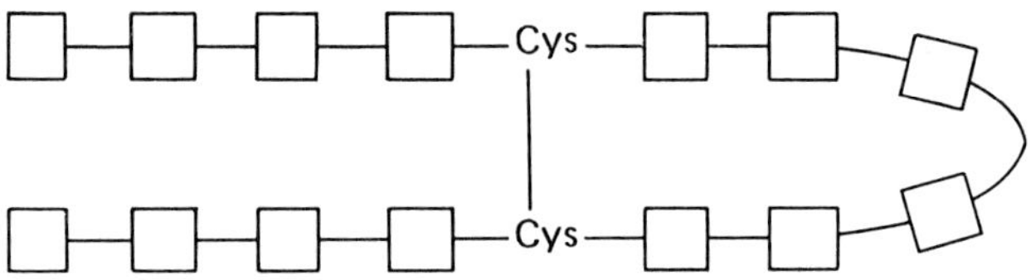

Salt links are simple ionic links – a positively charged group of one amino acid is electrically attracted to the negatively charged group of a second amino acid, either in the same polypeptide chain, or in a neighbouring one, thus:

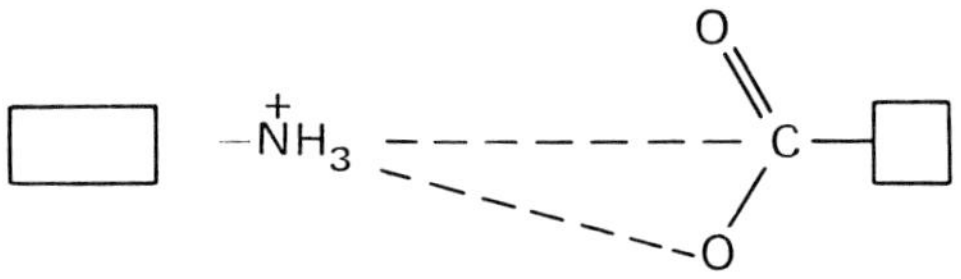

Salt link

Hydrogen bonds are a series of ionic links similar in nature to the salt link, each one being weaker than a salt link. There are so many such links that this type of bonding is of great importance to the hydrated protein structure. They are of the following general type:

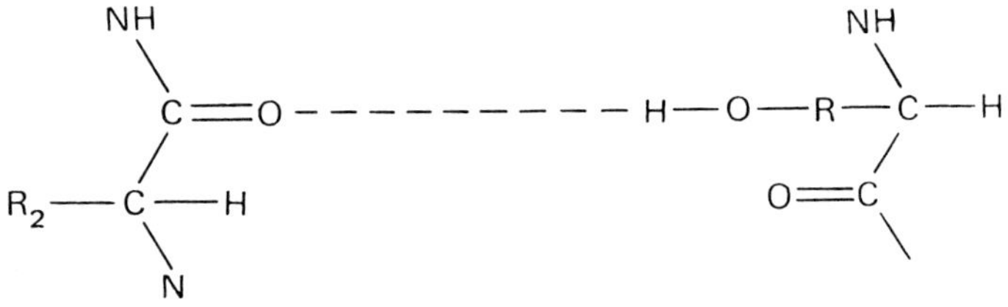

Van der Waals forces – portions of protein chain length are water attracting – hydrophilic. Other portions are water repelling – hydrophobic. If two hydrophobic portions are in such a position that they lie next to one another in a watery medium, their similar natures tend to repel water and attract one another so that they will tend to align themselves one to the other. As with hydrogen bonds, each individual force is relatively weak but two lengths of hydrophobic molecule can generate a considerable total attractive force.

These bonds determine the spacial configuration of the gluten molecules in a watery medium. The water is necessary if the salt links, hydrogen bonds and Van der Waals forces are to exist at all. The polypeptide chains of gluten do not exist as a long rod either poker stiff or infinitely flexible. A short length of the chain coils upon itself. The coils are kept in position by means of the hydrogen bonds, salt links and Van der Waals forces between neighbouring amino acids.

Work done in the USA has determined that glutenin and gliadin each have a similar coil or 'secondary structure' – about 20% alpha helix coil, the remainder being in the form of a random coil. The next step in building up the picture is to determine the spacial configuration of the coiled spring polypeptide chain units. The essential difference between glutenin and gliadin appears to be that the gliadin chain tends to be branched and folded back upon itself into a rather compact form whilst the glutenin takes the form of a long, unfolded, but flexible, spring. It is probable that in gliadin the disulphide bonds are largely intra-molecular whilst the glutenin polypeptide chains are linked one to another by disulphide links. Each polypeptide unit contains on average 2·3, -S-S- linkages and there is strong evidence to suggest that the glutenin molecule exists as an extended chain of sub units, thus:

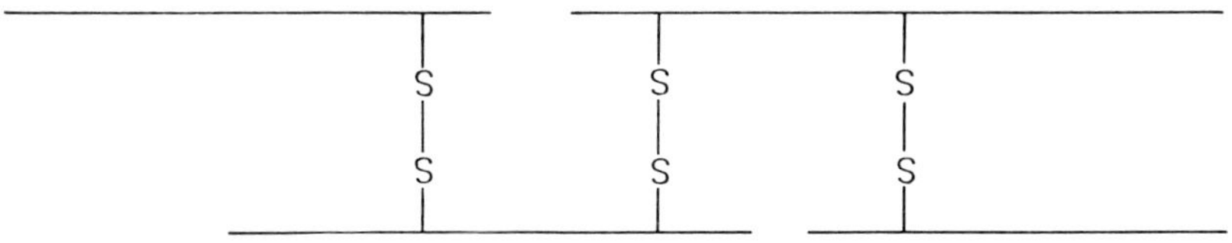

Dr Muller has outlined a theory to account for the structure of gluten. Gluten is a visco-elastic network. Dr Muller has postulated that it behaves as if it were similar in properties to rubber and that the 'statistical theory of rubber elasticity' can be applied to the gluten network. For a polymer to behave according to this theory the following three conditions must apply:

(1) The polymer must consist of long chain molecules with freely rotating links – i.e. glutenin molecules.

(2) Secondary forces between the molecules must be small.

(3) The molecules must be cross linked at a few places along their length, forming a three dimensional network.

A very important point is that in the application of this theory, the chemistry of the individual molecules – in this case the glutenin chains – is important. The theory can equally be applied to rubber, collagen or wool.

Assuming that the gluten structure is to be a glutenin network swollen in water, it can be treated as a 'rubber' swollen in liquid, eg rubber swollen in benzene, then the number of cross links per molecule can be calculated once the molecular weight of each molecule is known. Taking an average molecular weight of 1,000,000 the cross links/molecule will be in the order of 4·6 links per molecule for a weak flour and 5·8 for a strong flour.

It is the opinion of Dr Muller that the main difference between 'strong' and 'weak' glutens is that the stronger gluten has a higher degree of cross linking.

We can now postulate a sequence of changes as flour and water are mixed to form a dough by a conventional slow-speed mixer – and the dough is then 'developed' by bulk fermentation. We may then be able to deduce how a similar structure is produced by mechanical action in a high energy input mixer together with the requisite amounts and types of oxidant and fat.

Section 2 – Function of oxidant

Firstly, let us consider conventional mixing. Initially, a flour before mixing consists of protein wedges embedded in a network of starch granules. In the early stages of mixing the dough is sticky and 'short' with little strength and little or no elasticity. During this time it is thought that the dough is hydrating, i.e. taking water into the protein structure and bonding it by hydrogen bonding.

At the same time some water is being incorporated into that portion of the starch which is described as 'damaged', i.e. those starch granules which have been ruptured during the milling process so that the individual starch molecules are able to take water into their structure by hydrogen bonding. (Note that undamaged granules also take in a little water and swell slightly.)

This process allows the secondary structure of the gliadin and glutenin chains to develop. It is thought that the glutenin chains in the dry state are crosslinked to one another, within individual wedges. The hydrated wedges are dispersed throughout the dough. As the mixing continues after hydration the secondary forces, salt links, hydrogen bonds, etc., form non-specific bonds between the glutenin chains and a three dimensional network begins to be built up. However, such a structure would not exhibit elastic properties and would be subject to plastic deformation only, ie if it were stretched, as the glutenin chains slipped one over the other as secondary forces were overcome there would be no tendency for the structure to return to its original configuration. At the end of conventional mixing it is possible to demonstrate that some elasticity has been incorporated into the structure. Therefore, we must conclude that specific disulphide cross links have been formed between the glutenin molecules. That this structure is sufficiently developed to form bread after proving and baking, is demonstrated by the no-time conventional loaf. Furthermore, the structure is not the optimum one is equally clear when the improving effect on loaf quality of bulk fermentation is considered.

The building up of the optimum visco-elastic structure in the gluten is central to the whole theory. To understand this we must consider one further chemical reaction sequence:

Not all the cystine present in flour protein is in the cross-linked form Cys-S-S-Cys, about one in twenty cystine molecules is in a reduced form, thus Cys-S-H. This allows what is termed a disulphide/sulphydryl interchange to occur. During mixing, as proteins are moved relative to one another it is possible for sulphydryl groups to interchange with already formed disulphide bonds as shown:

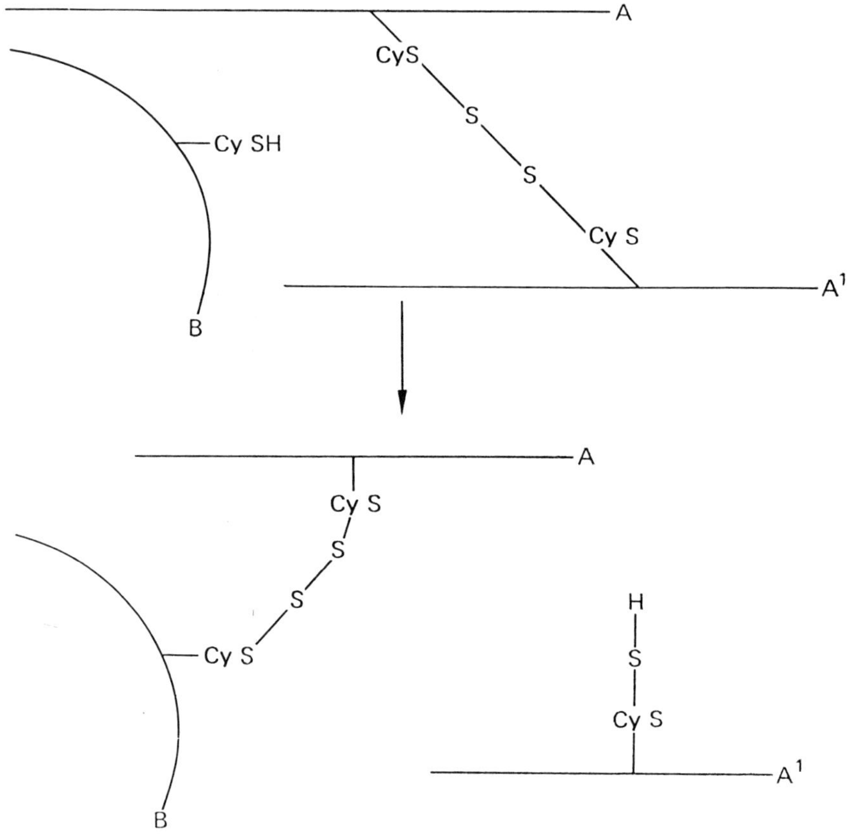

A, A1, B, = Protein Chains.
Cy S S Cy = Cystine
Cy SH = Cysteine

It is possible for the disulphide/sulphydryl interchange reaction to occur between any free sulphydryl group and disulphide cross link provided that the two are brought into contact and preferably if the disulphide bond is under some strain.

Thus, in summary, the mixing process commences with flour in the form of starch granules, some partly or wholly broken open, and protein which is largely unhydrated in discreet wedges and free water. At the end of mixing we have the dough piece – a three-dimensional visco-elastic structure which is a matrix of hydrated glutenin and gliadin incorporating hydrated swollen 'damaged' starch granules in which is embedded the undamaged slightly swollen starch granules. The elasticity of the structure depends upon cross-linked glutenin molecules forming a ribbon like basic network – linked together by disulphide/sulphydryl bonds. The great difference between the elastic structure of gluten and the dough which will undergo considerable deformation under stress is due to the discontinuity of the dough matrix where glutenin molecules are linked either to each other or via non-glutenin protein molecules by non-specific bonds such as hydrogen bonds. Once this type of bond is broken there is no tendency for the structure to revert to its original configuration.

Returning to the conventional dough at the end of mixing, its defect in breadmaking terms is that it is considered too resistant to stretching and not sufficiently elastic. The structural defects giving rise to the conditions are:

(*a*) *That the S-S- cross linkages which have formed may not be between glutenin molecules but between glutenin and non-gluten proteins – some form of equilibrium must occur thus:*

$Pr^1SH + Pr^2SS\ Pr^2$ — Contributes more to elasticity

$Pr^2SH + Pr^1SS\ Pr^2$ — Contributes less to elasticity

Pr^1 = non gluten protein
Pr^2 = glutenin

(*b*) *Those linkages which do not occur are not correctly situated to build up an ordered, extended network of the elastic type but occur randomly building up tangled, compact structures which are highly resistant and not very extensible.*

Lee and Lai (*Cereal Chemistry*, v. 46, p. 599) have demonstrated that an appreciable proportion of the SH groups present in glutenin remain during normal dough mixing 'masked' by the protein structure itself. The 'mellowing' effect of bulk fermentation would, therefore, appear to be due to further disulphide/sulphydryl interchange as the expanding glutenin containing sheets are stretched. The glutenin molecules are pulled into a more orderly and open linear coil form as existing -S-S-bonds become strained and are able to react with previously masked -S-H groups, which become available as the secondary protein structure is extended in the expanding dough films surrounding the growing gas bubbles.

The changes in position of disulphide bonds between glutenin molecules are thought to be due to:

(1) The reaction of non-gluten, often water soluble, proteins with strained S-S bonds between glutenin molecules

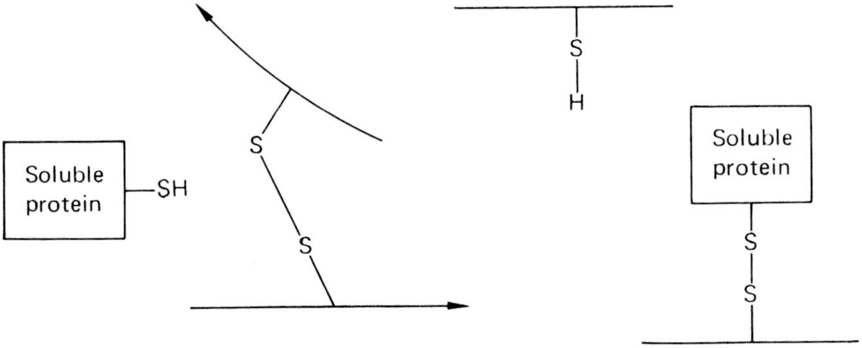

This does not in itself contribute to building up elastic properties in the structure but it will reduce the strain building up in a dough sheet forming the envelope of an expanding gas bubble. It also results in the presence in the glutenin chain of an S-H group capable of further reaction.

(2) If the strained -S-S- bond reacts with an S-H bond in a further glutenin chain, then it both reduces the strain in the network and at the same time directly contributes to increasing the elastic nature of the dough structure.

The result of these and similar reactions is the profound change which occurs in the physical characteristics of a dough during bulk fermentation – changes which the baker can easily detect for himself. The great relaxation of strain in the dough is coupled with a corresponding increase in both extensibility and resilience.

It has long been accepted that the incorporation of a low level of an oxidant such as ascorbic acid or potassium bromate into a conventional dough confers additional gas retention properties to the dough structure. It can be shown that approximately 7–10 ppm of potassium bromate is beneficial for most breadmaking flours and ascorbic acid has also been used at rather higher levels.

There are considered to be two possible reactions between the oxidants used in breadmaking processes and the dough in which they are included, both of which concern the disulphide and sulphydryl groups of the flour protein.

The two overall reactions are:

(a) The oxidant may link two sulphydryl groups thus:

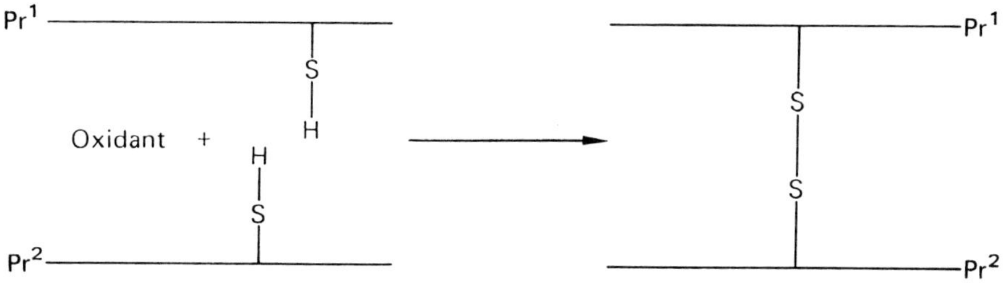

It may link together:
(1) two non-gluten protein sulphydryl molecules.
(2) a gluten protein with a non-gluten protein.
(3) Two glutenin molecules to each other.

Certain of the oxidants are also capable of reacting directly, when present at high concentration with a single sulphydryl group.

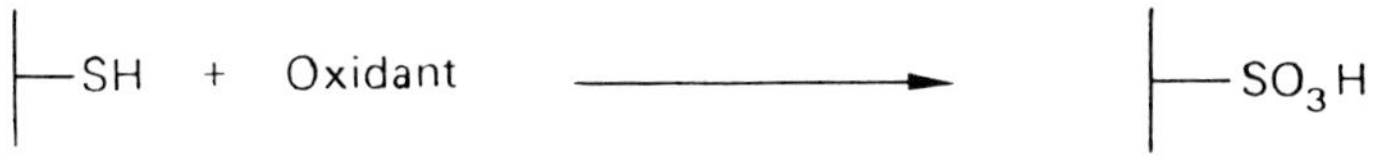

The group so formed being stable and no longer taking part in interchange reactions.

These various oxidants are considered to all take part in the first reaction but not all are able to participate in the second. Each has its own distinct rate of reaction, the significance of which will be discussed in detail when mechanical dough development is considered.

A small amount of oxidant which may be used with benefit in bulk fermentation processes appears to react with sulphydryl groups to take a portion of the soluble non-gluten protein sulphydryl groups out of the reaction system and also to increase the amount of glutenin cross linkage.

An excess of oxidant is detrimental in that it removes from the dough system too many of the mobile water soluble protein SH groups and also may form some cross links in the gluten. The strain in the glutenin sheets can not now relax due to disulphide/sulphydryl interchange as the dough expands and a bound structure results which is highly resistant to extension and rips open under pressure instead of expanding.

If we now turn to the mechanical development of dough the aim is to build up a structure similar to that of a conventional dough at the end of bulk fermentation. This is to be brought about by the combination of intense mechanical work and the chemical action of a high level of oxidising agent. It must be assumed that the effect of mechanical action is in some way to modify drastically the state of the protein, particularly of the glutenin protein. As with any dough mixing action the first step must be the hydrating of the protein and the establishment of the hydrated protein secondary and tertiary structure. The intensive mixing action is thought to accomplish this phase of dough formation very rapidly – in as short a time as 60–90 seconds. The conventional so-called 'high-speed' mixers substantiate the propostion – in that they can drastically reduce the time required for dough mixing as opposed to dough development. It has been suggested that the mechanical action then directly modifies the protein structure by physically rupturing -S-S- bonds so that interchange can then occur with the ruptured -S. groups. A more likely explanation concerns the 'masked' -SH groups. These are -SH groups present in the glutenin (about 50% of the total) which are not immediately able to react in a normal dough. They do not for instance react with oxidant – even strong fast acting ones such as potassium iodate. They will, however, react if the dough is dispersed in a strong urea solution. The urea nullifies the effects of the hydrogen bonds, etc., in building up protein spatial configuration, demonstrating that it is these forces which are responsible for a protein spatial configuration physically protecting the S-H groups from attack. During bulk fermentation the expanding dough sheets stretch the protein structure exposing a few of these S-H groups at any one time so that disulphide sulphydryl interchange may optimise the structure as previously described.

In the case of mechanical development there may be some -S-S- cleavage but the essential action is thought to be the stretching and opening out of the glutenin protein as secondary forces are overcome to expose the masked S-H groups to chemical attack. Thus there are at the one time large numbers of S-H groups in the glutenin molecules able to react with any other strained -S-S- bonds present in the structure.

The system is also in violent motion capable of producing such strained bonds and bringing reactive sites into contact at a very rapid rate. Further, the optimum type of mixing has been found to be that which produces a high rate of shear-stretching the dough rather than cutting it so that the glutenin chains are in the process of being stretched into an extended linear coil.

It is suggested that the correct mechanical amount and type of work aligns the glutenin chains in the correct spatial configuration for optimum dough condition and also exposes the S-H groups which are necessary to stabilise the dough in the state, by cross linking with the strained -S-S- bonds and possibly -S-S- bonds broken by mechanical action.

However, the system is not stable – a dough produced in such a manner which does not contain an oxidising agent at a much higher level than would be used in conventional processed dough does not produce satisfactory bread. The dough might appear to prove normally, but has poor gas retention properties and exhibits little or no oven spring during the baking process. The reason is simply that the optimum dough structure is never formed during development. The most mobile -S-H group containing entities are the water soluble non-glutenin protein molecules and it is these which would preferentially react with any available strained -S-S- bonds exposed during the mixing process. We must, therefore, consider the mode of action of the commonly used oxidants to see how they both prevent the weakening of the structure by the water soluble protein S-H groups and also help to build up the desired new inter-glutenin chain -S-S bonds. The three oxidising agents which have been most widely used in the baking industry for this purpose are potassium iodate, not permitted in Great Britain but has in the past been used in the USA, ascorbic acid and potassium bromate. Although the net effect of each used at its correct level is the same, the various rates of reaction of the three, and also their mode of action, varies to some extent.

Any of the oxidants is in theory capable of undergoing two reactions with the S-H group either with one such group thus:

$$PrS\text{-}H + \text{Oxidant} \longrightarrow PrSO_3H$$

or with two groups

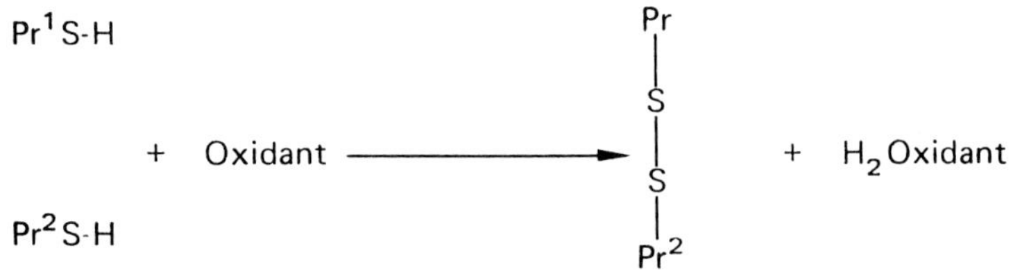

In the first case the S-H group is stabilised and can, therefore, no longer take part in disulphide/sulphydryl interchange. In the second case a new disulphide link may be formed.

The possible effects of oxidants in mechanically developed doughs can, therefore, be listed as:

(1) Oxidation of water soluble S-H protein groups to remove them from the system – this would benefit the dough structure by preventing them from preferentially reacting with the S-H groups of the gluten molecules exposed during the development period.

(2) Causing an -S-S- bond to be formed between a water soluble protein S-H group and a glutenin S-H group, this might well weaken the dough structure.

(3) Causing an -S-S- bond to be formed between two of the glutenin S-H groups exposed during the development period. This would increase the elasticity of the dough structure.

(4) The direct oxidation of an S-H group in a glutenin molecule to a stable form which is then unable to take part in further interchange reactions.

Thus the role of the oxidant is thought to be firstly to remove the water soluble protein S-H groups from the system. These groups will be the most readily reactable ones in the system so this must be the major reaction. The result is a shift of the balance of the reactions of glutenin molecules towards the formation of inter-glutenin -S-S- bonds rather than glutenin-soluble protein -S-S- bonds, thus producing a more elastic structure. It will also increase the degree of reaction of the 'masked' glutenin S-H groups exposed during development – both to increase the number of -S-S- linkages and also to stabilise some in a non-reactive form.

The overall effect is to produce a stable, stronger, more elastic gluten network capable of expanding without rupture, during the rapid growth of the gas cells during the early part of the baking process.

The three oxidants have widely differing reaction rates – potassium iodate reacts almost immediately. Ascorbic acid reacts at a linear rate, the reaction being completed during the normal processing and proof period of 60–90 minutes. Potassium bromate is rather unusual in that it appears that at levels of up to 60 ppm on flour weight it reacts in two stages – a rapid initial reaction of approx. one-tenth of the oxidant, followed by a rather slow linear reaction which is incomplete at room temperature even after several hours. The modes of action of potassium iodate and bromate are essentially similar during the mixing process in spite of their greatly differing overall reaction rates. It may be significant that potassium iodate gives its optimum effect in the region of 6–8 ppm on flour weight whilst bromate is effective at 60–80 ppm each as the sole oxidant in the system.

The rate of reaction of iodate is so swift that it must react totally during the development period. Its action must follow the four possibilities already described. Removal of the water soluble protein -S-H groups to allow the strained S-S bonds to react instead with glutenin -S-H groups (is considered to be) the principle reaction, but the high reactivity of the IO_3 group and its small size allow it to attack also the usually masked glutenin S-H groups exposed during development.

The effect of potassium bromate is much more complex. It may be assumed that the initial effect of potassium bromate is essentially similar to that of potassium iodate. During processing and proof the oxidant might well continue to act somewhat in the manner of a 'bulk fermentation' oxidant system. It has been shown that it also continues to act in the oven when the increase in dough temperature greatly increases the rate of reaction leading to an increase in the number of -S-S- bonds present in the dough piece during the early stages of baking.

Both the iodate and bromate exhibit a particular detrimental property when used in excess – iodate above approximately 12 ppm on flour weight and bromate above 90 ppm in a Chorleywood bread dough produce bread of very large volume with a weak soft (even sticky) crumb, a coarse texture with a tendency to form holes at the moulding lines. This detrimental effect must occur early in the production cycle – being common to both iodate and bromate.

The probable cause is that the non-gluten protein S-H groups are all or almost all removed from the reaction system by the oxidant. The glutenin SH groups are also attached in two ways – as per reactions (3) and (4) – as the level of oxidant increases the total number of SH groups reacted will increase and also reaction (4) becomes increasingly preferred to reaction (3).

The number of -S-S- bonds formed in the gluten may not be greatly increased. In fact as the concentration of oxidant increases and reaction (4) becomes more favoured they may even decrease. The result is a weak but truly elastic structure which is capable of expanding without rupture but offers less resistance to expansion than is optimum, leading to large weak-walled-cells giving the characteristic 'over-oxidised' effect.

Ascorbic acid is thought to have a similar overall effect to that of the two previous oxidants, although it acts at a rather slower rate than iodate. It can be shown that a dough, incorporating ascorbic acid as the sole oxidant, cannot easily be made to demonstrate the over oxidised effect of excess of iodate or bromate. It has been claimed that it is impossible to over-oxidise a dough by the action of ascorbic acid.

The reasons suggested for this phenomenon are that the ascorbic acid being a bulky molecule is not able to attack certain of the S-H groups in the glutenin chain and that this is further exaggerated because there is no initial rapid reaction whilst the dough is in the state of most rapid movement and the glutenin chains are most extended so that their S-H groups are most open to attack. Hence ascorbic acid is able to remove from the system the highly soluble non-glutenin molecules but is not able to cause too high a degree of glutenin cross-linking. It must be remembered that although the oxidant has a profound effect on dough structure in mechanical development processes producing a stable basic gluten film, disulphide/sulphydryl interchange reactions continue to occur during processing proof, and baking of the dough. In the case of potassium bromate and ascorbic acid the continued presence and activity of the oxidants modifies these reactions. In the case of potassium iodate it is the initial basic structure only which is effected.

Section 3 The function of fat

The presence of fat in Chorleywood doughs is essential to the production of acceptable bread.

In contrast to the position of oxidants, where a considerable amount of theoretical speculation has occurred, in the case of fat most people have contented themselves with a description of the benefit confirmed on the final loaf by the inclusion of fat, coupled with an examination of the type and amount of fat which confer the maximum benefit on the finished bread. The effect is easily demonstrated. Two doughs may be processed identically using any of the commercially available machines, following the procedure as outlined earlier, but omitting fat from one of the recipes. The doughs appear identical after mixing and we have ourselves been unable to detect any difference from normal in dough rheological properties either during mixing or at any stage up to the end of final proof. In practical experience the dough piece without fat appears to prove quite normally and as it enters the oven the dough has achieved the proof height one would expect. It is the first ten to fifteen minutes of the baking which are critical. This is the growth period of the loaf during which the rapid increase in loaf volume occurs due to the increased activity of the yeast and to the rapid expansion of the gas which is generated as the temperature rises. A graph of the increase in temperature at the centre of a 2 lb tin loaf against time for a mechanically developed dough on which is superimposed the increase in loaf height at the same time, demonstrates the normal state of affairs.

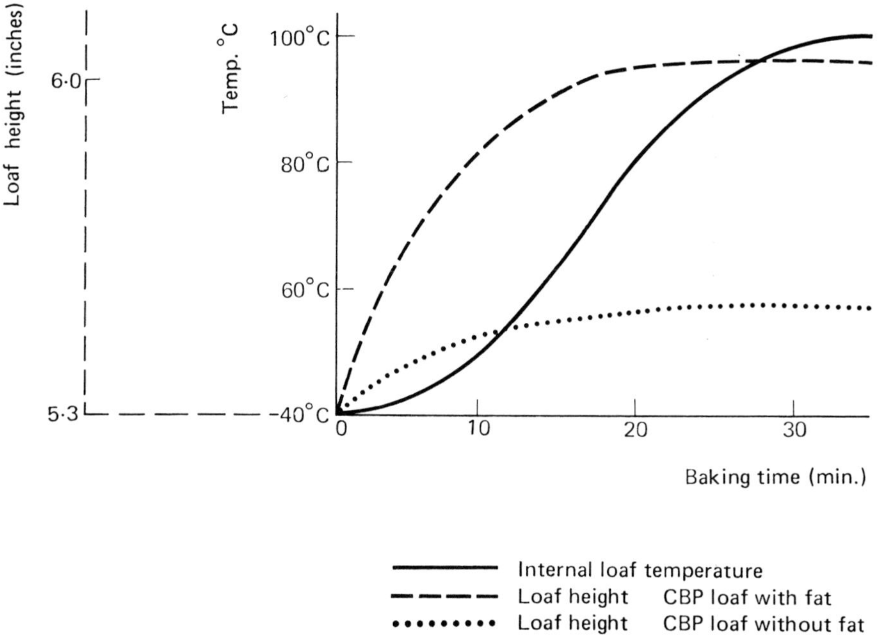

When fat is omitted the usual proof height is obtained. When the loaf is placed in the oven, the lack of fat becomes apparent. There is no growth in the oven, equally, there is no great collapse, the loaf merely bakes at about the same volume as it had at the end of the proof. (See graph page 63)

If we examine the baked bread, the lack of fat can be seen clearly for the great majority of flours, in a low volume loaf with poor crumb colour and a close dense crumb texture, which is especially deficient in crumb softness.

The two relevant components can now be considered. The great majority of flours conform to the behaviour as described – but there are occasionally flours which give satisfactory bread from a recipe containing no added fat. Oven spring is normal, and the general crust and crumb characteristics appear to be in no way unusual. The addition of extra fat does not appear to lead to any further improvements.

It would seem that we might have a considerable portion of the explanation if it were possible to discern the particular attributes of these atypical flours. Unfortunately, none of the usual chemical or physical flour tests seem to pick out any difference. It must be stressed that the 'few unusual flours' are not from a particular wheat variety or flour grist as far as we can tell. Similarly there are occasionally flours which seem to require excessively high levels of fat to obtain satisfactory bread, and even the optimum loaf is of a poor quality, although various factors such as a lack of cereal alpha amylase can contribute to such a loss of quality, particularly in a deficiency in oven spring.

Wheat flour analysis gives about 2% of flour as total lipid. When this lipid is extracted by butanol/water solvent systems the resulting gluten has greatly altered attributes. Lipid extraction with water, saturated in butanol, yields a flour which requires a fourfold increase in development time. It was necessary to enclose the doughball in a nylon bag during washing in distilled water to retain a gluten mass. The coherency of this gluten under strain is very small. The gluten is extremely fragile, with a very low elastic limit, i.e. it ruptures easily. More important there is no plasticity. Bread produced conventionally from flour after lipid extraction shows similar deficiencies to those present when mechanical dough development bread is made without fat. The original character of the bread can be restored by either re-introducing the original lipid into the formula or alternatively by introducing a sufficient amount of normal shortening to replace the flour lipid. We must assume that the 'odd unusual' flours might have peculiar lipid compositions but detailed analysis of this small fraction of the flour is necessary before any reliable conclusions can be drawn.

We now come to the main consideration, the amount and type of fat itself. Originally 0·7 % of commercial shortening on flour weight was used; as liquid oil has no improving effect, it would seem likely that the solid portion of the fat is of importance – at the end of proof, about 5–10 % of most commercial shortenings would still be solid. A natural step was to produce fats with a higher solids content, 15 to 30 % at about 35°C – these proved effective at 0·35 %.

These preliminary observations pointed the way to finding the optimum fat for the process. We now seem to be at the state of knowledge where we can tentatively conclude that there are three points of importance:

(a) The percentage of solids present in the fat.
(b) The state of dispersion of the fat.
(c) The length of the fatty acid chains which make up the fat.

A series of experiments has been done in the test bakery of the British Arkady to examine each of these three points separately. In the initial trials we limited our 'fats' to normal triglycerides of fatty acids at greater or lesser degrees of hydrogenation.

Plots of percentage solids of fats over a temperature range from 20°C to 60°C were obtained for a series of fat blends. The minimum percentage of fat on flour weight which gave the optimum fat response showed that fat A was equally effective at 4½ oz/sk as fat C is at 2 lb/sk and fat B at 1 lb/sk. Further increasing the amount of fat in any of the three cases did not lead to a great improvement in bread quality.

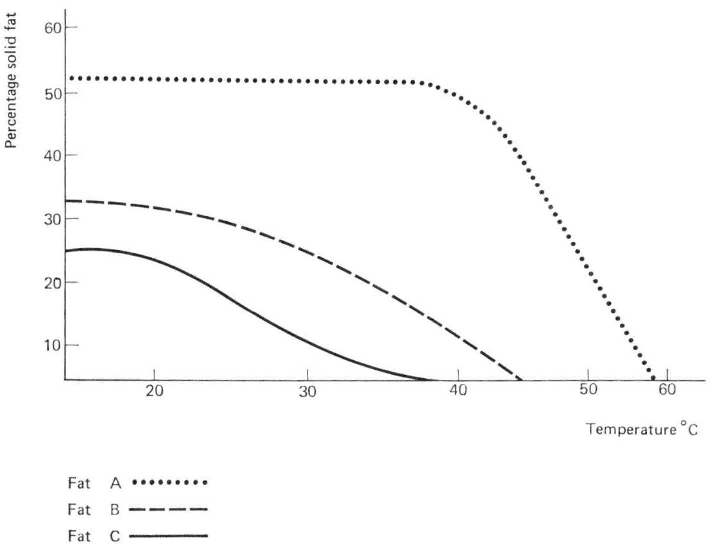

We conclude that the optimum fat effect, i.e. the maximum improvement in bread quality using the minimum quantity of fat, occurred when the fat was fully hydrogenated.

As has been stated, liquid oil has no improving effect even at high rates of addition so the effect of fully hydrogenated fats at various levels was studied by pre-dispersing the fat in liquid oil and adding the fine dispersion to the ingredients in the mixer immediately prior to mixing.

Bread was then made from each dough following standard mechanical dough development procedure: employing the same grade of flour from one flour mill, the flour being of the grade recommended for mechanical dough development and each batch was analysed to ensure as little variation as possible between batches. A control dough was included which contained only liquid oil at a rate of 2 lb/sk. When solid fats were to be pre-dispersed, the solid fat was melted and poured into liquid oil (again taken at 2 lb/sk) and the mixture allowed to cool. Solid fat is not appreciably soluble in liquid oil and sets up in the oil as a fine dispersion.

The resulting bread was examined after twenty-four hours for crumb softness and oven spring.

The usual pattern of results may be expressed graphically.

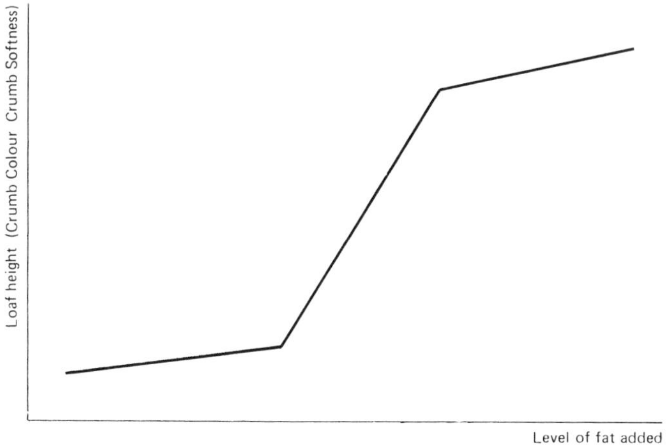

In each case the parameter being measured, loaf height, crumb softness or crumb colour appeared to be only slightly influenced until the weight of added fat reached a fairly narrow critical range. Within this range dramatic improvements in all parameters occurred, after which only marginal further improvement took place even with large increases in the level of added fat. The general pattern suggests some sort of surface effect, no improvement occurring till some unspecified dough component is fully coated or in some way reacted with the added fat. Once the layer is complete there appears to be no great benefit from the inclusion of further amounts of fat.

Fully hydrogenated triglycerides were very effective and the length of the fatty acid chain was also found to be important.

It is possible to confirm to some extent that it is only the hard fat which is effective, by experiments similar to those conducted at the FMBIRA, Chorleywood, where a series of trials were done in which hard fats were dispersed in mineral oil as the sole fat source, giving satisfactory bread. A variety of compounds have also been examined to try to establish which properties allow the correct growth of the loaf in the oven. Further research at Chorleywood has shown that a 'fat effect' can be obtained from straight chain hydrocarbons. A series of hydrocarbons with chain lengths C18 n-octadecane, C20 eicosane

C22 n–decosane and C24 n–tetracosane were dispersed in groundnut oil and added to doughs at a level of 0·7% on flour weight in a similar manner to our own work. The shorter chain lengths hydrocarbons gave a reduction in loaf volume but the longest chain had an effect parallel to that of glycerol tristearin. We have ourselves found stearyl tartrate to be equally as effective as the best triglyceride fats on a weight basis.

A further interesting observation in our own test bakery work was that sodium stearate or even stearic acid was effective, although not very efficient, on a weight basis as the sole 'hard fat' source whilst methyl stearate with a similar composition but being (a) less ionic and (b) of a much lower melting point, appeared ineffective even at levels of addition of up to 2 lb/sk.

Several papers describing fundamental work on this problem have been published by Dr Daniels and others, principally in the *Journal of Food Science and Agriculture*. It would be presumptuous to attempt to summarise all this effort in a short outline of this type, but I would refer to one or two of the many important observations.

When a wheat flour and water are mixed into a dough, a proportion of the naturally occurring wheat lipid is bound into the protein network. In the case of mechanically developed doughs this proportion is considerably higher than is the case of bulk fermented ones, although many factors such as vacuum level, etc., can greatly affect the final equilibrium. It may be that the added fat replaces the bound lipid in the protein structure, thereby releasing wheat lipid. The natural bound lipids contain a fraction which is more polar or water attracting than the triglyceride added fat which replaces them so that the nature of the protein structure is to some degree modified by the exchange, to become less water attractive, and the more water attractive lipids are released into the watery dough medium to give a dough more similar in free lipid composition to that of a bulk fermented dough.

To summarise

(1) The lipid present naturally in flour forms a necessary part of the structure of gluten – being especially important with respect to plastic deformation.

(2) In conventional processes to produce a satisfactory bread either this lipid must be present, or else its absence must be compensated for by the addition of triglyceride fat.

(3) For mechanically developed doughs. In the absence of added fat there is for most flours no oven spring in the early part of baking and the resultant loaf has a very close texture, lacking colour and being especially deficient in crumb softness.

(4) High melting point triglyceride fats are particularly effective as a fat source.

(5) A straight chain hydrocarbon of chain length C24 has an improving effect similar to that of fat but is less efficient on a weight basis.

(6) Distearyl tartrate is very effective in this process.

It is clear that much more work is still needed before the nature of the fat effect can be fully explained. However, the following considerations would seem to be of importance.

The critical stage appears to be in the first stages of baking when the dough structure is being subjected to forces which causes the gluten to be in a state of fairly rapid plastic deformation at a temperature up to about 55°C. Until this time dough rheological testing machines were not able to detect weakness in the gluten structure. The evidence would seem to suggest that it is the long non-ionic hydrocarbon chains which are the function groups in the added fat. The very small amount of fat necessary and the need for it to be in such a fine dispersion to be effective at a low level – approximately 1 part glycerol tristearin to 160 parts glutenin protein (on a dry weight basis) – would suggest that the fat is in some way directly incorporated into the protein structure, possibly by Van der Waals forces, where it forms an integral part of the gluten film giving stability to the structure. It may be that portions of the protein chain which are coiled or linked to naturally occurring flour lipid and are not normally exposed to the watery dough medium due to the relatively gentle action of fermentation are forcibly exposed by the severe action of mechanical dough development, and it is by being selectively absorbed at these points that the hydrocarbon chains in some way help to stabilise the structure. Each of the three factors, work level and intensity, oxidant type and level and fat type and quantity is of critical importance in a mechanical dough development system. It is established beyond doubt that the high rate and level of work input of mechanical dough processing profoundly effects the wheat gluten network in a dough when compared with a dough mixed in a slow-speed machine. The role of oxidant is complex but its overall effect is to allow the building of cross links [-S-S-] bonds between gluten molecules to strengthen and stabilise the structure. The role of fat is equally critical but as yet has not been fully defined although a direct surface reaction with the hydrated gluten network must be suspected.

Basic factors in the Chorleywood Bread Process.

Variable	*External View*
Work Level IN EACH LOAF 2lb./sk Lard Normal Oxidant	CONTROL  $2\frac{1}{2}$ watt hrs./lb · $3\frac{1}{2}$ watt hrs./lb. · 5 watt hrs./lb. · $7\frac{1}{2}$ watt hrs./lb. · 10 watt hrs./lb
Oxidant Level IN EACH LOAF 5 watt hrs./lb. work 2lb./sk Lard	CONTROL  No Oxidant · $\frac{1}{2}$ Normal Oxidant · Normal Oxidant · Slight Excess · Gross Excess
Fat Level IN EACH LOAF 5 watt hrs. /lb. work Normal Oxidant	CONTROL  No Fat · 1 lb./sk Lard · 2 lb./sk Lard · 6 oz./sk Optimum Fat · 4 lb./sk Groundnut Oil

Internal View	*Variable*
CONTROL  watt hrs./lb. · 3½ watt hrs./lb. · 5 watt hrs./lb. · 7½ watt hrs./lb. · 10 watt hrs./lb.	**Work Level** IN EACH LOAF 2lb./sk Lard Normal Oxidant
CONTROL  o Oxidant · ½ Normal Oxidant · Normal Oxidant · Slight Excess · Gross Excess	**Oxidant Level** IN EACH LOAF 5 watt hrs. /lb. work 2lb./sk Lard
CONTROL  No Fat · 1 lb./sk Lsrd · 2 lb./sk Lard · 6 oz./sk Optimum Fat · 2 lb./sk Groundnut Oil	**Fat Level** IN EACH LOAF 5 watt hrs./lb. work Normal Oxidant

PART III

Practice

Practical aspects of the Chorleywood Bread Process

In the following four chapters it is proposed to deal with the commercial production of bread by mechanical dough development processes. This will be discussed under the following headings:

(1) Chorleywood mixing machinery – This chapter will also briefly examine the ancillary plant required by the process.

(2) Raw materials – There are a number of excellent publications dealing with baking raw material. It is intended in this chapter therefore to concentrate on the special requirements of the particular process.

(3) Processing considerations – The main emphasis is inevitably on the production of a standard 28 oz white loaf using a batch mixing process. Processing modifications required for a continuous mixing process will be outlined and the production of small goods and special breads will also be touched on.

4. Chorleywood mixing machinery

The commercial development of the Chorleywood process has called for the design and production of a new range of bakery equipment.

The mixer

Its power requirements are far greater than those of a mixer intended for a bulk fermentation process. Even the 'high-speed' mixers intended for bulk fermentation dough mixing would require a minimum mixing time of at least twelve minutes to impart the necessary five watt hours per pound of mechanical work to a dough. The Chorleywood process requires that this work be imparted within at the most four and a half minutes. In addition it is necessary to incorporate into such a machine new control systems not previously required for bakery machinery, a device capable of accurately measuring the amount of work imparted to the dough, and in the case of plant machinery it is desirable to automate as far as possible the mixing sequence. The batch machines, particularly those of larger capacities, also require, to produce the optimum bread, a vacuum to be applied to the mixing chamber.

Ancillary equipment

Plant scale batch mixers require the two bulk ingredients to be fed to the machine at a rate sufficient to be able to recharge the mixer with the desired pre-weighed amounts of flour and water at the end of each mixing cycle. The cycle must also be arranged so that it is possible to introduce small ingredients, salt, yeast, Dynarex,* etc., to each batch of dough prior to mixing.

In the case of continuous mixers all the necessary ingredients must be continuously and accurately introduced at the desired rate to the mixing chamber.

A further possible problem is that as mechanical work is imparted

* One of Arkady's C B P Dough Conditioners.

to a dough there is an inevitable temperature rise. If five watt hours per pound is introduced in the relatively short mixing period this rise is in the region of 26°F and there is insufficient time for the heat to be dissipated. If the ambient temperature and hence the flour and mains water temperatures become too high, it may be necessary to provide a device to supply chilled water in order to control the final temperature of the developed dough.

Let us now consider individual items of machinery in some detail.

Mechanically developed dough production by means of a batch mixer
As the Tweedy is by far the most widely used batch mixer in the British

MIXING CAPACITIES

IMPERIAL

Mixer Model Type	*Capacity Cu. Ft.*	*No. of Mixes per hour*	*Charge per mix Minimum lbs.*	*Charge per mix Maximum lbs.*	*Maximum Dough Output per hour lbs.*
Tweedy					
35	2·071	8	7	60	480
70	3·819	8	14	121	968
140	7·374	10	50	235	2350
160	8·450	11	50	275	3025
200	10·00	11	75	340	3740
4400	10·00	12	105	340	4080
300	17·25	11	120	595	7140
6600	17·25	12	150	660	7260

METRIC

Mixer Model Type	*Capacity Cu. M.*	*No. of Mixes per hour*	*Charge per mix Minimum kgs.*	*Charge per mix Maximum kgs.*	*Maximum Dough Output per hour kgs.*
Tweedy					
35	·058	8	3	27	216
70	·108	8	6	55	440
140	·209	10	22	107	1070
160	·239	11	22	125	1375
200	·283	11	34	154	1694
4400	·283	12	50	154	1848
300	·493	11	55	270	3240
6600	·493	12	68	300	3300

Mixing capacities.

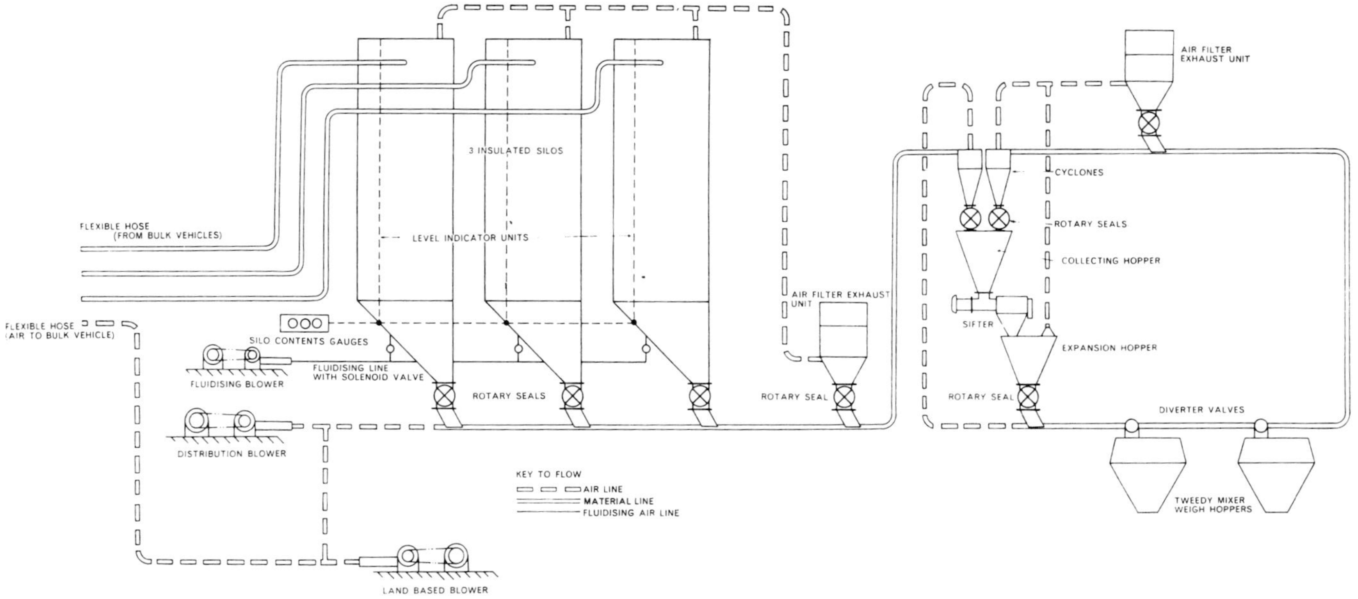

Flour storage and handling plant feeding two Tweedy high-speed mixers.

baking industry it will serve to illustrate this method of dough development. A range of similar machines exist to cater for a wide range of mixing capacity requirements (see table page 75).

The larger machines from the Tweedy 160 upwards are intended for plant bakeries and all the general comments – appropriate for automatic batch mixers – which have already been made, apply.

The main piece of ancillary equipment is the automatic flour-feed system. This is absolutely necessary if the mixer is to be fed with flour quickly enough to maintain adequate rate of dough production.

A typical automatic flour-feed system suitable for feeding one or more of the larger Tweedy mixers is illustrated opposite.

View of the automatic Tweedy 160.

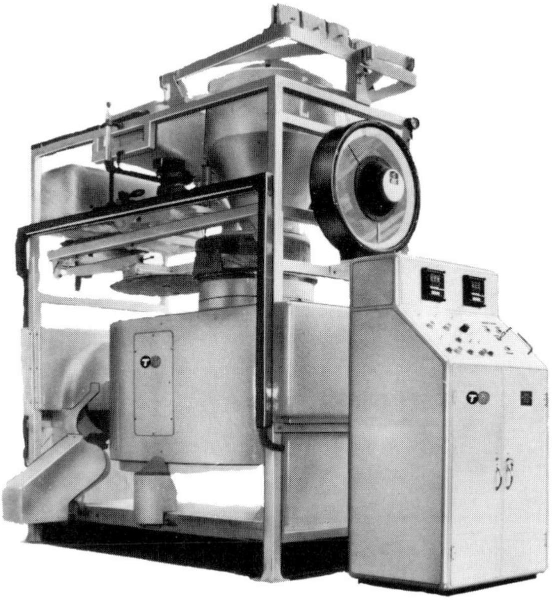

The siting of the machine itself is of some importance, principally to ensure that the dough can be speedily and efficiently transferred from the machine, after mixing, to the hopper of the divider for subsequent processing.

We may now consider the dough developing machine itself and examine the way in which it performs its complete mixing cycle. Typical of the range of plant production mixers is the Tweedy 160 (illustrated above).

Leading Particulars

Mixing capacities		*Electrical*	
Mixing chamber capacity	8·450 ft^3 (0·239 m^3)	Supply required for standard machine	388/440V, 3-phase, 50 Hz, 85 amp.
Bread Mixing		Water Supply	
Minimum charge/mix	50 lb (22 kg)	110 gall/hour (500 l/hour) tempered or chilled water for production of 3025 lb (1375 kg) of dough/hour.	
Maximum charge/mix	275 lb (125 kg)		
No. of mixes/hour	11		
Maximum dough output/hour	3025 lb (1375 kg)		
Confectionery Mixing		Flour Feed	
Cake batter charge/ mix	240 lb. (109 kg)	Feed rate	160 lb (72·6 kg) in 1·5 minutes when required.
Paste Short and Puff charge/mix	240 lb (109 kg)		
No. of mixes/hour	12		
Output/hour	2880 lb (1306 kg)	Height of delivery from floor	11 ft (3·35 m)
Dimensions			
Height	11 ft 3 in. (3·429 m)		
Length	10 ft 6 in. (3·200 m)		
Width	5 ft (1·524 m)		
Floor Loading			
Dead weight	3 tons 5 cwt (3302 kg)		

Outline of operation

The diagram on page 79 shows the machine in simplified form. The mixing chamber and motor are carried in a frame which can be pivoted about a horizontal axis to one of three fixed positions. These positions are:

(1) 'Full tilt' for ejection of the finished mix.

(2) 'Half tilt' for the manual addition of ingredients such as yeast, salt, etc.

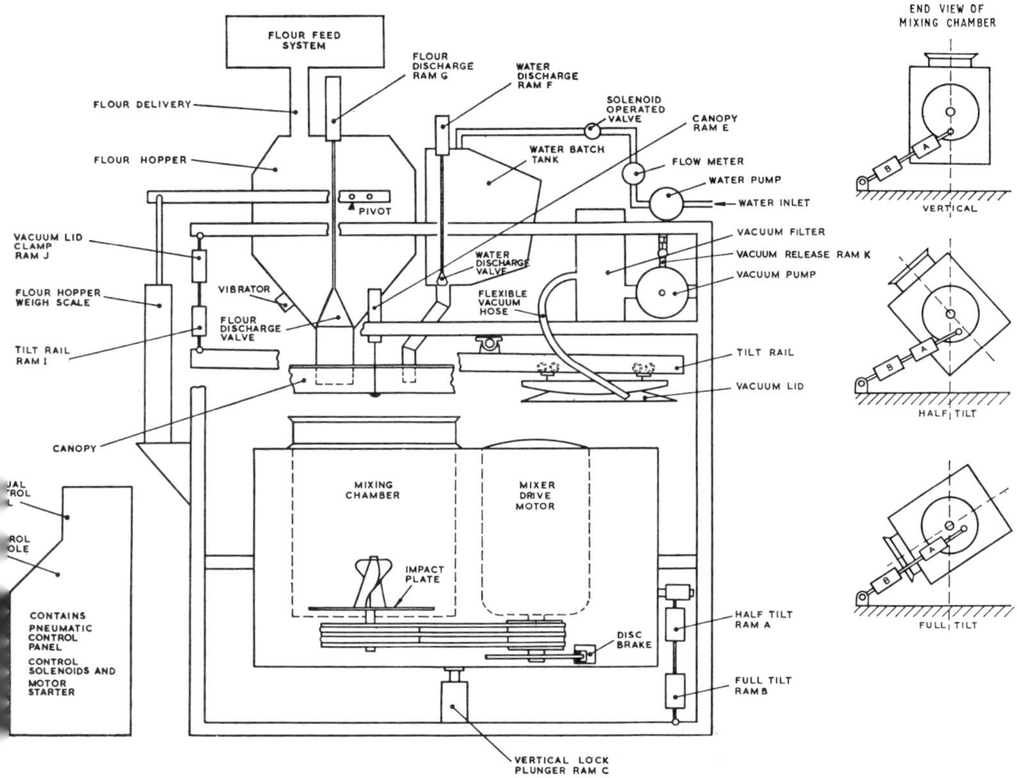

The Tweedy 160 Automatic Dough Mixer. Simplified diagram.

(3) 'Vertical' for the automatic addition of water and flour and for mixing.

The machine automatically performs the task of adding the correct quantities of water and flour for mixing doughs. These quantities are set into the control circuits of the machine prior to the mixing operation. Other dough ingredients are added manually when, early in the machine cycle, the mixing chamber is caused to pause at the half-tilt position as it is being turned from the full tilt to the vertical position.

When all the dough ingredients are in the mixing chamber, air is partly evacuated from the chamber.

The machine is designed to mechanically 'develop' dough by means of the Chorleywood process. In the process it is necessary to determine the amount of work that is required to be expended on the dough during mixing. The amount of work required depends upon the mathematical product of the weight of dough being mixed, which is variable, and an experimentally determined 'work factor', which is constant. The amount of work required is calculated by the operator and set manually into the control unit. The amount of work expended on the dough is measured and compared automatically with the pre-set value. When the set value and the measured value are equal, the mixing action is stopped.

When mixing is complete, the dough is ejected by automatic tilting of the mixing chamber to the full tilt position.

Automatic sequence of operations

The automatic sequence of operations is controlled by penumatic and electro-mechanical devices. The pneumatic control panel and electrical control equipment are housed in the control console.

Start of sequence

At the start of the sequence, the water batch tank and flour hoppers contain the correct quantities of their respective ingredients and the mixing chamber is at the full tilt position.

The sequence is started by pressing the CYCLE START push-button on the control console. This causes ram A to retract and turn the mixing chamber to the half tilt position. The chamber remains in the half tilt position for approximately five seconds to permit the manual addition of dough ingredients other than flour and water. The time for which the chamber is kept at the half-tilt position can be increased if required by means of a manual override control.

After five seconds have elapsed with the mixing chamber at the half-tilt position, the penumatic control unit causes ram B to retract. The mixing chamber is thus turned to the vertical position. At the same time, the disc brake is released.

The attainment of the vertical position is signalled to the control unit, which then causes the vertical lock plunger ram C to extend. The vertical lock plunger prevents excessive vibration of the mixing chamber when the mixing action is in progress.

When the mixing chamber is locked in the vertical position, rams E1 and E2 are caused to extend to lower the canopy over the mouth of the mixing chamber (ram E2 is on the side of the canopy opposite to ram E1 and is not shown on Fig. 4). The purpose of the canopy is to prevent the scattering of flour and water when these ingredients are discharged from the hopper and batch tank respectively.

Addition of water and flour

When the canopy has been lowered the water discharge valve is opened by means of ram F. The contents of the water batch tank are thereby discharged into the mixing chamber.

Ram G is then operated and the flour-hopper discharge valve opened to permit the contents of the hopper to fall into the mixing chamber. A vibrator, mounted on the hopper, is caused to operate to assist in the complete emptying of the hopper.

When the hopper is empty the operations directly concerned with the mixing of the dough or pastry are continued. Also, the recharging of the hopper and water batch tank is begun. The mixing sequence is described first.

Mixing sequence

After all the ingredients have been put into the mixing chamber, the canopy is raised by the retraction of rams E1 and E2. The control unit then causes ram I to extend thereby tilting the rails from which the vacuum lid is suspended. The vacuum lid travels on its rollers down the tilted rails until it reaches end stops, which results in the lid being positioned above the mixing chamber. Ram J is then caused to extend and the lid rails are tilted further thereby clamping the vacuum lid over the mixing chamber.

The vacuum pump is started and air is evacuated from the chamber. Approximately twenty-five seconds after the starting of the vacuum pump the mixing motor is started. The motor is started in 'star' to reduce the starting current. After four seconds the motor is switched to 'delta' and at the same time the measurement of energy expenditure, when mixing dough, or time, when making pastry, is begun.

The energy expended on the dough being mixed is measured by

means of watt-hour meter. The watt-hour meter is used to measure the electrical consumption of the mixer motor. This measurement is compensated in order to take into account electrical and frictional losses of the motor and bearings. Thus, only the work expended on the dough is measured.

When the work expended on the dough becomes equivalent to the amount of work manually pre-set, the motor is stopped.

When the motor has stopped the mixing chamber vacuum is released by the operation of ram K. Rams I and J are then caused to retract, thereby removing the vacuum lid from the mixing chamber and tilting the lid rail so that the vacuum lid is carried on its rollers clear of the mixing chamber.

The mixer brake is applied and rams A and B are caused to extend to turn the mixing chamber into the full tilt position. The contents of the mixing chamber are thus ejected. Assistance in ejection is provided by an 'inching' facility which permits the mixing motor to be switched on for short periods by means of a manually operated INCH push-button.

Flour hopper recharge sequence

The flour hopper is weighed by means of the weigh scale. Electrical contacts, in the weigh scale, close when:

(1) The flour hopper is empty.

(2) The flour hopper contains the full weight of flour for a single mix cycle.

(3) An intermediate weight which is used when two grades of flour are combined is contained in the hopper.

Weights (2) and (3) can be adjusted manually so that variations in mix weights can be accommodated.

After the flour has been discharged from the hopper the flour discharge valve is closed. (A signal is sent to the flour-feed mechanism which causes the hopper to be filled again after the mixer motor is started during a mixing cycle.)

It is possible to refill the hopper from one or both of two flour sources. The mode of feeding is selected by means of manually operated switches, BULK and SIFTER on the control console. If BULK is selected, flour is fed from a bulk supply into the hopper. This feed is stopped when the weighing complete contacts in the weigh scale are closed.

If SIFTER is selected, flour is fed from another supply (usually a bag feed sifter) into the hopper. This feed is stopped when the weighing complete contacts in the weigh scale close. If both BULK and SIFTER are selected, flour from the bulk store source is first fed to the hopper. This feed is stopped when the intermediate contacts in the weigh scale close. Then flour from the second source is fed to the hopper until the weighing complete contacts are closed.

With the intermediate weight facility it is possible to adjust the flour mix quality as required.

Water batch tank recharge

Water is delivered into the batch tank via a water flow meter by means of a pump. The water pump is switched on at the same time as the vacuum pump is started prior to the mixing action taking place.

The water flow meter produces electrical pulses the repetition frequency of which is directly proportional to the flow rate. These pulses are fed to a pulse counter on the control console. The counter is set manually to the required water quantity. When the flow meter pulse count reaches the manually pre-set water count, a contact is opened which causes the pump to stop and a solenoid operated water valve to close.

Emergency stop

An EMERGENCY STOP push-button is provided which makes it possible to stop the machine safely in mid-cycle.

Operating instructions

Calculation of watt-hour counter setting

Work factor = 0·4 hp min/lb
= 5 watt hours/lb weight of total ingredients

The watt-hour counter reads 1 unit per 10 watt hours.

Therefore:

$$\text{Watt-hour counter setting} = \frac{\text{total ingredient weight (lbs)}}{2}$$

Example:

Flour	160 lb	
Dynarex	1 lb	10 oz
Yeast	3 lb	
Salt	2 lb	12 oz
Water	97 lb	
	264 lb	

Total weight of ingredients = 264 lb

Watt-hour counter setting $= \frac{264}{2} = 132$

Setting up procedures

Watt-hour counter

The watt-hour counter is the right-hand counter on the panel facia. Set the three setting knobs to indicate the required figure.

Water counter

The water counter is the left-hand counter on the control panel facia. Set the three setting knobs to indicate the required figure.

Note: The standard calibration of the water counter is one unit per pound of water. Variations (e.g. one unit per quarter-litre) are indicated on the front of the counter.

Aquatrol probe

The Aquatrol probe and sight glass are mounted next to the batch tank at the front of the mixer. The procedure for adjusting the probe is as follows:

(1) Slacken the coupling nut at the top of the sight glass.
(2) Slacken the allen screw which holds the probe unit in position.
(3) Set the tip of the probe to the required level in the sight glass.
(4) Re-tighten the allen screw and the coupling nut.

Flour scale

The 'final weigh' and 'intermediate weigh' contacts on the weigh scale are adjusted as follows:

(1) Unlock the cover at the centre of the weigh scale and remove it.

(2) Rotate the lever marked FINAL until the black pointer on the weigh scale indicates the total weight of flour required.

(3) If a blend of sifter and bulk flours is required, slacken the coupling between the FINAL and INTERMEDIATE levers, and set the INTERMEDIATE lever to indicate the required weight of bulk flour on the subsidiary scale on the lever housing.

(4) Recheck the FINAL setting, lock the coupling, and replace the cover.

Timer

The timer is mounted on the paxolin panel, access to which is gained by opening the lower doors of the control console. The dial of the timer is calibrated in seconds.

To adjust the timer, set the pointers to the required figure by means of the central setting knob. During operation of the timer, the black pointer remains at the present figure and the red pointer moves back to zero.

Panel air pressure

The air-pressure gauge mounted on the control panel facia should indicate 80 psi. The pressure is adjusted by means of the valve at the bottom of the regulator, which is mounted in front of the pneumatic panel. The regulator is the second unit from the left.

Operating sequence *(see illustration, page* 86*)*

(1) Set the HALF-TILT HOLD lever on the control panel to HOLD.

(2) Depress CYCLE START.

(3) When the mixer is at half tilt, add the pre-weighed fine ingredients, e.g. salt, yeast, oxidant or proprietary additives.

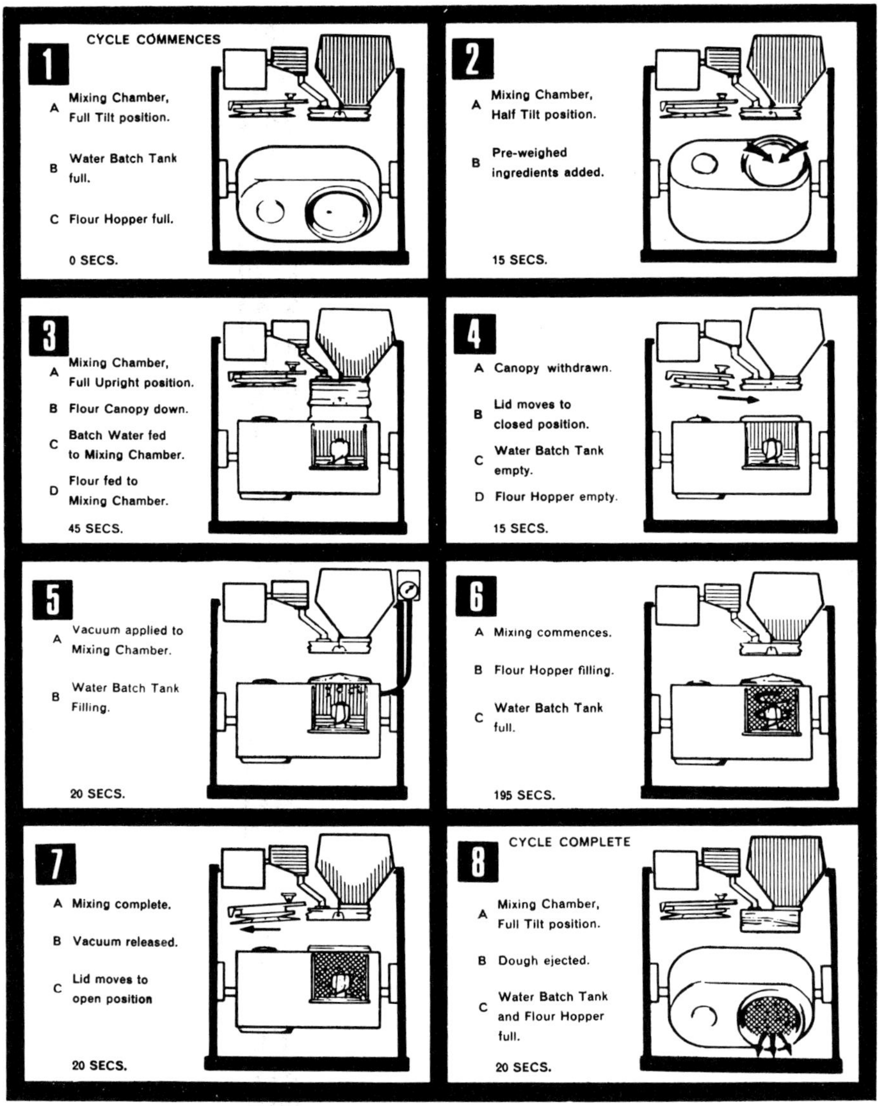

The Tweedy 160 Automatic Dough Mixer. Operating sequence.

Note: The mixer will remain at half-tilt for as long as the HAFT-TILT HOLD lever is at HOLD. If fully automatic operation is required, step (1) of this procedure should be ignored, and instead a check made that the lever is at NORMAL. Under these circumstances the mixer will rise to half tilt and, after a delay, continue to vertical. The delay is normally set to be about five seconds; it can, however, be altered to suit bakery requirements (see maintenance; checks and adjustments).

(4) When mixing is required, set the HALF-TILT HOLD lever to NORMAL. This allows the cycle to continue.

(5) When the vacuum motor starts, check that the water counter is recording (if vacuum is not being used, check that the water counter starts recording before the mixer motor starts).

(6) When the mixer motor starts, check that flour is being metered by the pointer on the weigh scale.

(7) After mixing has finished and the mixer has come to rest in the full-tilt position, press MIXER INCH on the control panel and keep it depressed until the dough has been ejected.

(8) Repeat from step 1.

Note: If the dough is not required immediately, set the HALF-TILT HOLD lever to HOLD before the mixer motor stops. On completion of the mix, the mixer will come to half-tilt and remain there until the lever is restored to NORMAL. (Tweedy doughs should not be delayed by more than five minutes – see Emergency Stop Procedure).

Time measurement procedure

If a time-controlled mix is required instead of an energy-controlled mix, carry out the following procedures before starting the production cycle.

(1) Set the timer to the required figure (see setting up procedure).

(2) Switch on the key-operated AUXILIARY TIME CONTROL switch on the control panel facia.

Aquatrol water measurement procedure

If for any reason it is necessary to use the Aquatrol unit rather than the water counter to control the batch tank water level, carry out the following procedure:

(1) Set the Aquatrol probe to the required level (see setting-up procedure).

(2) If the batch tank already contains more water than is required, remove the surplus by means of the drain valve.

(3) Switch on the key-operated AUXILIARY WATER CONTROL switch on the control panel facia.

(4) If the batch tank contains less water than is required, depress WATER MANUAL on the control panel.

Complete weigh override procedure

If it is required to deliver to the mixing chamber less flour than there is in the hopper, carry out the following procedure:

(1) Carry out steps 1 to 4 of the production cycle procedure.

(2) When the FLOUR VALVE operation sequence lamp comes on, observe the pointer on the weigh scale.

(3) When the required weight of flour has been delivered, depress WEIGHING COMPLETE (OVERRIDE) on the control panel facia.

(4) Complete the production cycle procedure.

Emergency stop procedure

A. Plant breakdown

In the event of an emergency arising from a plant breakdown (oven, prover, etc.) it may be necessary to suspend dough production. If a dough is in the process of preparation all that is necessary is to set the HALF-TILT HOLD lever on the control panel to HOLD. This allows the machine to finish its cycle but retains the mixing chamber in the half tilt position, thereby preventing dough discharge into the system.

B. Mixer breakdown

If it is necessary to stop the Tweedy 160 because of a malfunction or other emergency:

DEPRESS EMERGENCY STOP on the control panel.

The emergency stop valve removes main air from the pneumatic system, and the main air pressure switch stops the mixer motor and vacuum motor if mixing is in progress.

The dough can now be cut manually from the mixing chamber if required.

After an emergency stop, two reset methods are available:

(1) To continue the cycle, depress RESET on the control panel. The cycle will continue only if the mixer motor had not started at the time EMERGENCY STOP was depressed.

(2) To cancel the remainder of the cycle and return the mixer to full tilt, depress CYCLE RESET on the pneumatic panel then depress RESET on the control panel.

Warning: Tweedy doughs that have been delayed by more than fifteen minutes should not be used through the plant in bulk. They can, however, be added to subsequent mixes in quantities of about 17 lb per mix without detriment.

Shutdown procedure

(1) Before the last mix:

(a) Set the WATER switch to STOP.
(b) Set the FLOUR switches to STOP.

(2) After the last mix:

(a) Set all switches on the control panel to STOP.
(b) Switch off the main isolator.
(c) Open the batch tank drain valve.
(d) Carry out the daily routine maintenance schedule.

A number of machinery manufacturers now offer batch mechanical dough development machines. Although there are variations in machine design, the problems presented to the manufacturers are the same:

(1) Feeding of ingredients to the mixer.
(2) Cooling feed water to the mixer if necessary.
(3) Adequate control systems to ensure that the correct level of work is imparted to the dough.
(4) Dough discharge for further plant processing.

The leading British manufacturers of batch mixers, apart from Tweedy of Burnley Ltd, are:

Baker Perkins Ltd.
G. & R. Gilbert Ltd.
Mono Universal Baking Machinery
The Hobart Manufacturing Co. Ltd.

Mechanically developed dough production by means of a continuous dough developer

Although the CBP was conceived as a batch process, a number of machines were also designed to incorporate a continuous dough development step. Direct panning has never been carried out successfully in the British baking industry, but continuous development followed immediately by dividing has found a place. The only machine at present in wide commercial use is the Oakes continuous mixer modifier; its production cycle will therefore serve to illustrate this method of dough production.

The Oakes continuous mixer modifiers have been produced in five sizes:

The 8D 15/8 with a maximum dough throughput of 1800 lb per hour,
The 8D 30/10 with a maximum throughput of 3150 lb per hour,
The 8D 30/12 with a maximum throughput of 3370 lb per hour,
The 10D 50 with a maximum throughput of 4950 lb per hour, and
The Twin 8D 30/12 with a maximum throughput of 6750 lb per hour.

Further details of the performance of these machines are shown in the performance chart (below):

Model	*Dough Production*				*Flour Usage*				*Power Input at 0·4 hp*		*Approximate Dimensions*				*Approx. Weight-lb.*
	lb./hr.		*lb./mins.*		*Kgs./hr.*		*Sacks/hour*		*Mins./lb.*		*A*	*B*	*C*	*D*	
	Min.	*Max.*	*Min.*	*Max.*	*Min.*	*Max.*	*Min.*	*Max.*	*Min.*	*Max.*					
8D 15/8	900	1800	15	30	408	817	2	4	6	12	4′ 5″	3′ 6″	9′11″	2′ 6½″	3800
8D 30/10	1150	3150	19	53	523	1430	2·5	7	7·65	21	4′ 8″	3′ 9″	8′ 3″	3′ 7″	5000
8D 30/12	1150	3310	19	56·2	523	1530	7·5	7.5	7·65	22·5	4′ 8″	3′ 9″	8′ 9″	3′ 7″	5200
10D 50	1800	4950	30	82·5	817	2250	4	11	12	33	4′ 10″	3′ 9″	10′ 2″	3′ 8″	6700
Twin 8D 30/12	1150	6740	19	112·4	523	3060	2·5	15	7·65	45	4′ 8″	3′ 9″	8′ 9″	3′ 7″	10400

Performance of the continuous mixer/modifiers.

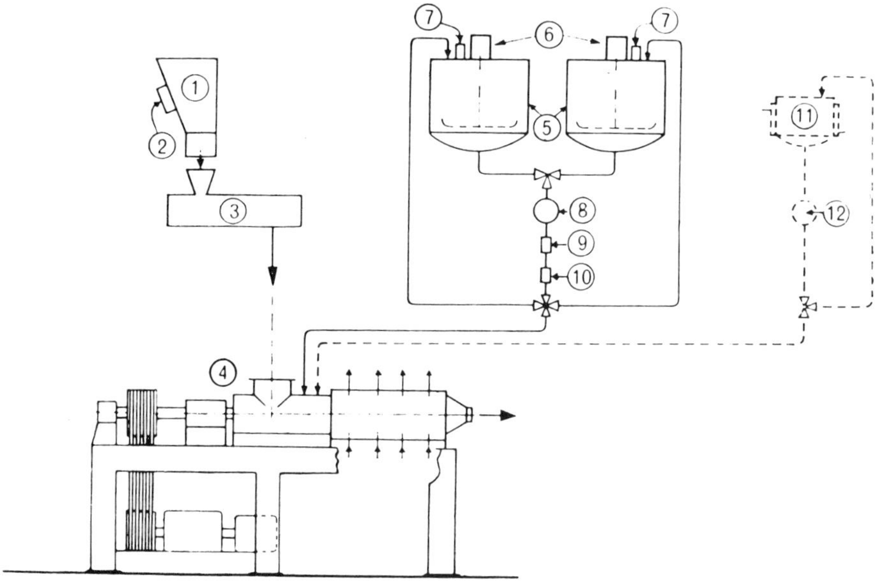

Top, Oakes continuous mechanical dough development installation.

Above, typical flow diagram for the Oakes continuous dough development installation

Typical plant layout

A commercial Oakes continuous mechanical dough development installation designed for the Chorleywood Bread Process is shown on page 91. Also illustrated on page 91 is a typical flow diagram for this type of plant.

Flour from bulk storage or sacks is fed from a hopper (1) by means of a vibratory flour feed (2) to a constant weigh feeder (3) and thence via a small feed hopper directly into the mixer/modifier (4); two liquor tanks (5), each of 75 imperial gallons capacity, are provided for the preparation and storage of the liquor which comprises water, salt, yeast and improver. Each tank is fitted with an agitator (6), a low-level alarm system (7) and a further minimum flour alarm system is also incorporated. Facilities are also installed for the re-circulation of liquor back to the hold tank.

The liquor is pumped by a positive displacement pump (8) through an in-line filter (9) and then injected directly into the mixer/modifier via a manually controlled flow-meter (10). The fat injection system consists of a thermostatically controlled tank (11) of 15 imperial gallons held at a temperature such that the molten fat can be accurately metered via the fat pump (12) directly into the mixer/modifier. (However, the fat feeding

Good-quality loaf produced from the Oakes system
(a) internal view *(b) external view*

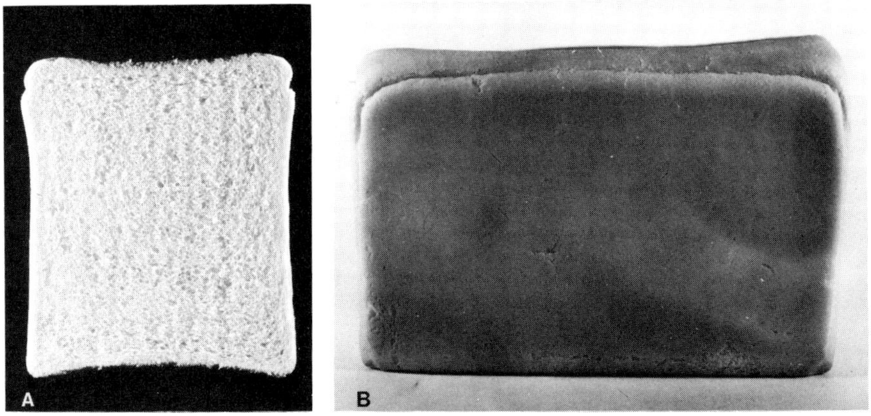

and injection equipment can be completely eliminated when using Dynarex.)

The liquor and fat are injected through separate points immediately after the entry point of the flour.

Oakes mixer/modifier construction

The 8D 30 range of mixer/modifiers consists of a central shaft driven by a 30 hp totally enclosed fan-cooled electric motor via an infinitely variable speed constant hp gear box and reduction gear box. On the shaft is an accurately machined screw feed which lightly mixes the flour liquor and fat and transports them to the main barrel of the unit where the mixing and modification of the dough takes place. This section consists of a series of water-jacketed stators secured by tie bars and having a number of elements protruding towards the central shaft. Inside and in between each stator are rotors which are keyed to the central shaft and which may be varied in design according to the texture required. The design of both the rotor and stator sections is such that the minimum resistance to flow is maintained while imparting the correct mixing action. All wetted parts of the mixer/modifier are of food grade stainless steel and all moving parts are enclosed in stainless steel sheeting. The hygienic straight-through construction facilitates in-line cleaning and is

The Oakes continuous automatic dough divider.

specifically designed for quick and easy dismantling. The dough produced by the mixer/modifier is extruded in the form of a continuous ribbon which facilitates easy transfer to the subsequent dough processing equipment.

Oakes continuous automatic dough divider

The combination of conventional dough-dividing equipment with the Oakes continuous mixer/modifier has enabled a greater degree of dividing accuracy to be attained. This is mainly attributed to the inertness of mechanically developed dough at this stage combined with the constant head of dough in the divider hopper due to the continuous feed from the mixer/modifier. It is an established fact however that harmful effects on dough quality may be produced by conventional dividing because of the difference in characteristics between bulk fermented and mechanically developed doughs. The Oakes continuous automatic divider has been developed to eliminate these effects, and in addition statistical analyses carried out during commercial production with this divider coupled directly to the mixer/modifier have shown an increased degree of accuracy compared with conventional methods. Tests carried out with the prototype divider in which batches of 100 random 2 lb samples were weighed have given a Standard Deviation of 0·14 oz or better. Conversion from 1 lb to 2 lb pieces or vice versa may be carried out easily whilst the machine is operating, thus eliminating any down time during these changes.

Plant operation

The ease of plant operation is enhanced by the fact that the major controls are all contained in one panel. This panel is fully interlocked and consists of stop and start buttons and indicator lights for all individual pieces of equipment, i.e. liquor agitators, liquor pump, fat pump, flour feed, mixer/modifier, energy input control, indicating watt meter, dough conveyor, alarm systems and continuous plant. These are in turn controlled by a master switch which may be set for either manual or automatic control of the plant. The interlocking of the panel is such that when operating on automatic control the flour feed cannot commence until the liquor and fat feeds are operating. Furthermore, loss of liquor feed for any reason causes the flour feed to stop automatically thus minimising the possibility of blockages during production runs.

An example of the start up and check procedure for the Oakes 8D 30/12 mixer/modifier is as follows:

Conway flour feeder

First decide the sackage per hour. Divide the total poundage by 60, this gives pounds per minute. Then divide this figure by 10, this will give the poundage setting for the Tare bar (10 = belt speed per minute).

e.g. 6 sacks per hour

$$= \frac{1680}{60} \text{ lb per hour} = 28 \text{ lb.}$$

$$\frac{28}{10} = 2{\cdot}8 \text{ lb this is the Tare bar setting approximately 2 lb 13 oz.}$$

Next, calculate the liquor requirements. Take the following typical recipe.

Per 280 lb (1 sack) flour
160 lb water
6 lb salt
6 lb yeast
3 lb Dynarex
Total weight: 175 lb or 17·5 gallons.

The flour weigher is set to run at 6 sacks per hour, therefore

$6 \times 17{\cdot}5$ gallons = 105 gallons per hour.

Next, calculate the work input requirement. Take the total dough weight per hour, divide this by 60, this gives pounds per minute. Multiply this by the work input factor, this will give an hp figure; multiply by 0·746, this will give the kw figure; to this add the No Load kw figure:

e.g. 6 sacks per hour
1680 flour
1050 liquor
2730

$$\frac{2730}{60} = 45{\cdot}5 \text{ lb per minute}$$

$45{\cdot}5 \times 0{\cdot}4$ hp per minute per lb = $18{\cdot}2$ hp $\times 0{\cdot}746$ = $13{\cdot}6$ kw + No load – say 3 kw at 200 rpm.
Total work input 16·6 kw – say 17 kw.

In the example given, the following settings would result:

Flour feed settings	=	2 lb 13 oz
Liquor flow rate	=	105 gpm
rpm	=	200
Total kw	=	17 kw

Slight variations from these figures may be necessary, but they form a sound basis on which to start. Other important factors are flour/liquor temperatures for a work level of 0·4 hp per minute per pound. It is not usually possible to control the flour temperature in a bulk silo, therefore the water temperature must be controlled; it may need to be cooled by chilling in the batch holding tanks. A simple rule of thumb method is as follows: 120°F minus the flour temperature gives the desired water temperature for a final dough temperature after development to 0·4 hp per minute per pound of 86°F. If development to 0·5 hp per minute per pound is required, the factor becomes 108.

e.g. at 0·4 hp per minute per pound
Final dough temperature required 86°F.
Flour temperature 75°F
Liquor temperature required $= 120 - 75 = 45$°F.

A rotor speed of 200 rpm is quoted, this may vary from machine to machine, the variation of rpm when optimum dough consistency has been obtained is the means by which the required work input kw is obtained.

It has also been noted during recent work that work level inputs in the region of 0·45 to 0·475 hp per minute per pound can give better results than 0·4 hp per minute per pound, the main objections to these higher work levels is the resultant increase in temperature. However the work has also shown that dough temperatures in the range of 88–90°F produce very acceptable bread products and allow for a slight reduction in the high yeast levels normally required by the Oakes mixer/modifier. The Oakes equipment is also designed to allow further automation to be introduced as required, i.e. it is possible for instance to allow automatically for varying flour properties, in particular, the water absorption, by controlling the liquor input to maintain a constant energy input.

The Oakes continuous mixer/modifier coupled with the automatic dough divider has two great advantages. It is best used for the prolonged production of a single type of bread, especially standard 1 lb

12 oz white tin bread when, if conditions of working are correctly maintained, excellent and consistent results may be obtained. The second great advantage concerns the automatic divider which permits very accurate control of dough piece weight variation.

Compared with batch mixers, these advantages must be balanced against the following drawbacks:

(1) It is difficult to make major changes quickly in bread type from say white to brown bread.

(2) Due to synchronisation problems, it has been found difficult to feed conventional intermediate provers, therefore a series of belt conveyors have been found beneficial, in most instances the intermediate proof time has been reduced to between 30 seconds and 2 minutes. This has in turn made it necessary to increase the yeast levels used in Oakes mixer/modifier produced doughs above that normally used in doughs produced in the Oakes mixer modifier above that normally used in Chorleywood Bread Process batch mixers. The usual level is in the range of 5½ to 6½ lb per sack, even when dough temperatures of 88°F are employed.

(3) The levels of water contained in a dough produced on the Oakes mixer/modifier are normally lower than those in a similar dough produced on a batch type Chorleywood Bread Process mixer. This may be due to the shorter residence time in the Oakes mixer/modifier compared with batch machines. Under normal conditions, the residence time in the Oakes mixer/modifier is in the range of 1·25 to 1·75 minutes whilst batch mixing times are normally in the range of 2·5 to 3·25 minutes. The quantities of water involved may be anything for ¼ to 1 gallon per 280 lb flour.

Both batch and continuous dough development processes present the baker with doughs of similar characteristics which differ in important respects from the dough prepared by a mixer which is designed to precede a bulk fermentation process.

This has in turn been responsible for changes in both raw materials and dough processing conditions which the baker must appreciate if he is to ensure that the bread he produces is of a consistently high quality, and is produced in the most economical way.

5. The role of raw materials in the Chorleywood Bread Process

The change from bulk fermentation to mechanical dough development has resulted in changes in either type or quantity, or both, of virtually all of the majoi raw materials used by the baker in commercial bread production.

The flour miller, the yeast manufacturer and the producers of those small ingredients, loosely classed as improvers, have all needed to re-think and re-tailor their products to suit the new process.

Flour

Firstly, let us look at the bakers' major raw material, wheat flour. The first major economic advantage claimed for the Chorleywood Bread Process was that, compared with a bulk fermented dough produced from the same flour, it was possible to increase the water content by about one gallon per sack (i.e. from approx. 60 to 63% of flour weight). It was later found that it was possible to maintain the bread quality obtained from bulk fermented doughs whilst reducing the percentage of 'strong' and hence expensive wheat in breadmaking grists, thus giving further economics in raw material costs.

During the period 1965–70 the percentage of Canadian wheat decreased by 30% whilst Australian wheat imports doubled. The percentage of English native and similar weak wheats also increased.

The world shortage of wheat coupled with the effect of the EEC common agricultural policy has now put severe economic pressure on British millers to incorporate high levels of wheat grown within the boundaries of the European Economic Community in their breadmaking grists.

English native and French wheats (there is a surplus of French wheat which the French farmers or millers wish to export as wheat or flour) have become increasingly attractive due to the general rise in the price of wheat on world markets together with the long-term effects of the CAP import levy system as the United Kingdom becomes fully integrated into the EEC. The levy system that fixes the price of wheat imported from outside the EEC, would, under normal conditions, be expected to appreciably increase its cost to the miller.

The inclusion of medium protein (filler) wheats such as Roumanian and Australian has greatly diminished. Indeed Australian wheat has almost disappeared from the United Kingdom market.

Grists are becoming limited to English native or EEC wheats blended with good quality Canadian or United States wheat.

The future may well see a further reduction in total protein and, even with the skill of the miller in blending his wheats, a more variable raw material for the baker.

The Chorleywood Bread Process has already made great demands on the miller both to develop suitable grists for the new process and also to institute adequate quality control systems. In particular it was necessary to ensure that the water absorption of flour produced for the process should vary as little as possible from batch to batch, as delivered to the baker. The dough development cycle is very short, and dough processing commences almost immediately after development, so that the bakery plant cannot be adjusted to cope with big variations in dough consistency.

A typical CBP flour analysis would be:

Moisture	13–14·5%
Protein	11–12%
Damaged starch	25–30 farrand starch damage units
Total alpha amylase	7–12 farrand total amylase units
Hagberg falling time	275–325 seconds (7 gm sample)
Water absorption	17½–18 gallons per sack
Farinograph stability	4–7 minutes
KJ colour grade figure	2–3 units
Oxidising agent	10–15 ppm potassium bromate

The baker might be presented with such a report and needs some acquaintance with the figures and their significance if he wishes to gauge the suitability of a particular flour for the process or to account for a deficiency in its performance.

The moisture content rarely varies outside acceptable bounds, over-dried or very moist flours are scarcely ever met in commercial practice. All the remaining figures are based on a moisture content of 14%.

Protein

Protein content is possibly the single most reliable guide to general flour type, a protein content of above 12% is in no way detrimental to bread quality though it may contain a higher proportion of expensive wheat than is necessary.

As the protein falls below 11%, it becomes more difficult to produce bread of a good quality, particularly tin bread, and it becomes increasingly important for the miller to control all the remaining flour properties.

Damaged starch

There are a number of popular misconceptions about what is meant by this term. Starch is 'damaged' as starch granules pass through the rolls during the milling process.

There is no 'water-resistant' envelope to starch granules waiting to be split open to allow water to penetrate the interior, nor are many of the granules totally disintegrated; what does occur is that some granules are to a greater or lesser extent broken into smaller fragments which are then capable of absorbing much more water than the compact structure of the intact granules. One more myth must be exploded at this point, there is no evidence at all to suggest that there is any increase in the level of starch damage due to the mixing action of any of the high-speed mixers employed in the Chorleywood process. The miller alone is able to influence damaged starch level by controlled manipulation of the flour mill.

With this preamble let us look at starch damage as it concerns the baker. The maximum level of starch damage in a flour intended for a bulk fermentation process is determined by the need for the miller to balance the increased initial water absorption against the inevitable breakdown of the damaged starch by the amylases in the flour during the bulk fermentation period, and the consequent decrease in water absorption prior to dividing and processing in the bakery auto plant. The Chorleywood process being a no-time process does not present this problem. The dough reaches the final proof stage within at most thirty minutes after leaving the mixer. Hence it is possible to process a dough which is not only initially softer but one in which there is a significantly higher level of starch damage, i.e. an increased amount of water may be incorporated into the starch phase.

The majority of CBP flours fall in the range of 25–30 farrand starch damage units. Too low a level (20–25 units) is not detrimental to bread quality but gives a rather low water absorption. About 25–30 units is usual. As the level approaches 35 units, more water can be added to the dough. Unfortunately although it is possible to incorporate high levels of water at the mixer and to process the resultant dough, during the subsequent baking process the dough cannot incorporate the water fully into the denaturing protein and gelatinising starch, and this results in a grey, soggy, even water logged looking loaf crumb. As the starch damage level approaches 40 Farrand units this danger increases and calls for increasing skill from the baker if good quality bread is to be produced. As a rule the higher the level of protein in the flour, the higher level of damaged starch it can accept without loss in bread quality.

Farrand's work on starch damage has helped the miller to measure, and so control, starch damage so that he can offer the baker a flour with a controlled consistent water absorption, the importance of which we have already noted. (Farrand has worked out a system by which the water absorption of a flour can be estimated by a knowledge of the protein level, moisture content and damaged starch level alone.)

The miller will also 'treat' the flour, bleaching it and also adding an oxidant and possibly fungal enzymes. Often CBP flours contain higher levels of oxidant, almost invariably potassium bromate, than was usual for bulk fermentation flours. This seems rather odd, as the baker will in turn be adding 60–70 ppm of oxidant at the dough-mixing stage.

Diastatic enzymes

Flour contains natural enzyme systems, cereal alpha and beta amylase which are capable of breaking down the amylose and amylopectin molecules of starch into sugars on which yeast can feed. The miller is able to measure the level of enzyme activity by methods such as 'Farrand's total alpha amylase method' and, if necessary, supplement the enzyme activity with similar enzymes prepared from a fungal source.

Once again the miller strives to keep the level within limits which he thinks acceptable to the baker. A total of 7–11 Farrand total amylase units is thought to be in the optimum range, although some millers omit any amylase supplementation, letting the baker add amylase in the form of malt to suit his own needs.

For the baker the picture is more complicated. He may be given a total amylase value by the Farrand method, but this does not tell him how much fungal and how much cereal amylase is present. It has been observed that flours with an adequate alpha amylase activity can give bread of poor volume by the C B P, if all that alpha amylase is in the form of added fungal amylase, and the flour contains little or no cereal alpha amylase (this may occur when there is an increased use of Australian and similar wheats which are very short of natural cereal alpha amylase enzymes). The miller does not usually add diastatic malt to a flour at the mill. The baker may, therefore, be required to do so should a shortage of cereal alpha amylase become apparent.

The Hagberg falling time is an arbitrary scale which measures the level of cereal alpha-amylase only. If the test is based on a 7 gramme flour sample the time should be in the region of 270–320 seconds. A high value, above 350 seconds, indicates a shortage of cereal alpha-amylase, possibly resulting in a lack of volume in the finished loaf.

Even an excess of fungal amylase (15 Farrand Units and above) in conjunction with overproof and bad transfer between prover and oven has been implicated in the handbag fault in single-piece tin bread.

To return to less contentious properties the flour colour, acidity and of great importance, extraction rate, as measured by the KJ colour-grade figure, are as they were for bulk fermentation flours and only rarely stray from the prescribed bounds.

The baker may use the Farinograph curve together with the protein percentage to gauge the type of grist which the miller has used, but again a word of caution – it is possible by carefully controlling flour properties during milling, particularly the damaged starch level, to give misleadingly high water absorptions and apparently good farinograph stabilities which are not primarily due to the protein content of the flours.

By and large in Britain the baker is well served by the flour miller. The majority of flours now offered for Chorleywood bread production have been carefully matched to the requirements of the process. Flour-mill quality control has made it possible to keep constant those factors which affect dough production and bakery properties, in particular water absorption. None the less, flour is such an important and complex raw material that it is necessary for the baker to understand how its various properties might affect dough processing and bread quality.

Yeast

The second supplier of raw materials to the baker is the producer of yeast. Here again the new process has posed new problems which are not always appreciated by the rest of the baking industry. The nature of the problem and the way it has been overcome is dealt with admirably by an article in *The Arkady Review* by H. G. Sykes of the Distillers Yeast Company, which is here reprinted in full:

'Traditionally, the function of yeast in a fermenting dough has been threefold. In the first place, the gas produced stretches the gluten strands and both physical and chemical changes take place. As a result the dough is able, in the final stages, to retain the gas produced, giving bold, well-risen loaves. Secondly, it is the gas produced during proving and baking which aerates the dough to give a palatable texture. Thirdly, the yeast itself and the by-products of fermentation contribute to the mild but characteristic flavour of well-made bread.

'During the past few years breadmaking processes involving the mechanical development of dough have become widely accepted, particularly by the large producing units. Already the majority of the bread made in this country is produced by this technique and it seems likely that the proportion will continue to increase.

'In these processes the first function of yeast noted above is now less important. The question of bread flavour is so complex and controversial an issue that I do not propose to tackle it in this article. There is, however, one point which might be noted. This is that the total amount of gas produced by fermentation in the new short processes does not differ very greatly from that produced in the longer conventional methods of breadmaking. There remains perhaps the most vital function of yeast, that of aerating the dough during final proof and baking.

'The elimination of bulk fermentation necessitates a high rate of gas production within the first hour or so after mixing if the proof period is not to be unduly prolonged. This is achieved by using high levels of yeast and high dough temperatures. These changes impose conditions upon the yeast which are quite different from those obtaining in the normal 3–4-hour bulk fermentation process.

'In order to explain the behaviour of modern baker's yeast in these processes, and the advances which have been made in its performance, it is first necessary to consider the complex mixture of different sugars present in a bread dough and the ways in which various types of yeast deal with them.

'Normal white flour contains only very small quantities of the simple sugars glucose and fructose together with a little sucrose. It also contains a larger and very important quantity of more complex sugars such as raffinose, glucodifructose and fructose-containing polysaccharides. When dry, it contains little or no maltose. Whenever the flour is wetted to make a dough, the diastic enzymes or amylases present in the flour begin to break down a proportion of the starch to give the sugar maltose.

'When presented with this mixture of sugars, baker's yeast first ferments the glucose and fructose, at the same time rapidly breaking down the sucrose by the action of the enzyme invertase to produce further small quantities of these simple sugars. Certain types of yeast are also able to attack the more complex sugars which are broken down to simpler forms and fermented. In all cases, maltose is not fermented until the supply of simple sugars is nearing exhaustion. Maltose therefore accumulates in the dough during the early stages of the process. The fermentation of maltose will eventually commence and will then normally rise to a rate considerably faster than the rate at which fresh maltose is being produced by the diastatic enzymes. Sooner or later, depending on the amount of yeast present, the dough temperature and the diastatic activity of the flour, the supply of sugar becomes inadequate to sustain the maximum rate of fermentation and gas production falls to a low level governed by the rate at which new maltose is being produced.

'Until a few years ago, all the baker's yeast produced in this country and, indeed, throughout the world, was of a type which could not readily ferment the more complex sugars in flour. After utilising the simple sugars, this yeast had then to adapt its enzyme system to maltose fermentation. This adaption cannot take place instantaneously. The yeast must, at this stage, have, in addition to sugar, a host of other essential nutrients and must devote a part of its energy to the synthesis of new enzymes. In conventional breadmaking processes involving say three hours of bulk fermentation at about 80°F with yeast usage of around 3 lb per sack, this characteristic was not very important. The yeast then had sufficient time to adapt itself to maltose fermentation and a steadily increasing rate of gas production occurred during the fermentation period as shown in Figure 1(a) on page 106. As the rate of yeast seeding is increased the simple sugars are utilised more rapidly and a drop in gas-production rate occurs during the transition to maltose fermentation. A typical gas-production curve using this yeast at the rate of 5 lb per sack in a dough at 80°F is shown in Figure 1(b). The higher the rate of yeast seeding and the higher the dough temperature, the more pronounced becomes this characteristic fall in gas production. Thus, in a typical mechanically developed no-time dough using 6 lb of yeast per sack with a dough temperature of 85°F–90°F, the gas-production curve takes the form shown in Figure 1(c). It now becomes obvious that this type of yeast would perform very inefficiently under such conditions. Gas production falls to a relatively low level during what would be the critical final stages of proof and early stages of baking. Further, the addition of even more yeast does not improve matters. The initial rate of fermentation will certainly be increased but the fall in gas production during adaption to maltose fermentation will become both earlier and of greater extent thus cancelling the earlier gain.

'The deficiencies of this type of yeast were realised many years ago by the Distillers Co. Ltd. Bakery processes were tending to become shorter and, as time became an increasingly important factor, it was clear that a faster yeast with more versatile fermentative characteristics would eventually be required. The research effort of the Yeast Division was, therefore, directed to the development of such a yeast.

'Baker's yeast belongs to the family of single-celled plants known as *Saccaromyces cerevisiae*, of which there are innumerable different strains showing widely varying fermentative behaviour. By suitable manipulation, it is possible to cross different strains to produce completely new hybrids. One thus aims to breed in the best characteristics of both parents and at the same time to eliminate their weaknesses. Although this simple explanation may give the impression that the procedure is quite straightforward, it is, in fact, an extremely difficult, time-consuming and often fruitless task. However, after an extensive programme of hybridisation and selection, combined with the most detailed study of different methods of growing the yeast, success was finally achieved. A new strain of yeast was developed which was not only more active than the original, but fermented all the sugars in flour with almost equal facility. It then transferred to maltose fermentation

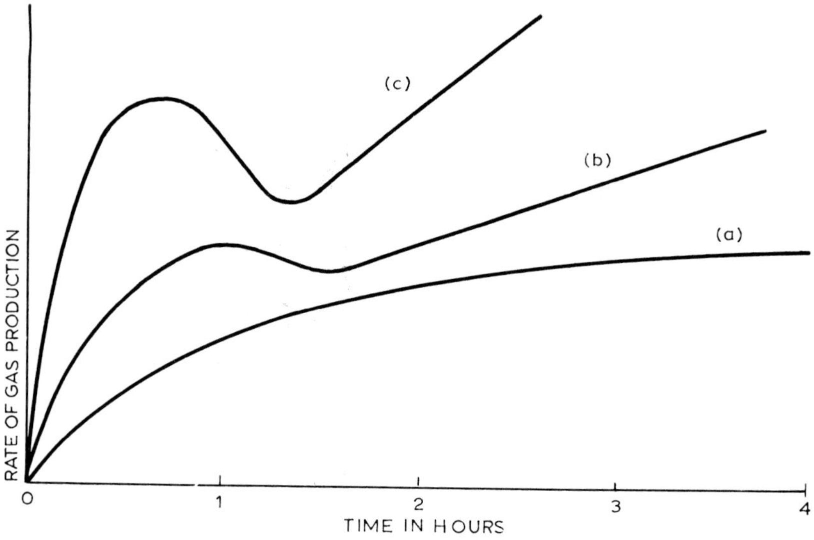

Fig. 1

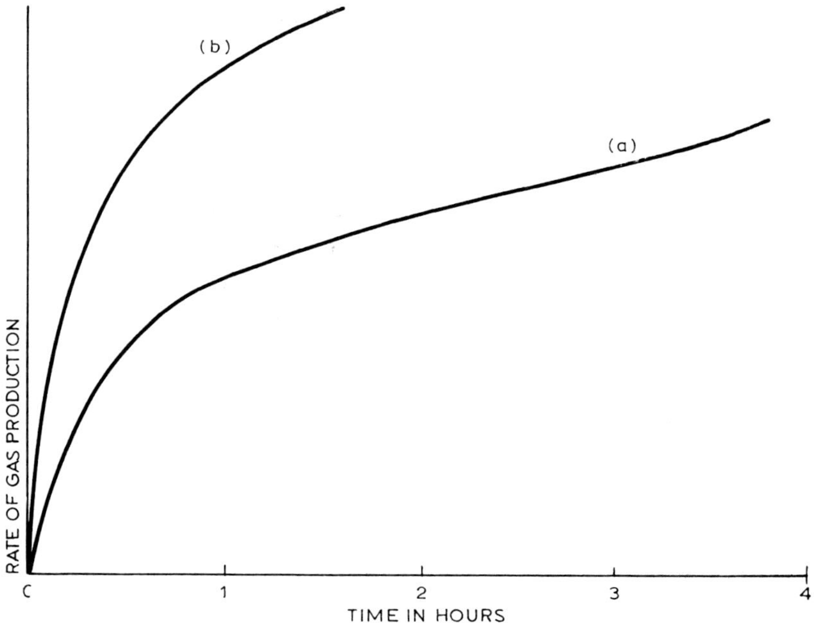

Gas-production curve. **Fig. 2**

with little or no hesitation. It was stable and could be produced with consistently high activity. Once the new culture had been adequately tested it was put into commercial production and the benefits of its higher and more versatile activity passed on to the baker.

'A typical gas-production curve given by this yeast used at the rate of 5 lb per sack in a dough at 80°F is shown in Figure 1. Even when used at the rate of 6 lb per sack in a dough at 90°F a rapidly and steadily increasing rate of gas production is maintained during the first and now critical 1½ hours as shown in Figure 2.

'This yeast has, therefore, fermentative characteristics which are ideally suited and tailor-made to the requirements of the new processes. Thus the problem which might have been a considerable stumbling block to the introduction of fast, no-time doughs was in this instance anticipated and solved before it arose.'

Dough conditioner

The third group of suppliers of raw materials are those loosely classed as 'Bread Ingredient Manufacturers'. The British Arkady Company, a prominent supplier of this type of ingredient since 1920, has found that the many problems presented by the Chorleywood process have been offset by the new opportunities it offered.

With the advent of the CBP a specified amount and type of both fat and oxidant have become basic ingredients as essential to the dough composition as the flour, salt and yeast. For the ingredient producer, many of the problems of the CBP had already been encountered in the various continuous development systems undergoing plant trials in the late 1950s. The British Arkady Co Ltd at that time decided to develop for such processes a specific complete product to complement Ambirex, its enzyme-active soya-flour-based complete improver for bulk fermented conventional doughs.

Ambirex was (and is) a free-flowing powder, with yeast foods, the correct oxidant type and level, and also fat, the optimum fat for the particular process, in finely dispersed powder form on an enzyme-active soya flour and therefore fully functional base.

Detailed investigation of the fat requirements of mechanically developed doughs showed (see Chapter 3) that, provided the correct fat blend was used, then considerably less than the 2 lb per sack of white shortening originally specified in the BBIRA Report No. 59 was sufficient to produce the optimum bread. Further, the fat blends containing as they did a high proportion of high melting point material were suited to the production of a powdered product. The oxidant requirements were also re-examined. The two oxidants available were ascorbic acid and potassium bromate, each was used as the sole oxidant followed by various blends of the two. The total oxidant level of 75 ppm on flour weight was confirmed as being in the correct region, but the best results, both in performance and economically, proved to be a mixture of roughly equal proportions of the two.

Once these two basics had been established, it was possible to build them into a complete improver, including with them those ingredients which were of benefit to both bulk fermented and mechanically developed doughs.

Two of the 'Arkady salts', ammonium chloride and calcium sulphate, retained their place strictly on merit. Ammonium chloride is traditional yeast food acting as a nitrogen source to speed and regularise the rate of gas production in the dough.

Calcium sulphate is only slightly soluble in water, although its solubility is greatly increased in a salt solution of the strength present in bread dough. It serves as a source of calcium ions which are incorporated into the dough protein and strengthen the gluten structure to some extent.

Both salts are used at a level of a few ounces to the sack; each has a small but quite discernable effect on general bread quality, though increasing the levels gives no further benefits.

The correct functional level of enzyme-active soya flour is incorporated into the product. Full fat soya contains 40% protein, 20% oil, roughly 33% carbohydrates and 7% moisture.

The soya bean oil present is in mycells within the flour particles and includes approximately 4% of the natural emulsifier lecithin. The mycell structure and natural anti-oxidant in the plant effectively protect the oil from rancidity for very long storage periods. The protein is not denatured because the flour is not heat-treated and for the same reason the natural enzyme systems are not inactivated.

The benefit of the oil and protein fractions is a joint one. The protein and oil plus lecithin combine to improve the quality of the crumb of the baked loaf. There is an increased softness and resilience in the crumb structure giving the cut slice a silky surface appearance and a soft but not soggy feel when compressed by hand. The undenatured protein has also the more prosaic virtue of increasing the water absorption of the dough. (Enzyme-active full-fat soya flour can be expected to take at least its own weight of water in a Chorleywood dough.)

One particular enzyme system, the lipoxidase enzyme system, also has a specific beneficial property: it acts as a natural bleaching agent, decolorising the yellow pigments normally present in wheat flour, thus giving a whiter loaf.

It is a well-known fact that wheat flour can be and has been bleached chemically by such materials as chlorine, chlorine dioxide and benzoyl peroxide. This type of treatment has been carried out by flour millers to improve the colour of their flour. However, treatment may not always be desirable.

An examination of the patent literature of 1930 reveals some of the very early work done in the Arkady Laboratories to effect the natural bleaching of flour through the agencies of high-speed mixing and enzyme-active soya flour. The relevant patent numbers covering this work are BP Nos. 342,697–343,193 and 343,677. Enzyme-active soya flour, or an aqueous extract of this flour, was added at a level of up to 2% of the wheat-flour weight to a dough made from bleached or unbleached flour. A dough so made was subjected to a fast mixing action which continuously exposed varying parts of the dough to the oxygen of the atmosphere. Oxygen was transferred to the wheat flour, via the soya flour, bringing about the necessary bleaching effect.

Where the process consisted of a sponge and dough, the enzyme-active soya flour was added to the sponge made from half the flour and all the water. Once again rapid mixing at this stage was continued until the necessary bleaching had been achieved and the batter had acquired the desired consistency. The remainder of the flour was incorporated on slow speed. Great stress was laid upon the fact that an auto-oxidisable material (soya flour) be included in these high-speed mixing processes for optimum effect.

In 1932 the name lipoid oxidase was coined for the soya bean enzyme which transferred atmospheric oxygen to wheat flour and brought about an observable bleaching action. Since this time the name has been modified to lipoxidase.

The American patent literature of 1943 also showed a series of patents on the bleaching action of soya, namely USP Nos 1,957,333–7. More recently the Rank-Hay patent, BP No 646,311 of 1950 showed that enzyme-active soya flour could be used to good advantage in the preparation of good bread from unbleached, untreated flour.

Well now, what sort of reaction does this lipoxidase enzyme perform? Before answering this question, a brief examination of the function of an enzyme would be helpful. An enzyme is a biological material which helps a chemical change to take place but which remains unchanged at the end of the reaction. In every case, only a small amount of enzyme is required to catalyse a reaction. For a reaction to take place there must be a substrate and, in the case of lipoxidase, this is the wheat flour oil (more precisely the unsaturated fatty acids linoleic and linolenic). There must also be the reactant material, in this case oxygen. If one or both of these factors becomes limiting (i.e. the substrate is in short supply, or the oxygen is used up), then the reaction will stop. Conversely, if the oxygen concentration is increased, then the reaction can be carried out more rapidly. At this stage, time can be considered as an important factor. If the normal state of diffusion of oxygen is operative the reaction will be very slow because of the time taken for the oxygen to arrive at the site of active lipoxidase and then be transferred to the wheat flour. Constantly changing the exposed surface of a dough, by high-speed mixing, will speed up the reaction. The mechanism of the lipoxidase activity can be described as follows:

Atmospheric oxygen is transferred to the unsaturated fatty acids of the flour oil through the agency of the enzyme. A peroxide of the unsaturated fatty acids is formed and this undergoes a further coupled reaction whereby the oxygen is transferred to the corotenoid pigment of the flour. The bleaching effect results from this sequence of enzymatic reactions.

It has been suggested that the peroxides formed as an intermediate product in the foregoing sequency may also be available for the oxidation of the sulphydryl (-SH) groups of the gluten giving a maturing effect on the gluten. More positive proof of this mechanism is still required.

In the case of the Tweedy and similar CBP mixers which mix either under partial vacuum or in the mixing barrel of the Oakes where the enclosed environment again restricts the available oxygen, the bleaching action is still considerable due to the high-speed action which continually exposes new dough surfaces and enzyme to the oxygen which is available.

From these ingredients the complete Chorleywood additive for standard white bread is built up. It must contain sufficient of the optimum fat type, correctly dispersed, to give a total fat response for all flours (see Chapter 3).

As one can use much lower levels than two pounds of fat per 280 lb of flour if the correct fat is selected, it becomes possible to include sufficient yeast food, ammonium chloride and calcium sulphate and enzyme-active soya flour, together with the best oxidant system to make up a complete additive at a convenient addition rate (2–3 lb per sack). The baker now needs only to weigh and add salt, yeast and improver for each dough, making the dough maker's job easier and reducing the possibilities of error. The single improver addition guarantees that the basic fat and oxidant requirements of the dough system are correctly met, paradoxically though the Chorleywood Bread Process is critically dependent on fat and once the correct fat type is used then one can obtain bread of the highest quality with much lower levels of addition than is normal in the case for bulk fermented doughs.

The remaining array of raw materials traditionally used in the wide variety of breads produced by the British baker may be incorporated into mechanically developed doughs usually with only minor alterations from their mode of use in bulk fermented doughs. These are best examined in the passages of the book dealing with variety and speciality bread.

The net effect on bakery ingredients of the introduction of the Chorleywood Bread Process has, in fact, been the opposite to what might have been expected. One might suppose that the new breadmaking system with its particular demands in raw materials and process parameters would greatly increase the complexity of all facets of dough processing.

From the baker's viewpoint, in the case of raw materials the reverse is true. Provided he chooses wisely he is able to obtain a breadmaking flour which is specifically processed to consistently be of the correct type and possess the correct parameters to produce high quality bread by the Chorleywood Bread Process.

The small ingredients have been developed and refined till the addition of one complete composite ingredient guarantees that all the essential functional materials are incorporated into the dough in their correct proportions.

Thus an elegantly simple formulation: flour, salt, yeast, Dynarex and water only, in their correct proportions, are now capable of producing bread of an unvarying high quality.

Note

The Farrand method for damaged starch and the Farrand method for determining the total alpha amylase are both described in a paper by E. C. Farrand in *Cereal Chemistry*, Vol. 41, 1964, page 98.

6. Processing white tinned bread from dough produced by the Chorleywood Bread Process

Batch mixers

The first basic essential to the correct and consistent processing of a bread dough is that the dough, as it leaves the mixer, should consistently be in the optimum state for the production of bread of a high and unvarying quality.

Individual raw materials have already been discussed, but we must now consider their correct proportions. In commercial practice, levels of major ingredients do not vary greatly in the bread dough.

Most batch mixers are named according to either the maximum amount of flour which the machine is able to mix successfully, or, in the more modern machines, it is related to the maximum weight of dough that the mixer can produce in one cycle.

Take for example the Tweedy 280. This machine is capable of mixing one sack (280 lb) of flour per cycle. The level of salt varies very little, in almost all bakeries it is between 5 lb 8 oz and 6 lb per 280 lb of flour. Yeast quantities tend to vary rather more than this, dependent on the volume of the loaf required and also, to a larger extent, on the particular bakery conditions. An average would be 5 lb to 280 lb of flour with a spread of between 4 lb 8 oz and 6 lb 8 oz.

The essential oxidants and fats are usually added in powder form as part of a composite ingredient which may also contain yeast foods and enzyme-active soya flour, etc. Dynarex is the most widely used product and the optimum level is 3 lb per 280 lb flour. Depending on flour type and particular bakery conditions, this too can vary. Except for very unusual circumstances, no less than 2 lb 8 oz and no more than 3 lb 8 oz may be used in commercial practice without the quality of the finished bread being adversely affected.

Some bakeries have used levels of Dynarex as low as 2 lb, together with added fat as an 'insurance policy', but this is both uneconomic and bad practice.

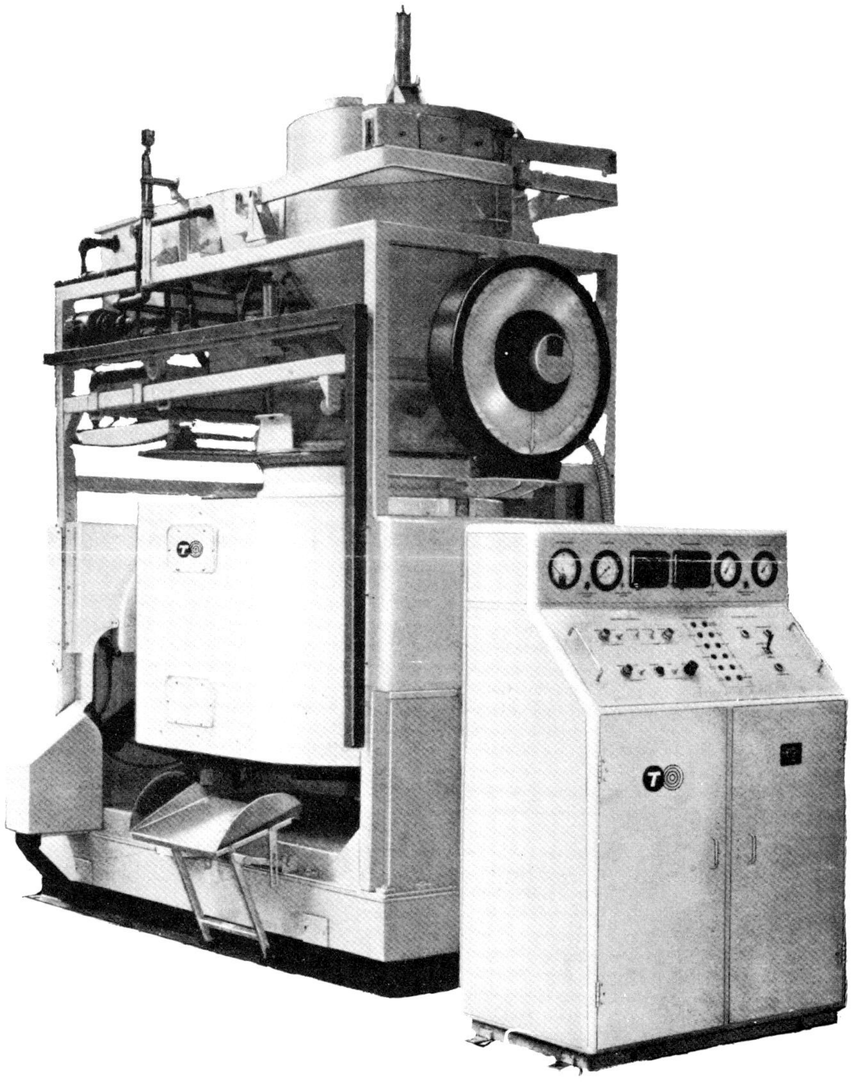

The Tweedy 280 Automatic mixer.

Proprietary additives such as Dynado are also available. This is used at 2 lb per 280 lb flour and does not contain soya flour.

The water level in a dough can vary considerably according to the flour used, but the great majority of flours of the correct CBP bread-making quality require between 17 and 18½ gallons per 280 lb flour.

A typical standard recipe for the production of 28 oz bread by the Chorleywood Bread Process is:

	lb	oz
Flour	280	—
Salt	5	8
Yeast	5	—*
Dynarex	3	—
Water	180	—*

*Varies within the range previously discussed.

Once the basic formula has been decided, a number of other fundamental decisions must be made.

1. Work level

As previously stated, 5 watt hours or 0·4 hp minutes per pound of dough or 11 watt hours per kilo of dough is the normal work level used for bread in this country and was indeed the level prescribed in the original Chorleywood report.

Watt hours are the usual method by which the energy being put into the dough is measured. When the baker requires to calculate how much development a particulaı dough requires, it is fairly straightforward. For instance, take the recipe above and total up all the ingredients, ie 280 lb flour, 180 lb water, 3 lb Dynarex, 5 lb 8oz salt and 5 lb yeast equals 473 lb 8 oz. Disregard any ounces in the recipe and then multiply the amount of ingredient in your dough by the amount of watt hours for which you are mixing, i.e. $473 \times 5 = 2365$. On the larger machines, the watt hours are usually registered on a three figure or $\times 10$ basis and therefore the end unit figure is again disregarded. The figure to set up for this particular dough is 236. A more simple way of calculating work level (provided 5 watt hours is being used) is just to divide the total pounds of dough in your recipe by two, i.e. $473 \div 2 = 236$. For all practical purposes, the figure set up on the counter can be varied 5% either way without having a noticeable effect on the finished bread quality. In many bakeries unnecessary adjusting of the watt counter is carried out by force of habit, but like varying fat and oxidant, varying work level is not good practice (the basic principles are there to be adhered to). The most useful contribution adjusting the watt counter can have is that of helping to control dough temperature. Energy develops heat and, when mixing by this process, the large amount of energy expended causes the temperature of the ingredients in the mixer to rise by 5·2°F for every watt hour per pound of dough used. Adjusting the work level down to say 224 (5 %) can help to reduce the dough temperature, but not by much more than 1½°F.

2. Dough temperature

The optimum temperatures of Chorleywood Bread Process doughs ex mixer lie between 84°F and 88°F (most bakeries work to a dough temperature ex mixer of 86°F to 88°F). Bread is produced at temperatures of up to 92°F, but this is unwise because dough soon becomes sticky and may 'go over the top', i.e. cannot be handled through a plant. Lower temperatures than 83°F tend to require more yeast and take longer in final proof. As on most plants, the final proof times are governed to no longer than sixty minutes, therefore using lower dough temperatures is not a practical proposition. One or two people with the correct facilities have used very low temperatures (for Chorleywood Bread Process) – 82°F – and produced bread with a whiter crumb and a greater water quantity, but, because larger provers are required, very few are able to take advantage of these marginal improvements.

3. Vacuum level

The level of vacuum is a vital factor and the practical limits to which it may be normally adjusted lie between 15 and 20 in. of mercury for 28 oz four-piece bread. The lower the vacuum level the more open the texture of the bread, and the higher the vacuum the closer the structure becomes up until 23 in. when a deterioration in bread quality occurs, showing itself by blistering in the crust surface and a gradual breakdown of internal structure as vacuum is increased. One-piece bread generally requires less vacuum than four-piece bread for two reasons:

(a) that a more open texture is normally required, and

(b) when a slight excess of vacuum is used, the strains put on the dough piece shows itself by exaggerating any Swiss-roll effect created during moulding.

The ideal level of vacuum for one-piece bread is felt to be about 12–15 in. hg.

Having discussed optimum recipe, work level and vacuum level before mixing the dough, another parameter must also be considered – dough water temperature.

4. Water temperature

This is governed, obviously, by the flour temperature in the bakery and the dough temperature required. It is also governed, in the case of Chorleywood Bread Process, by the work level to be used in the dough.

To calculate the water temperature for a CBP dough is quite simple. For a conventionally fermented dough the method adopted is to double the required dough temperature, and subtract the flour temperature. The result is the correct water temperature. A similar rough calculation can be made for CBP doughs bearing in mind that a significant temperature rise occurs in the dough during mixing. This temperature rise is always 26°F for 5 watt hours or 5·2°F for 1 watt hour. The calculation to obtain the correct water temperature for a CBP dough mixed to 5 watt hours is:

> Required temperature 86°F. Subtract 26°F from 86°F = 60°F, double this = 120°F. From 120°F subtract the flour temperature, e.g. 70°F. The water should be taken at 50°F.

Therefore, provided the doughs were mixed to 5 watt hours per lb, a Major Factor can be used to calculate water temperature. This is 120°F – if the flour temperature is taken from this the correct water temperature for a CBP dough is obtained.

The flour temperature in bakeries varies considerably according to conditions in the bakery, the efficiency of the bulk flour system and the temperature at which the flour is delivered in the tankers, etc. Generally it varies between 65°F and 90°F.

The temperature of mains water in bakeries can vary from 40°F in the winter and 75°F in the summer. It is therefore necessary for most large bakeries to install a water-chilling unit. These are usually part of the 'package deal' for large fully automatic mixers and embrace features (a water services cabinet) which enable the baker to adjust water temperatures from about 35°F upwards to 70°F. Care should be taken to ensure that the pipe work from the chiller unit to the mixer is adequately insulated so that there is no gain in temperature during water transfer from the chiller to the mixer. We can assume that water temperature can and must be controlled properly if the correct dough temperature and the finished quality of the bread are to be consistent.

5. Mixing time

Mixing time is directly related to the work level being put into the dough. Other factors can also influence this, principally the dough consistency. The tighter the dough, the quicker it will mix, because there is a greater resistance in the mix and hence work is put into the dough more quickly. A soft dough takes longer to mix. The time it takes to mix a dough can be a very reliable guide as to its consistency. Another factor which has to be considered is the amount of dough being mixed in the machine. If 140 lb of flour is being mixed in a 280 machine, this certainly does not mean that it will only require half the mixing time.

The time taken to put five watt hours into a dough when the machine is fully loaded varies between 2 minutes 45 seconds and 3 minutes, 10 seconds, according to machine type and impact plate configuration. When half quantities are mixed to five watt hours per pound it may take about 2 minutes 15 seconds to 2 minutes 30 seconds.

It has been shown that a deviation in dough consistency measured over an hour's production, equivalent to a change in water requirement of one pound for a sack dough, will alter the mixing time by an average of two seconds. Various quality-control devices, notably the Rank Pullen meter, can now be used to control dough consistency very accurately by carefully measuring the variation in mixing time. A careful dough-mixer man with a stop-watch can perform a similar function, but many bakeries still mix to five watt hours with a single predetermined water level, relying on the consistency of their particular flour supply.

Having established the recipe and all the other parameters, a fully automatic machine can then be set to go through the mixing cycle described in section one of this chapter.

After the dough is ejected from the machine it should go directly into a divider hopper. Giving the dough any rest before dividing is to be avoided at all costs.

6. Divider and auto-plant

Two major points must be noted when producing Chorleywood Bread Process doughs:

(1) It is absolutely essential not to allow a Chorleywood Bread Process dough to be in the divider hopper for longer than eight minutes, otherwise deterioration in bread quality will result. The whole of the dough-producing system should ideally be tied up to the level of dough in the divider hopper. Before the Chorleywood Bread Process it was common practice to maintain the dough level in a hopper to the absolute maximum, i.e. about 1500 lb of dough in a nine-sack plant. For a Chorleywood dough the maximum quantity of dough in the divider should never exceed 700 lb. An electronic probe in the head, which will set off an alarm when a low level is reached, is a worth-while addition to the plant. Even a red line to mark the maximum quantity of dough remaining in the hopper before the next is to be discharged is better than nothing. Some modern plants have a probe in the divider which will set off the normal mixing sequence and will never allow excess dough in the hopper. The best method of control is the automatic counting of the number of dough pieces as they are divided.

(2) Divider accuracy is increased considerably when making Chorleywood Bread Process doughs as against conventional systems. This is because the dough contains very little gas and has, therefore, a very uniform density, unlike a gassy fermented dough. It has been found that dividers normally tend to wear out more quickly when dealing with dead doughs, but hitherto no major alteration to the knife-and-ram principle of volumetric dividing has taken place except in continuous mixers.

From the divider the dough pieces (some of which are check-weighed) should then pass to a *conical moulder*. This piece of equipment is important for two reasons:

(a) It gives the individual dough pieces some semblance of crumb direction.

(b) It helps put the divided dough piece into a shape which can be easily handled by the moulder.

The dough pieces then pass by means of a conveyor and pusher bar to the intermediate or first prover. This part of the make-up plant has had to be changed from when conventional processes were used. For Chorleywood Bread Process the first proof time on batch production should not be lower than five minutes and not exceed ten minutes. Six to eight minutes is the average first-proof time used in plant bakeries

Top, Tweedy 300 mixer with related divider/auto plant.
Above, twin moulders with automatic four piecing and tinning attachment.

today. Most of the first provers have been modified from the ones used in conventional production which used to run for up to twenty minutes. This modification involves the elimination of one rung of the first prover. It is extremely important that too much dry or cold air should not be allowed to circulate in the first prover, otherwise excessive skinning of dough pieces will occur; this problem is greater in Chorleywood Bread Process doughs because of their higher temperatures. Perhaps the best modification that could be made to the first prover is the control of temperature and humidity so that the doors at the top of the prover, which are often left open, could be closed at all times, except for cleaning purposes or under very adverse ambient atmospheric conditions (cloths and other internal parts must be cleaned and laundered weekly).

7. Moulding

After being in the first prover for approximately six minutes, the dough piece passes through the final moulder where the finished texture and cell formation of the baked loaf are created. The moulder also shapes the dough piece into the particular tin size that is required. Until the advent of the Chorleywood Bread Process three major types of moulding machines were available:

(1) Spindle moulder.
(2) Drum moulder.
(3) Universal moulder.

Spindle moulders have been found to be almost totally unsuitable for this type of dead dough and consequently very few are in use today. Drum moulding is being carried out quite successfully, but these machines have gradually been replaced by the Universal type which has a much gentler action and is very suitable for Chorleywood Bread Process type doughs. This type of moulder consists of two or three sets of rollers into which the dough is fed, a curling chain, a pressure board and a set of cutting knives for producing four-piece bread. It is of vital importance that each of these facets is carefully controlled if the best bread is to be produced. The settings are totally different than any which were used for conventional systems.

Typical settings for this type of moulder are:

Four-piece bread

	Top rollers	0·230 in.
	Bottom rollers	0·100 in.

Pressure board – measurement above belt at outside of the board

	First pillar	$1\frac{1}{2}$ in.
	Second pillar	$1\frac{5}{16}$ in.

Guide rails – $15\frac{1}{2}$ in. at both ends

One-piece bread

	Top rollers	0·285 in.
	Bottom rollers	0·130 in.

Pressure board – measurement above belt at outside of the board

	First pillar	$1\frac{3}{4}$ in.
	Second pillar	$1\frac{5}{8}$ in.

Guide rails – 11 in. at first adjustment
– $6\frac{1}{2}$ in. at second adjustment

The above settings are for Chorleywood doughs in optimum condition, therefore setting will need slight adjustment to suit dough consistency and tin shape in the bakery.

These settings are a rough guide and will vary according to the manufacturer. The manufacturer may mark the setting on the moulder on some arbitrary scale, but the quoted measurements can be checked by Feeler gauges or by simply using bakers plastic scrapers which are usually readily to hand in the bakery.

The curling chain can be adjusted marginally to suit the size of dough piece and the knives for four-piece have to be adjusted to give either four even pieces or, better still, the two outside pieces being marginally heavier than the inner ones.

Automatic four-piece panning devices are becoming more popular and, although this type of machine has not been quite perfected, the consistency and size of dough pieces are extremely important if 98% satisfaction is to be obtained. Of course, when moulding is completed it is extremely important to select the correct tin size and shape. Two or three examples of the internal measurement of pan for four-piece, one-piece and one-piece farmhouse bread are set out below:

For four-piece 28 *oz white bread*

	Length top	8 in.
	Length base	$7\frac{1}{4}$ in.

Width top	$4\frac{7}{8}$ in.
Width base	$4\frac{1}{4}$ in
Depth	$5\frac{1}{8}$ in.

For one-piece 28 *oz white bread*

Length top	$8\frac{3}{4}$ in.
Length base	$7\frac{3}{4}$ in.
Width top	$5\frac{1}{8}$ in.
Width base	4 in.
Depth	4 in.

For 'Farmhouse' 28 *oz white bread*

Length top	7 in.
Length base	$6\frac{21}{32}$ in.
Width top	5 in.
Width base	$4\frac{21}{32}$ in.
Depth	$2\frac{3}{8}$ in.

Tin treatment and coatings and the type of greasing emulsions used can also affect finished bread quality. This will be dealt with in the chapter on bread faults. One of the main points to watch during moulding is that dusting flour should be at a minimum and excessive draught should be avoided, when the dough piece is being sheeted. After panning or tinning up the dough pieces pass into the final prover.

8. Final proof

The conditions in the final prover are important; it is particularly important not to have excessive skinning taking place and that no hot or cold spots exist in the prover. Normally Chorleywood Bread Process final proof of doughs takes between 45–59 minutes according to the type of plant and rate of throughput. The temperature of the final prover ought to be within the range of 100–120°F. The Relative Humidity is usually best between 70–85%. Most people seem to prefer the conditions about 105°F and 75% R/H. During this period the dough piece gasses freely and proves to just below tin height. (This varies according to tin height.) It is then transferred either automatically or manually to the oven; transfer is of critical importance and care must be taken not to bang or damage the fully proved dough piece as it is in a very delicate state.

Top, automatic prover.
Above, discharge end of travelling oven.

9. Baking

Many types of oven are used in plant bread production in the UK and each manufacturer has different recommendations.

Both gas and oil-fired ovens are widely used. The baking time for a 28 oz baked loaf is usually between 26–40 minutes. The quicker baking times occur because of the use of turbulence in the oven chamber. The baking temperatures again vary according to the type of oven in use, but they also vary from section to section in individual ovens and from manufacturer to manufacturer. For example, the temperature of the three sections of a nine-sack oven with turbulence may be 420°F front, 446°F middle and 390°F rear. Temperatures can be between 390°F and 460°F. The use of steam in baking is quite important because this can help control loaf volume and finished crust character. Normally steam at up to 8 psi in the first third of the baking chamber is used.

It is extremely difficult to be specific when baking is discussed as no two ovens are alike, but in general very little change has taken place in baking technique since the days of conventional doughs. One trend which certainly needs to be avoided is underbaking.

10. Cooling

From the oven most of the larger bakeries pass the baked bread to an automatic de-panning and then to a cooling system. They are humidity and temperature controlled. It normally takes at least 2 hours 40 minutes to cool the centre of the loaf down to 75–80°F., which is required for optimum slicing conditions. Some coolers can take up to 3½ hours to cool bread to this temperature; if bread is cooled in atmospheric conditions, 4½ hours at least is required, although there is a tendency in practice to slice the bread when it is too warm, a state which does lead to problems. The shelf life of the loaf is greatly affected by the conditions under which it is cooled. If the temperature of the storage atmosphere is below 65°F for any period of time, certainly more rapid staling occurs. If bread is not cooled properly, then its susceptibility to mould growth is greatly increased.

Automatic de-panning system.

11. Slicing and wrapping

Finally, slicing and wrapping takes place when the bread is in its correct condition; for large 28 oz bread the slicing technique has not changed for many years, perhaps the only changes since the development of the Chorleywood Bread Process are that the bread may have a higher volume (this can sometimes cause problems), and that Chorleywood process bread is definitely softer and possibly more difficult to slice. Slicer blades do need to be changed more frequently, but the advantages of greater shelf life far outweigh any such considerations. Wrapping is all part of the same machine, and, if the blades are set correctly and the wrapping paper is of the correct quality, little or no problems exist here.

CONTINUOUS MIXERS

Oakes mixer

Some modification in processing technique is required when making pan bread on this continuously fed mixer.

The slurry tanks are where the first major difference occurs. In the normal Oakes system, two brew or slurry tanks are positioned close to the developer head. These tanks vary in capacity but it is usual to make up sufficient slurry to allow approximately forty minutes' running time in each tank. The weighing in of the various ingredients is quite important if a thorough distribution is to be obtained (without lumps). The usual procedure is to run the doughing water into the tank; when the level of water reaches the high-speed stirrers the dough conditioner (Dynarex) should be added. Salt and yeast may be added at any time during the filling of the tank, but again it is probably better to empty the salt just after the dough conditioner. Any other ingredients such as malt flour and milk powder, which are difficult to disperse in this large amount of water, should be pre-dispersed in a small measured quantity of water. The water so used should be included in the total measure of the liquor.

A typical formulation for a nine-sack tank would be:

50 lb	salt
50 lb	yeast
27 lb	Dynarex
1440 lb	water

If fat is required, this is added directly into the barrel of the mixer by a constant displacement pump.

Two other points on ingredients are: it is more usual to use granular yeast in this type of mixer because it is available in bulk and consequently simpler to handle. It has been found that dough produced on this type of mixer does not normally have the same water absorption as a CBP batch mixer; the drop in water absorption is difficult to quantify but could be approximately 5 lb per 280 lb flour.

The optimum dough temperature is the same as for batch mixers, i.e. 85°F–87°F.

When the dough emerges from the special divider head (described earlier), the piece is put through a conical moulder in the usual fashion.

Generally this type of continuously mixed dough is given much shorter first proof time than a batch processed dough; in practice this varies between thirty seconds in open conveyor belts to approximately four minutes in a much shortened conventional first prover. Moulder settings and other production points remain the same.

It is interesting to note that most Oakes mixers are used to produce one-piece bread. The finished texture of the loaf appears more spherical than in a batch mixer loaf, probably due to the mixing action. It is also probable that the shorter first-proof time is used to keep this more rounded cell from becoming too open. No vacuum is applied to this type of mixer and therefore the control of texture is obtained by varying the first proof, by altering dough temperature and by altering configuration or throughput of the mixer. The throughput of the mixer is, of course, extremely critical and it is vitally important to ensure that the residence time in the mixing barrel is sufficient to both hydrate the mix and develop the dough correctly. (See section on Oakes mixer.)

7. Production of speciality breads and small ferments

The production of brown bread on CBP is very little different from that of 28 oz white bread. One or two points which should be considered can make the difference between success and failure.

Flour: Normally blends of wheatmeal and white flour are made to achieve the type of texture and volume required. A blend of 75% wheat meal and 25% white flour is most common, but this can vary according to local taste. As much as 50% white flour is used in some areas and none in others.

One fairly common fault found in CBP brown bread has been low volume; this is usually associated with the use of older wheatmeal flour; it is most important, therefore, to ensure that stocks of wheatmeal are turned round quickly and kept for a maximum of ten days only.

The oxidant requirement for brown bread is normally higher than for standard bread, consequently specialised brown-bread products are made – such as Panado and Darpan – which, apart from having the correct oxidant and fat blend, also contain a level of dry caramel colour and flavours which eliminate the inconvenience caused by using sticky syrups and caramel.

Two other production points worth mentioning are that vacuum is not always required in brown bread doughs because the texture of the finished bread is not required to be as fine as that of white bread. A work level of 4 to 4½ watt hours per pound is needed when 100% wheatmeal flour – i.e. coarse wheatmeal – is used in the recipe.

Working at the lower work level does tend to give a more resilient crumb which is much less likely to give the crumbly characteristic common in much wheatmeal bread.

The Bread and Flour Regulations permit only ascorbic acid as the sole oxidising agent in wholemeal bread and, as most of the wholemeal produced is of the proprietry type, it is worthwhile contacting the manufacturers of the particular flour blends for their recommendations in the manufacture of this type of bread by the Chorleywood Bread Process. Generally it is necessary to work to low work levels of 3½ watt hours per pound of flour and give a little bulk time (10 minutes) before processing.

Germ meals

Hovis and Vitbe are the most common germ meals available. In this case the law allows the use of additives such as Dynarex. Again, for the most satisfactory results, it is worthwhile contacting the respective millers of the flour for their recommendations for Chorleywood bread production.

High-protein, gluten bread, etc.

The proposed amendments to the 1963 Bread and Flour regulations are likely to eliminate the class of bread at present designated 'gluten bread', a bread containing at least 16% protein on a dry weight basis. High protein bread will be retained i.e. bread containing at least 22% protein on a dry weight basis. There may be special labelling requirements for this type of bread depending on the type of protein used to increase the total protein content of the bread.

Processing details are supplied with appropriate recipes.

High-volume bread

During recent years the production of this type of bread has become very popular. In fact, one could argue that the CBP, together with the use of modern dough conditioners, have made its production possible. The use of these, extra yeast and sometimes a little fat, sugar oı milk powder are the only formulation modifications necessary.

Generally, two types of this bread are produced:

(1) The type which claims to be an aid to slimming as part of a calorie controlled diet, i.e. makes claims such as 'Slice for slice contains less calories than normal bread'. Usually this bread is scaled at 10 oz into a normal 1 lb bread tin.

(2) A 1 lb piece of dough scaled into either a longer 1 lb tin or into a 2 lb farmhouse tin.

The production method is similar to that of normal 32 oz bread and generally the problems which occur in production are similar.

One problem which does occur more frequently is that of holes and open texture. This is, of course, associated with stretching the dough piece to greater limits. It is therefore extremely important to ensure that the moulder can handle 10 oz or stretch the 1 lb dough piece out to a 2 lb tin. Many moulders will not do this adequately. Therefore, bakers often either mould a 20 oz piece and split it in the pressure board or cross pan the 1 lb piece which covers up rather than eliminate the problem. It is very important to allow the dough piece to grow in the oven rather than prove to the maximum height.

For recipes, see Chapter 8.

PRODUCTION OF MORNING GOODS

The production of morning goods from a mechanically developed dough is just as straightforward as that of pan bread. The same basic rules apply, but there are a number of formulation modifications and special production points which are worth noting.

Formulation

A range of ingredients has been developed specifically to assist in the production of CBP morning goods. This class of emulsifier-based improver, correctly used, is capable of conferring superb gas retention and consequently excellent volume on all types of morning goods, not least in CBP produced goods.

The fat and oxidant requirements are slightly different from white-pan bread production, and the small ingredients must be adjusted by the improver manufacturer to ensure that the optimum result is obtained.

Oxidant requirement

For morning goods, the level of oxidant is usually lower than it is for white pan bread. The reason is that some semi-automatic plants available for the production of Viennas, teacakes, etc., take about twenty-five minutes to work off a CBP dough. This can lead to undesirable 'over oxidation' effects if too much oxidant (over 60 ppm) is used. Some of the older plants and small hand-operated systems take much longer and therefore further adjustments ought to be made to suit the speed at which the dough can be worked off. Ideally, small dough batches, worked off quickly, lead to the most consistent results. The one exception to this rule will be discussed later.

Fat requirement

Most types of morning goods contain sufficient fat for there to be an adequate fraction of high melting point fat for the needs of the CBP apart from any specialised small ingredients. It is none the less sensible to ensure that the necessary small amount of specialised fat essential to the CBP is present in such a small ingredient as an insurance policy. If one can use for this purpose a specialised fat or emulsifier, with its additional benefits, so much the better.

Yeast

As for any no-time dough, extra yeast has to be used compared to a one-hour to a one-and-a-half hour dough system. When very high fat and sugar level articles are being produced, the retarding effect of these two ingredients may be considerable, so yeast levels do vary from 5 to 12 lb per 140 lb of flour in all types of articles. It is most desirable to include the maximum amount of water which the plant can handle to achieve the best results for almost all types of morning goods. This will be discussed in more detail later.

An exception to this arises when very high fat levels are in use – over 18 lb of fat per 140 lb of flour. Increased water compared to a bulk fermented recipe will then cause the dough to become slack and unmanageable.

Fat and sugar

These two ingredients may be coupled together, particularly as they are used in similar proportions in the richer type of articles such as cookies, bridge rolls, doughnuts, etc. A good general rule for these ingredients is that neither of them should be used at levels above 18 lb per 140 lb flour. The richest article one would normally expect to mix by a CBP machine would contain 18 lb sugar and 18 lb fat per 140 lb of flour. This probably accounts for about 95% of morning goods production. Obviously some bakers may wish to include higher levels of fat and sugar in speciality lines. In such cases, the yeast level may have to be increased considerably and the water level cut; both steps will clearly make the process less economic.

Flour

For most types of morning goods, the flour grades commonly used for CBP white bread production are quite adequate. For high-volume goods, 'Crusty Bread' and Viennas, and for Scotch morning rolls, a slightly better grade is preferable, possibly the flour grade recommended for bulk fermented standard white bread. A number of bakers, particularly in Scotland, still use flours containing high proportions of Canadian wheats – especially for Scotch morning rolls. In these cases it is essential to ensure that there is adequate cereal amylase present and an addition of light malt to the recipe may be necessary.

The remaining ingredients, such as egg, milk powder, dry gluten and spices, have a similar effect to that which they have in conventional processing and may be used as and when desired with no ill-effects or special precautions.

Fruit

One of the most difficult problems encountered in the production of morning goods by the CBP has been the incorporation of fruit. In the Tweedy machine this has been overcome and it is now possible to produce a very heavily fruited article, i.e. 140 lb of mixed fruit to 140 lb of flour, using a specially developed plate and a two stage mixing process.

The plate itself is expensive and is only worthwhile if it is intended to produce a good number of doughs incorporating high levels of fruit. For the baker who only wishes to produce a small number of fruited doughs, then the high-speed mixer can cope either by judiciously 'inching' the fruit into the dough after completing the dough development cycle or by tipping the developed dough into conventional mixing equipment in which the fruit can be added.

Processing

Work level

Conventionally processed morning goods have traditionally been made from fairly short time doughs. If one assumes that the work level required for a dough should be related to the corresponding bulk fermentation time of a conventionally mixed dough, then it might be expected that the work level imparted to such goods would be less than the 5 watt hours per pound required for white bread.

In practice it has been found that for Vienna goods, morning rolls, Yorkshire teacakes (i.e. the leaner small ferments), between 4·75 and 5 watt hour per pound gives the best results. For fruited teacakes, cookies and bridge rolls, a lower work level is desirable, say 4 watt hours per pound. Very high fat levels combined with a comparatively high dough temperature – 86–88°F – cause a 'softening off' of these richer doughs during the mixing period.

Vacuum level

The desired texture (crumb-cell size) of morning goods varies considerably throughout the U K. All bakers accept that Vienna goods and French bread must be mixed under atmospheric conditions. The vacuum level applied to other types of morning goods can vary between 0–18 in. hg. Although most bakers mix all morning goods atmospherically, for larger doughs it is advantageous, with the exception of Viennas, to employ normal vacuum levels.

Processing subsequent to mixing

Viennas, French bread and similar items which require an open texture are generally left for ten minutes in bulk before processing further in order to obtain their characteristic open texture. Generally inferior articles result if processing takes place immediately after mixing. However, it is also vital that once dough processing begins, the whole of the dough is divided within fifteen minutes, i.e. the total time in bulk of any of the dough should not exceed twenty-five minutes. This is because of the damaging effects of high levels of oxidant if processing is delayed. Such goods show typical 'over-oxidation' features.

All other types of morning goods should be divided immediately after mixing and the dough completely worked off within twenty-five minutes if the best results are to be obtained to stay. It is always advisable to mix the smallest dough that is practically possible.

Following dividing, as with white bread processing, conventional make-up plant is all that is necessary. Intermediate or first-proof times on most automatic roll plants are notoriously short. Some have been modified so that there is no first proof, but the usual period is between six and eight minutes' rest.

The largest single problem encountered in morning-goods production is a large hole under the top crust of flattened or pinned-out articles. This is directly related to the unsuitability of the autoplant to process properly the new type of dough presented to it.

The CBP morning-goods dough, after being divided, is in a highly delicate condition and is very sensitive to any excess pressure. The pinning unit in the roll plant, and to a lesser extent hand rolling, inevitably puts considerable pressure on the dough piece. If the first-proof time can be extended to between ten and fifteen minutes to allow the dough to recover from dividing before it is pinned out, then goods of the Yorkshire teacake type can be well pinned out with only a slight risk of the appearance of the ubiquitous hole. Another important factor if doughs are to be pinned out successfully is to aim to produce doughs which are as soft as is practically possible. Once again the limiting factor is that the automatic plants in the UK are not often designed to handle soft doughs and even when they are the operative will take out a pint or two of water at the first sign of 'doubles' or sticking in the divider or moulding cups. If the hole problem persists even with the longest first-proof and softest dough possible in a particular plant, there are a few further minor plant adjustments which can be made. Reduction in work level, reduction of oxidising agents, taking pressure off the pinner and finally taking top heat off the front burner of the ovens will all help.

For some reason the problem does not seem to occur in Scotch rolls, possibly because some are batched (baked off together).

All morning goods which are handled after the moulding cups – such as fingers – also require first proof, but this is not normally necessary for goods which remain ball shaped.

The proof and baking conditions of CBP produced morning goods are not normally different from the corresponding bulk fermented processes.

Production of CBP morning goods is now carried out in considerable quantities. Provided the basic rules are adhered to, very good results can be obtained. Most people also find considerable improvement in both consistency and production economics.

8. Recipes

On the following pages are a number of basic bread and morning-goods recipes, all of which are widely used in commercial bakeries throughout the United Kingdom.

Obviously it is impossible for all the recipes to be suitable for every bakery without some adjustment, particularly in water and yeast quantity. Personal taste and local conditions will also play an important part in whether or not these recipes exactly suit a particular bakery's requirements.

Any of them would therefore make a good starting point for any new line one might consider putting on in the bakery or if one is just starting up a CBP mixer.

For more details of production methods, etc., it is important to consult the appropriate chapter on morning goods, pan bread, etc.

All of the following recipes may be adapted for use in smaller machines and a simple division of the recipe will make them suitable for Tweedy 35–70 or 140, or at the other end of the scale the 300 and 350 machine. The quantity of flour stated in the recipes is the ideal for the 280 mixer, but in many cases morning goods and speciality bread are made in smaller quantities because the demand for these products is considerably less than normal pan bread.

Another point about the recipes is that except where stated a normal CBP flour may be used.

Pan bread

	lb	oz
Flour	280	—
Salt	5	8
Yeast	5	8
Dynarex	3	—
Water	175	—

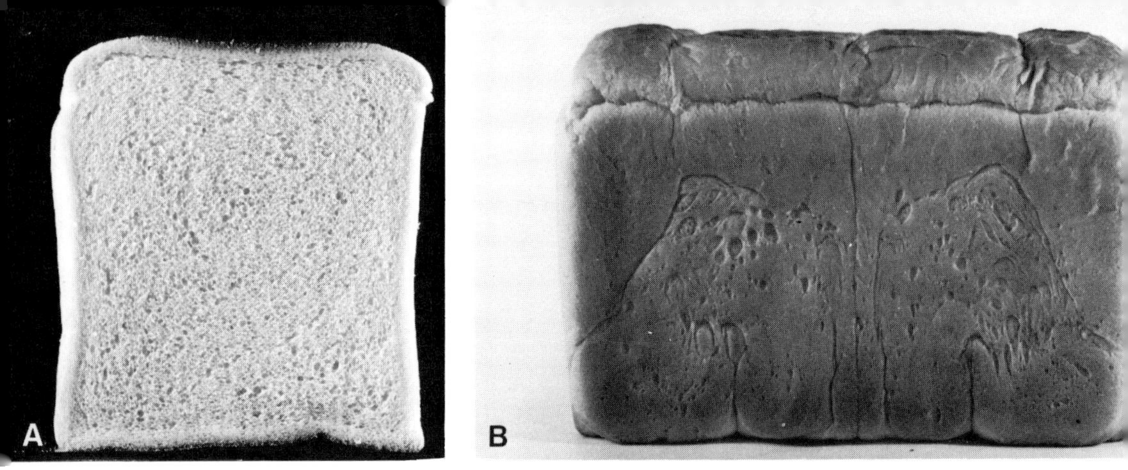

Pan bread, (a) internal and (b) external view.

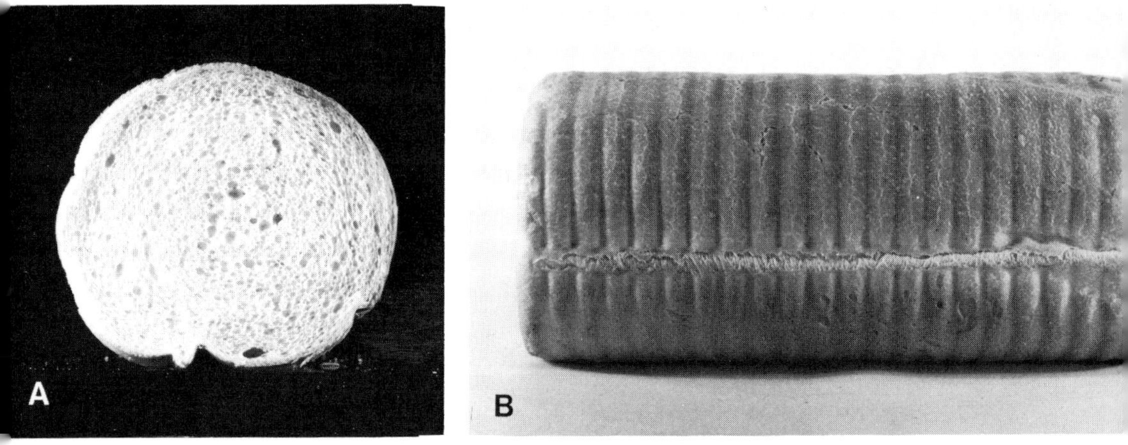

Milk bread, (a) internal and (b) external view.

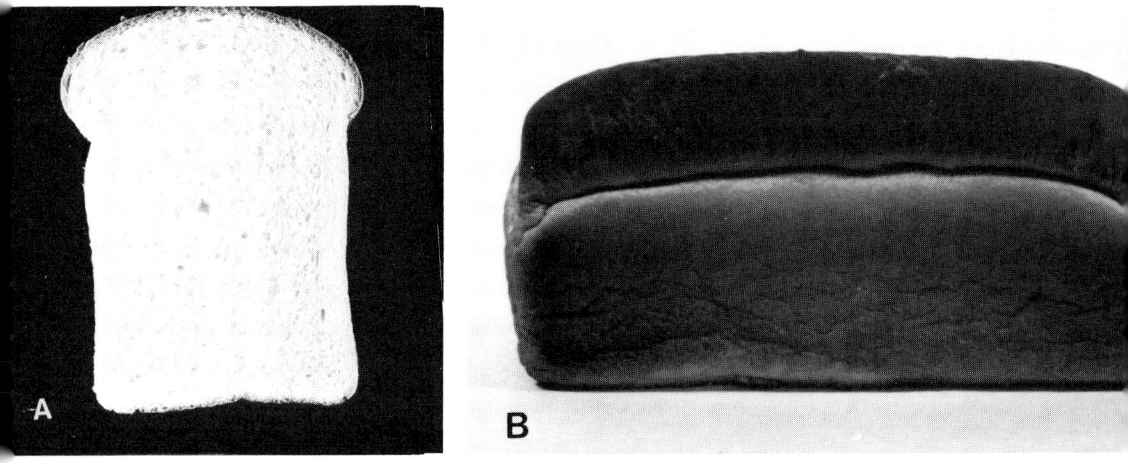

Skimmed milk bread, (a) internal and (b) external view.

Production points:

Work level	5 watt hours
Vacuum	17 in. Hg
Watt meter reading	234
Dough temperature	86°F

Follow the production method laid down in the chapter on processing. The level of yeast may have to be lowered if box bread is to be produced.

Pan bread – suitable for toasting

	lb	oz
Flour	280	—
Salt	5	8
Yeast	5	8
Dynarex	3	—
Fat	2	—
Skimmed milk powder or Cascade	4	—
Water	175	—

Production points:

Work level	5 watt hours
Vacuum	17 in. Hg
Watt meter reading	237
Dough temperature	86°F

Follow normal production method.

Milk bread

		lb	oz	lb	oz
	Flour	280	—		
	Salt	5	8		
	Yeast	6	—		
	Dynarex	3	—		
	Full cream milk powder	17	—		
or	Skimmed milk powder			12	8
	Butter			5	—
	Water	185	—	185	—

Production points:

Work level	5 watt hours
Vacuum level	17 in. Hg
Watt meter reading	248°F
Dough temperature	86°F

The above recipe will conform to the regulation which allows the bread produced to be called 'milk bread' or 'milk bread containing whole milk solids'.

An alternative recipe may be used which contains skimmed milk powder and not butter. This must be called 'skimmed milk bread', 'separated milk bread', 'lactein bread' or 'milk bread containing skimmed milk solids'.

Skimmed milk bread

	lb	oz
Flour	280	—
Salt	5	8
Yeast	6	—
Dynarex	3	—
Skimmed milk powder	17	—
Fat	5	—
Water	187	—

Production points:

Work level	5 watt hours
Vacuum level	17 in. Hg
Watt meter reading	250
Dough temperature	86°F

Note.

(1) It is most important to use a source of milk powder which has had a high heat treatment or the bread will be low in volume.

(2) In order to overcome any binding effect that milk powder may have, it is desirable to use a quantity of lard or shortening in conjunction with Dynarex.

Oven-bottom bloomers, (a) internal and (b) external view.

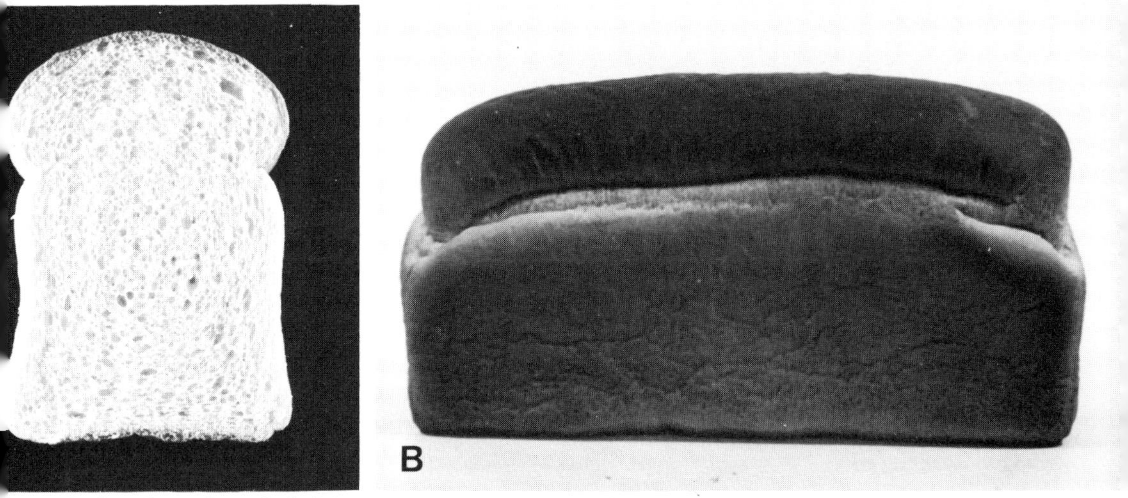

High-volume bread, (a) internal and (b) external view.

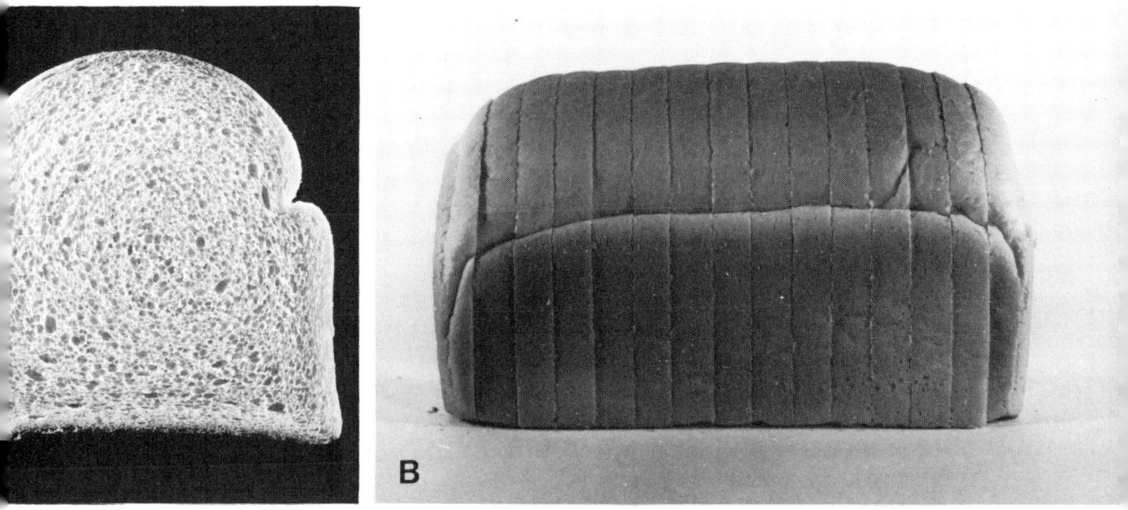

Danish bread, (a) internal and (b) external view.

Oven bottom bloomers, etc.

	lb	oz
Flour	280	—
Salt	5	8
Yeast	5	8
Dynacrust or Spiral	3	8
Water	168	—

Production points:

Work level	$4\frac{3}{4}$ watt hours
Vacuum level	12 in. Hg if possible
Watt meter reading	231
Dough temperature	86°F

(1) Dynacrust or Spiral are additives which help crust retention, but the correct baking conditions are of paramount importance if a good crust is to be obtained.

(2) The lower water absorption and work level are used generally to improve handling properties and to improve boldness of the loaf.

(3) Vacuum level is difficult to adjust but if a more open texture is desired then it is necessary.

High-volume bread

	lb	oz
Flour	140	—
Salt	2	12
Yeast	4	—
Spiral	2	8
Gluten	1	—
Fat	1	—
Water	87	—

Production points:

Work level	5 watt hours
Vacuum level	17 in. Hg
Watt meter reading	120

Dough temperature	86°F

Process normally.

(1) Because this dough is to be worked off into 10 oz or 16 oz pieces, it is important that smaller doughs should be made and worked off within ten minutes (max.) of mixing. It is important to adjust the baking conditions if small loaves are made and also to underprove rather than overprove.

(2) The 1 lb or 2 lb of gluten may be eliminated if a better grade of flour is in use.

(3) This dough may be worked off into 2 lb farmhouse tins or large 1 lb breads which are normally lidded, or in 1 lb bread tins and scaled at 10 oz tin size.

(4) No dietary claim may be made for this type of loaf, but if the baked bread weighs less than 10 oz and attains the volume of a normal 14 oz loaf, it is possible to state: 'Slice for slice this loaf contains less calories than ordinary bread.' No reference to slimming must be made.

Danish bread or other small crusty bread

	lb	oz
Flour	140	—
Salt	2	12
Yeast	2	12
Spiral	2	8
Fat	1	—
Milk powder or Cascade	1	—
Water	87	—

Production points:

Work level	5 watt hours
Vacuum level	17 in. Hg
Watt meter reading	117
Dough temperature	86°F

(1) This type of bread is normally produced either, as a tin loaf, with the dough piece scaled at 1 lb into a large farmhouse pan, or for family bakers on baking trays batched together and dusted liberally with flour.

(2) The normal working-off procedure is adopted.

A 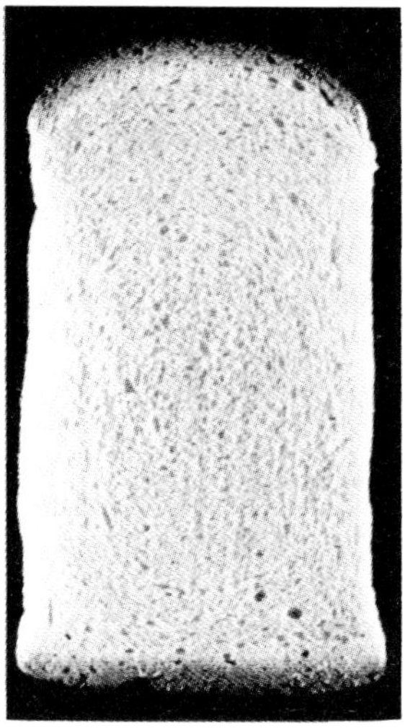 B 

Scottish batch bread, (a) internal and (b) external view.

Scottish batch bread or square bread

	lb	oz
Strong flour	280	—
Salt	7	—
Yeast	4	8
Dynarex	1	8
Water	155	—

Production points:

Work level	3·75 watt hours
Vacuum level	'variable'
Watt meter reading	168
Dough temperature	83°F
First-proof time	15 minutes
Final-proof time	35 minutes
Baking time	80–90 minutes according to oven.

(1) A good strong Canadian flour is mostly used, this being necessary to give a fine upstanding loaf; it is advisable when making batch bread from mechanically developed dough to use a good strong flour as any inclusion of a weaker flour may give rise to 'binking'.

(2) Because of the higher dough temperatures used, 82–83°F, there is naturally less tolerance than a conventional dough, but in a high-speed mixer only one sack at a time is mixed as against 2 or 2½ sacks conventionally. Therefore, control of the dough is considerably easier and divider weighing more accurate, resulting in better yield; also there is no fermentation loss.

(3) Where prover/oven plants are in use, the production of mechanically developed dough batch bread is somewhat easier than when a transfer stage from prover to oven, or from setters to drawplate is used. Due to the more delicate nature of the dough, as in the case of tin bread, greater care has to be taken in handling the setters during transfer. Obviously the bakeries vary tremendously in set-up, therefore the above recipe will produce excellent mechanically developed dough batch bread, but some slight alteration may be necessary.

N.B.

Very few large bakeries are producing Scottish batch bread on CBP as yet.
It is felt that some variations in quality still require ironing out before higher proportions are made. The few bakeries producing are satisfied with the results.

Irish batch bread

	lb	oz
Flour	280	—
Salt	6	8
Yeast	4	—
Dynarex	1	12
Water	160	— to 170 —

Production points:

Work level	4·5 watt hours
Vacuum level	variable
Watt meter reading	200
Dough temperature	84°F
First-proof time	8 minutes
Final-proof time	20 minutes
Bake – between	70–85 minutes very approx.

A Vitbe 14 oz loaf, (a) internal and (b) external view.

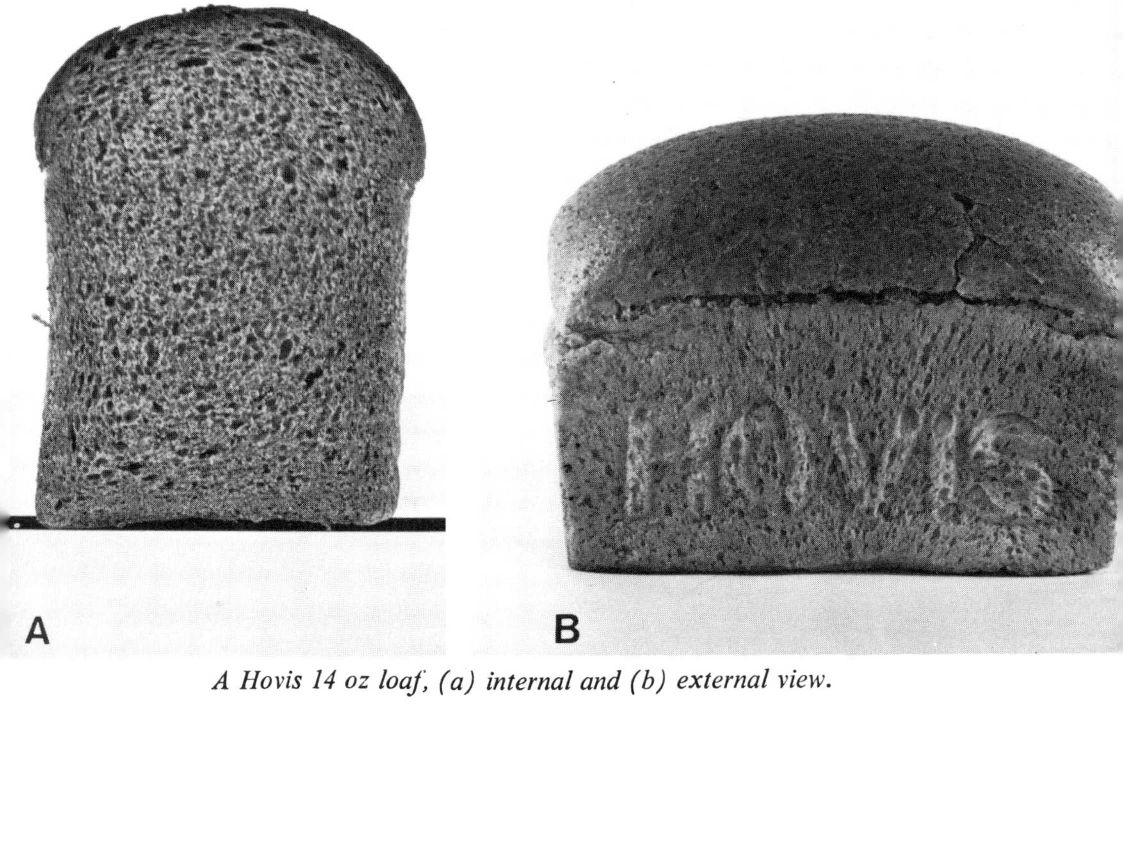

A Hovis 14 oz loaf, (a) internal and (b) external view.

The variability in water quantity is due to the use of flours of normal CBP grist in Northern Ireland, whilst in Eire approximately 70% of native wheat has to be used in their grists.

Note

The production of Irish batch bread on CBP is now fairly common throughout Ireland, but a few minor faults still require ironing out. It is felt that this comparative success may be due to the difference in height of the Irish loaf as compared to its Scottish counterpart.

National Vitbe recipe – wheat-germ bread

By mechanical development

	lb	oz
Vitbe meal	280	—
Water	170	—
Yeast	6	—
Lard	9	—
Dynarex	3	—
Malt flour	1	4
Wembrun	3	—

Countdown (Tweedy) 190
Dough temperature 86°F

Hovis wheat-germ recipe

	lb	oz
Hovis flour	280	—
Yeast	6	8
Bread fat	2	—
Dynarex	3	—
Water	184	—

Dough temperature 84/86°F

Mixer	Tweedy
Vacuum	Off
Primary proof	7 minutes
Final proof	45 minutes @ 110°F relative humidity 75%
Baking time	30 minutes

High Protein Bread

'New Slimcea White Bread'

	lb	oz
New Slimcea No-Time Blend	35	0*
White Flour	140	0
Salt	2	8
Yeast (approx)	7	0
Water (approx)	112	0

Dough temperature	86°F.

Yeast quantity variable according to bakery conditions

Work level	$5\frac{1}{2}$ watt hours per 1 lb of dough
Vacuum	20 in. mercury.
Scaling weight	$11\frac{1}{2}$ oz
Intermediate proof time	10 minutes
Final-proof time	50 minutes
Final-proof temperature	105°F
Baking time	30 minutes
Oven temperature	450°F – 500°F

New Slimcea Brown Bread

	lb	oz
New Slimcea Brown No-Time Blend	35	0*
Wheatmeal flour	70	0
White flour	70	0
Salt	2	8
Yeast	7	0
Water	110	0

Dough temperature	86°F.

Yeast quantity variable according to bakery conditions

Work level	$5\frac{1}{2}$ watt hours per 1 lb of dough
Vacuum	20 in. mercury.
Scaling weight	$11\frac{1}{2}$ oz
Intermediate proof time	10 minutes
Final-proof time	50 minutes
Final-proof temperature	105°F

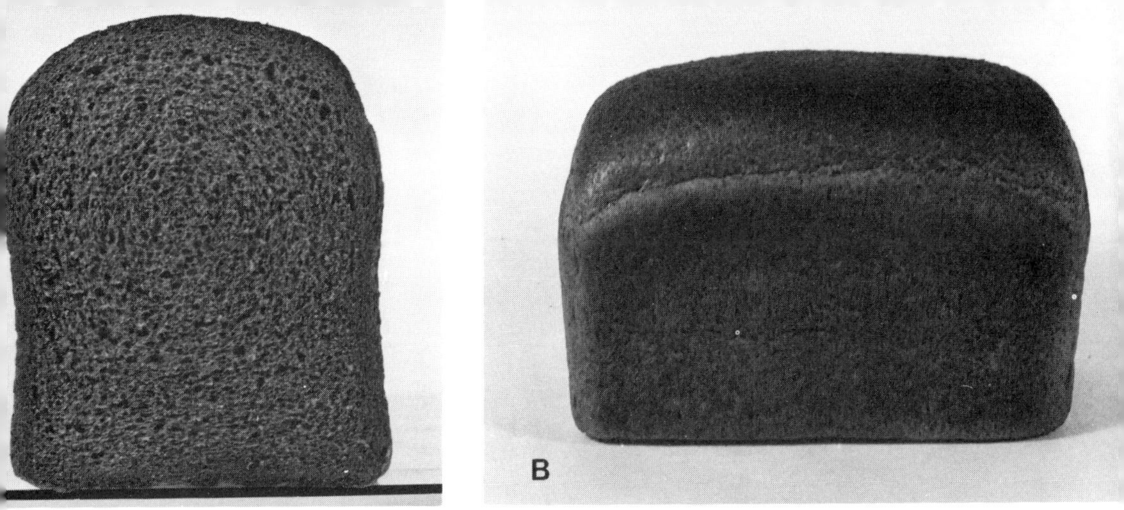

Brown bread, (a) internal and (b) external view.

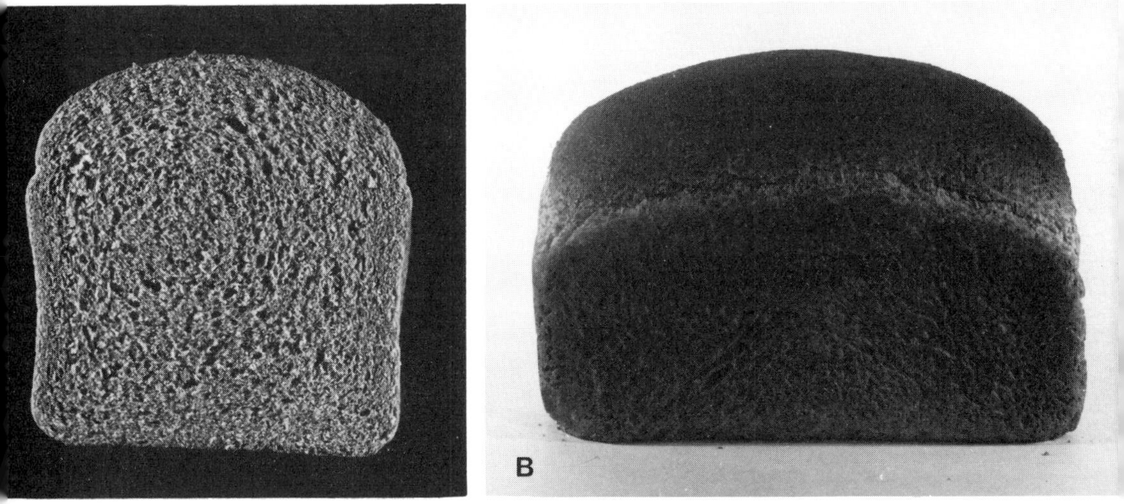

Wholemeal, (a) internal and (b) external view.

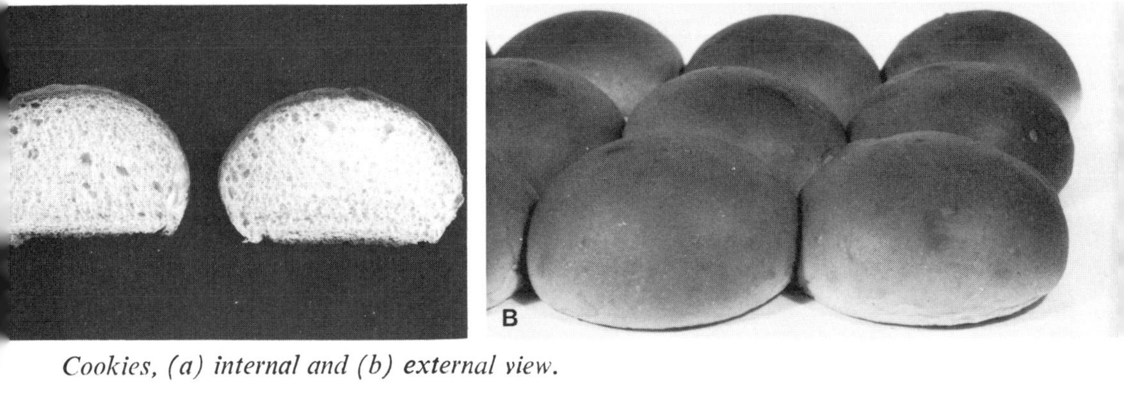

Cookies, (a) internal and (b) external view.

Baking time	30 minutes
Oven temperature	450°F – 500°F

**Note* these recipes are constituted so that the resultant bread may be designated, 'High Protein Bread', i.e. so that the level of protein is at least 22% of the total dry solids weight. In order to ensure that the correct level of protein is present in the finished loaf it is essential to adhere to the recipe recommended by the pre-blend manufacturer.

'Slimcea' breads are manufactured by Procea Nutrex Limited.

Brown bread

	lb	oz
Wheatmeal flour	210	—
Baker's flour	70	—
Salt	5	8
Yeast	6	—
Darpan	3	—
Water	185	—

Production points:

Work level	$4\frac{1}{2}$ watt hours
Vacuum	– operational
Watt meter reading	216
Dough temperature	86°F

(1) Darpan is a specially designed additive for brown bread which contains colouring and flavouring materials, together with the necessary fat and oxidant system for CBP.

(2) The proportion of wheatmeal flour can be varied; if more volume or lighter loaf is required, up to 50% white flour may be used. The work level may then be increased to 5 watt hours per pound.

(3) Fresh wheatmeal flour must be used.

(4) The working off procedure laid down for standard CBP production is suitable for brown bread.

High-volume brown bread

	lb	oz
Wheatmeal flour	70	—
Flour (bakers' grade)	70	—
Salt	2	12

Yeast	4	—
Spiral	1	4
Darpan	1	4
Dry gluten	1	—
Fat	1	—
Water	90	—

Production points:

Work level	5 watt hours
Vacuum level	17 in. Hg
Watt meter reading	121
Dough temperature	86°F

Follow normal CBP procedure – see production points on white high-volume bread.

Wholemeal bread

	lb	oz
100% wholemeal flour	70	—
Salt	1	6
Yeast	2	—
Dynacrust	1	—
Water	45	—

Production points:

Work level	3·5 watt hours
Atmospheric mixing	
Watt meter reading	51
Dough temperature	84°F

The above recipe will conform to the bread and flour regulations appertaining to wholemeal bread in the UK. Ascorbic acid is the only oxidising agent permitted if the bread is to be described as 'wholemeal'.

Normally only small quantities of this type of bread are made. Extra yeast and atmospheric mixing help give a little extra volume.

Dynacrust is the only product within the Arkady Range which may be used in this type of bread.

Cookies and plain teacakes

	lb	oz
Flour	140	—
Salt	2	—
Yeast	7	—
Spiral	1	8
Fat	16	—
Sugar	16	—
Cascade	2	—
Water	82	—

Production points:

Work level	4 watt hours
Vacuum level	optional
Watt meter reading	105
Dough temperature	86°F

For articles which are to be pinned out, a soft dough is required and at least twelve minutes first proof is necessary. Articles which are to remain round do not require this first proof.

Fruited buns or teacakes

	lb	oz
Flour	140	—
Salt	2	—
Yeast	8	—
Spiral	1	8
Fat	16	—
Sugar	16	—
Cascade	2	—
Water	82	—
Currants	32	—
Sultanas	32	—

Colouring and essence – as required

Production points:

Work level	4 watt hours
Vacuum level	optional

Fruited buns.

Watt meter reading	105
Dough temperature	86°F

(1) The fruit may be added during the last fifteen seconds of mixing in the Tweedy using the normal plate.

(2) Care should be taken when adding essences; it is preferable to add them into the fruit.

Scotch morning rolls

	lb	oz
Strong flour	140	—
Salt	2	8
Yeast	5	—
Spiral	2	8
Water	85	—

Production points:

Work level	5 watt hours per pound
Vacuum level	optional
Watt meter reading	117
Dough temperature	86°F

Scotch morning rolls.

Work the dough immediately into heads; allow to recover for ten minutes, divide, mould and rest for a further 10–15 minutes and then pin on to trays. Final proof time is about sixty minutes. Bake for 8–10 minutes at 500°F.

Yorkshire teacakes

This recipe will also be satisfactory for hamburger rolls

	lb	oz
Flour	140	—
Salt	2	12
Yeast	6	—
Spiral	2	8
Fat	6	—
Sugar	2	—
Cascade	1	—
Water	85	—

Production points:

Work level	5 watt hours
Vacuum level	optional
Watt meter reading	120
Dough temperature	86°F

Yorkshire teacakes.

Work the dough off immediately. Give at least twelve minutes first proof before pinning out gently. Prove and bake.

Vienna rolls

	lb	oz
Flour	140	—
Salt	2	12
Yeast	6	—
Spiral	2	8
Water	85	—

Production points:

Work level	5 watt hours
Atmospheric mixing	
Watt meter reading	117
Dough temperature	86°F

(1) Leave the dough in bulk for ten minutes before processing normally.

(2) Work off the dough within twenty-five minutes of completing the mixing cycle if consistent results are to be obtained. Prove normally, then bake in steam for ten minutes and a dry oven for a further ten minutes.

Vienna rolls.

Vienna batons

	lb	oz
Flour	140	—
Salt	2	12
Yeast	5	—
Spiral	2	8
Water	82	—

Production points:

Work level	5 watt hours
Atmospheric mixing	
Watt meter reading	116
Dough temperature	84°F

If an open texture is required, leave the dough in bulk for ten minutes and then work off normally, giving ten minutes first proof before putting through a baton moulder. Prove normally.

It is most important to have an adequate steam supply in the oven, otherwise bursting will take place.

If an 8 oz baton is being produced, the baking conditions should be for ten minutes at 450°F with steam in the oven at 7 lb per square inch. Evacuate steam completely and then bake for a further fifteen minutes.

Vienna batons.

Hot cross buns

	lb	oz
Flour	140	—
Salt	2	—
Yeast	8	—
Spiral	1	8
Fat	16	—
Sugar	16	—
Cascade	2	—
Water	82	—
Colour	As required	
Bunspice essence	Approx. 8 oz	
Currants	45	—
Sultanas	45	—
Peel	10	—

Production points:

Work level	4 watt hours
Vacuum level	optional
Watt meter reading	104
Dough temperature	86°F

Hot-cross buns.

(1) The level of spice and fruit will vary considerably from area to area.

(2) Bunspice essences are commonly used, but it is possible to use mixed spice, cinnamon, etc. These tend to have a retarding affect on yeast. Care should be taken in the selection of essence, as some tend to break down the dough if too high a level is used or the dough takes a long time to work off.

(3) It is advisable to add the fruit in a conventional dough mixer when the dough has been developed, otherwise a high level of damage would occur. There is an impact plate specially designed for the incorporation of fruit in the Tweedy (see Chapter 4, Section 3).

Brown and serve bread

		lb	oz
Flour		280	—
Salt		5	8
Yeast		4	8
Dynarex		3	—
Water	(approx.)	172	—

Production points:

Mix to 5 watt hours per pound of dough. Dough temperature 88°F.

Vacuum 15 in. depending on the type of texture. 'Home-made' type bread may be mixed atmospherically.
Normal first-proof time. Final-proof time 10% less than normal, approximately 48–52 minutes.
Bake at 300/320°F for 40–45 minutes, 1 lb pieces. Cool. Brown at 470°F for 10–12 minutes.

Many large bakers tend to use their normal pan bread recipe for this type of bread and adjust their oven conditions accordingly. It is extremely difficult to give general guidance about these conditions. (See beginning of chapter.)

PART IV

Problems

9. Problems associated with raw materials

To the baker the first indication that there is a problem is often a defect in the finished bread. The aim of this chapter is to relate some of the faults found in the loaf to their possible cause or causes. It should always be borne in mind that a particular fault may be brought about by one of a number of root causes, that subsequent incorrect processing or bakery conditions may aggrevate the fault once it has been introduced into a dough piece and it may often be that a combination of adverse circumstances is responsible.

It may be necessary to examine the dough ingredients, conditions within the mixing chamber, the dough consistency, defects in function and setting of processing plant and, equally important, the time taken for each phase of production.

It is proposed to concentrate mainly on the production of standard white bread, paying particular attention to batch dough development. Also, a few of the most widespread and intractable defects which are thought to have a number of interrelated causes will be discussed in greater depth.

Problems peculiar to continuous developers have been briefly discussed in the appropriate sections of the book, as have faults occurring in morning goods.

The three major factors, raw materials, dough developer conditions and processing have each been already examined. Each will now be reviewed, emphasising the most widely found defects, how they may be recognised in the finished loaf and what steps might be taken to overcome them once they have been correctly diagnosed.

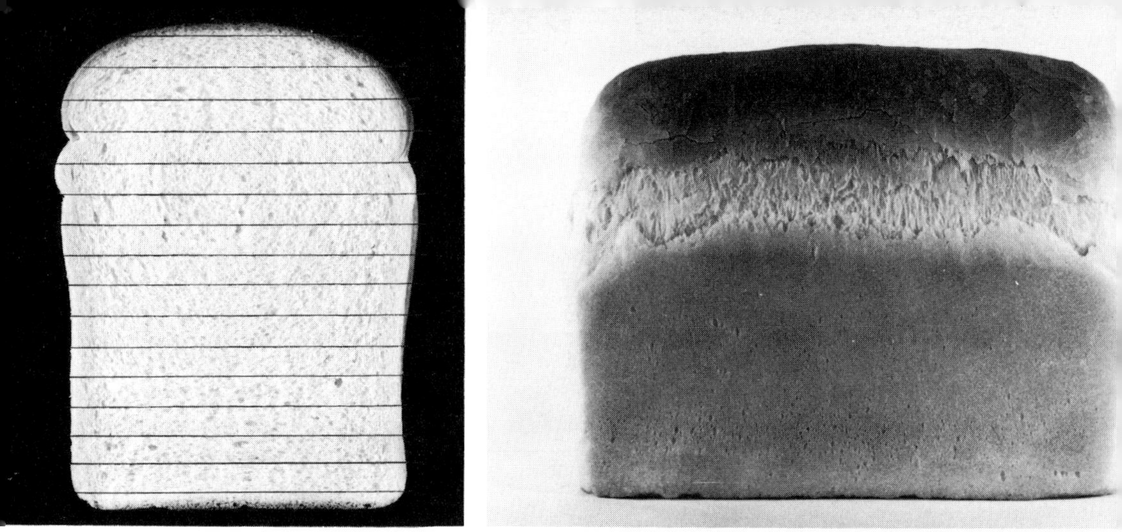

A good-quality loaf, produced commercially by the CBP batchmaking process, (a) internal and (b) external view.

Raw materials

It is perhaps natural that the baker's principal raw material – wheat flour – should be one of the first factors to be suspected when defects occur in the finished loaf. As has already been stressed, reputable millers can and do in the main provide a raw material which consistently maintains the parameters required for the production of good bread by the Chorleywood Bread Process.

None the less, there are occasionally faults which are directly attributable to failings in wheat quality. These may be due either to the incorrect selection of wheat or to incorrect processing at the mill. The single best guide to the suitability of a flour for use in the CBP is the amount of protein present in the flour. The 11–12% suggested in Chapter 4, section 2, has been established and demonstrated by a decade of industrial experience as being both technically suitable and economically acceptable.

It has been found that low-grade, very high protein Canadian flours (see illustration page 166) can produce doughs which, when developed to 5 watt hours per pound, have a highly resilient elastic feel and give rise to bread with a fairly normal internal appearance, but which has a low volume and a very resilient crumb feel. The price and availability of such flours makes this a largely academic problem – should it occur, there are three suggested solutions. The flour may be replaced by a more suitable one, it may be blended with weaker flour, or the processing may

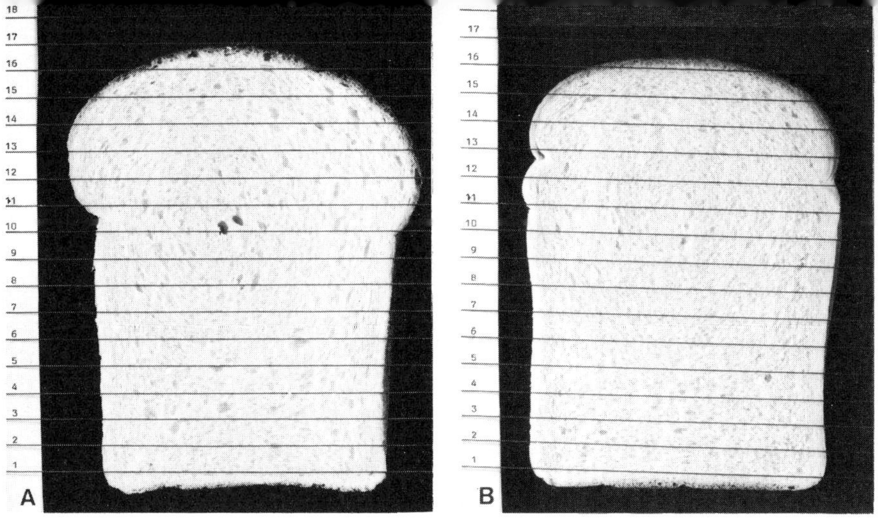

Loaf A is made from bulk-fermented dough made from a flour of $12\frac{1}{2}\%$ *protein.*

Loaf B is a CBP loaf made from a flour of $11\frac{1}{2}\%$ *protein.*

be modified, i.e. the work level increased, to develop more fully the dough protein.

There is always economic pressure on the miller to contain as far as possible the price of flour. The entry of the United Kingdom into the EEC and the phased introduction of the CAP levy system for cereal prices has greatly intensified this pressure. All wheats will become progressively more expensive and there will be a significant additional levy on any wheat imported from outside the EEC countries.

The result will inevitably be that wheat grists will change, increased levels of weaker wheats will be used and protein percentages will drop. This may lead to the production of flours in which the shortage of protein could be detrimental to the quality of the final bread. It is difficult to quantify a precise minimum protein percentage below which satisfactory bread can no longer be produced. For standard white tin bread one might suggest that a protein content of below 10·5% (see illustration page 166) would result in bread of a quality lower than usual.

The finished loaf exhibits a number of defects, due to the inadequate gas-retention properties of the dough. It is lacking in volume with a poor, ragged oven break. The crumb has a poor colour and the texture tends to be open and uneven, lacking both softness and resilience.

There is no simple remedy to the problem. Ideally, the answer would be to blend the flour with a percentage of high protein breadmaking flour, such as Canadian Manitoba. This may be difficult, but even a low percentage of such flour (10–20%) can lead to quite distinct improve-

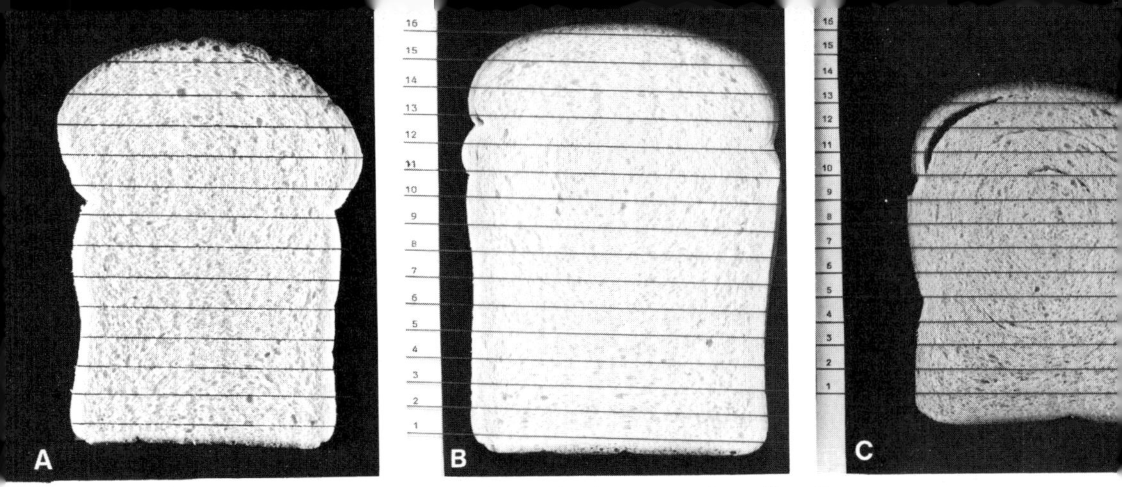

Loaf A is produced from a very high-protein Canadian flour.
Loaf B is the standard CBP loaf.
Loaf C is produced from flour with a protein content of 9·5%.

Note. All three loaves were produced using standard CBP methods and ingredients.

ments in overall bread quality. In the longer term it is possible to develop dough conditioners, such as are at present used in high-volume and speciality goods, to bolster the quality of standard white bread. However, the baker will have to be prepared to pay rather more for these sophisticated materials than he does for the present range of additives. Modifications to dough processing are not greatly beneficial, although cutting the work level as far as possible down to 4½ watt hours per pound may help.

The European wheats, which are expected to be increasingly used, in addition to being low in protein are also 'soft milling' wheats. They are not easily damaged during the milling process, giving flours with a

A loaf produced from a flour of normal protein level (11·5%) and a high level of damaged starch (40 farand units).

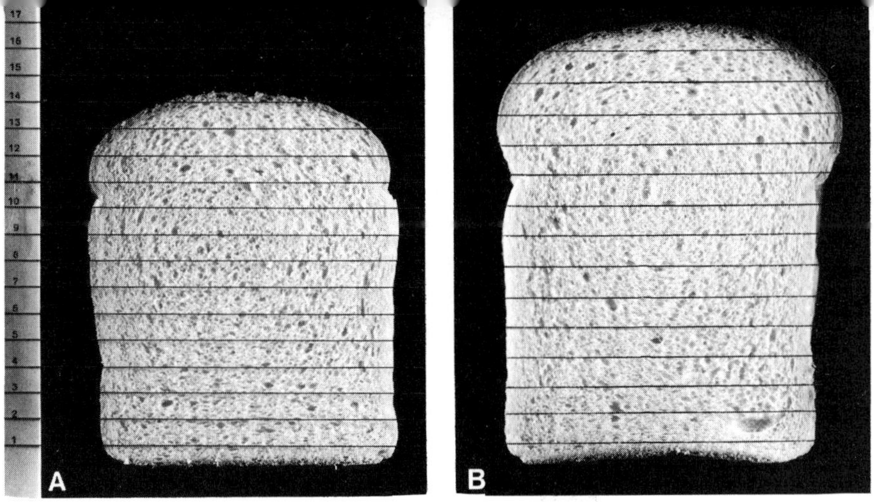

Loaf A was made from a flour with a Hagberg falling time of approximately 400 seconds.
Loaf B was produced from the same flour with the addition of 8 oz to the sack of 60–65° Linter malt.

low level of starch damage. The low protein and low level of starch damage combine to produce flours with a low water absorption. It is an unfortunate fact of life that as flour prices increase the water levels in the dough are likely to decrease. The baker must resist the temptation to try to maintain yields under these conditions. A low protein flour made into a dough containing too much water further reduces bread quality and multiplies production problems. (See illustration page 170.)

A further grist problem which has in the past been of considerable importance, but is now more of academic than practical interest, is that of a shortage of cereal alpha-amylase. The hard vitreous wheats, particularly the Australian ones, were found suitable for inclusion into CBP flours, the protein quantity was in the right range and it was possible to impart to them a high level of starch damage. However due to the climatic conditions in Australia, these wheats contain little or no natural cereal alpha-amylase. Flours which are deficient in cereal and alpha-amylase will not produce satisfactory bread by any no-time dough process. The main defect is a lack of oven spring leading to a lack of volume in the finished bread. The internal crumb is not unacceptable, although the lower than average specific volume leads to a rather poor softness. Flours with Hagberg falling times of above 350 seconds (on a 7 gm sample) are suspect. In extreme cases flours with a Hagberg falling time of 400 plus seconds were for a time used in the United Kingdom.

If the problem is just one of lack of cereal alpha-amylase, usually the incorporation of between eight ounces and one pound to the sack of 60–65° Linter malt can produce an apparently miraculous cure to volume defects (see illustration page 167). Although malt flour is often considered to be a small ingredient added by the baker, its use is so directly concerned with the properties of the wheat flour to which it is added that it is opportune to mention it at this point. The most widely used type of light (enzyme active) malt in use in British bakeries is 60–65° Linter SRB (straight run barley) malt. It should be added only when there is evidence that there is a shortage of cereal alpha-amylase in the flour. It is not advisable to add malt to CBP doughs just as a matter of course.

A further potential source of trouble for the baker was also highlighted by the inclusion of Australian wheats to the United Kingdom bread flour grists. These wheats made it relatively easy for millers to introduce high, and on occasion, excessive levels of starch damage to flours.

Starch damage levels of above 35 Farrand units can give rise to water absorption of between 18 and 19 gallons per sack (180–190 lb of water per 280 lb of flour) but bread quality inevitably suffers unless there is sufficient protein present (at least 12·5% is required for a starch damage level of above 35 Farrand units). The defect in the bread shows as a grey crumb with an open texture; it is initially soft but weak and tends to stale rapidly. The dough is characteristic. It is initially rather sticky as it leaves the developer but rapidly tightens in the divider to a normal consistency, though it has a rather dead, inelastic feel. It is again difficult to correct such a defect – one cannot reduce greatly the water content in the dough or else it becomes too tight to mould correctly.

Again, employing the best available dough additives helps by improving overall bread quality. However, the best solution lies with the baker – he must insist that in the final analysis bread quality must take precedence over yield and that the miller must provide him with the appropriate flour.

The problems associated with Australian wheat may no longer trouble the baker but it is most probable that they will be replaced from time to time by rather more serious ones, due to an excess of cereal alpha-amylase activity in the breadmaking flours available. The increased use of wheats grown within the EEC, with the variable climatic conditions of Western Europe, will result in wider variations in cereal alpha-amylase than was the case before the introduction of the Common Agricultural Policy into the United Kingdom.

In years when there are wet harvest conditions in Western Europe, the miller will either have to buy an increased percentage of wheat from outside the EEC which would be subject to an appreciable import levy or else the baker will have to accept flour containing a higher level of cereal alpha-amylase than is at present considered satisfactory.

The optimum range is above 250 seconds Hagberg falling time (on a 7 gm sample). As the level of cereal alpha-amylase increases above this level, the well-known symptoms of excess cereal alpha-amylase begin to appear. The first effect is that the slicer blades require changing more frequently than usual, they become blunt and tear the crumb, due to a build-up of dextrins on the cutting edge. In more extreme cases the cut crumb surface feels first soft and damp, then sticky to the touch. The loaf crust takes on increasing colour, the crumb colour becomes poorer and its quality deteriorates, becoming sticky and losing resilience.

It is very difficult to suggest effective steps to counter this problem. There is, as yet, no acceptable flour treatment which will reduce the level of cereal alpha-amylase in a flour, nor is there a magic ingredient to cure the fault. The baker's main hope must rest with the skill of the miller in blending the wheats available to him to keep the cereal alpha-amylase within usable limits.

Since work on this book began the implications of using increased levels of European wheats in United Kingdom breadmaking grists have become so immediate, and important, that the subject has been discussed more fully in the Chapter on New developments – in the section 'The EEC and the United Kingdom baking industry'.

It is worth noting that in the production of some lines of lean morning goods, particularly Scotch morning rolls, where a high volume is required, strong, sometimes all-Canadian, flours may be used. Here again there may be a deficiency in cereal alpha-amylase, and such recipes often benefit from the inclusion of 8 oz to 1 lb per 280 lb of flour of light malt (60–65 L).

Flour faults are fortunately infrequent, but if the baker does suspect this raw material it is essential that he should ask for, and be able to fully comprehend, a flour report whose parameters are relevant to the process he is employing.

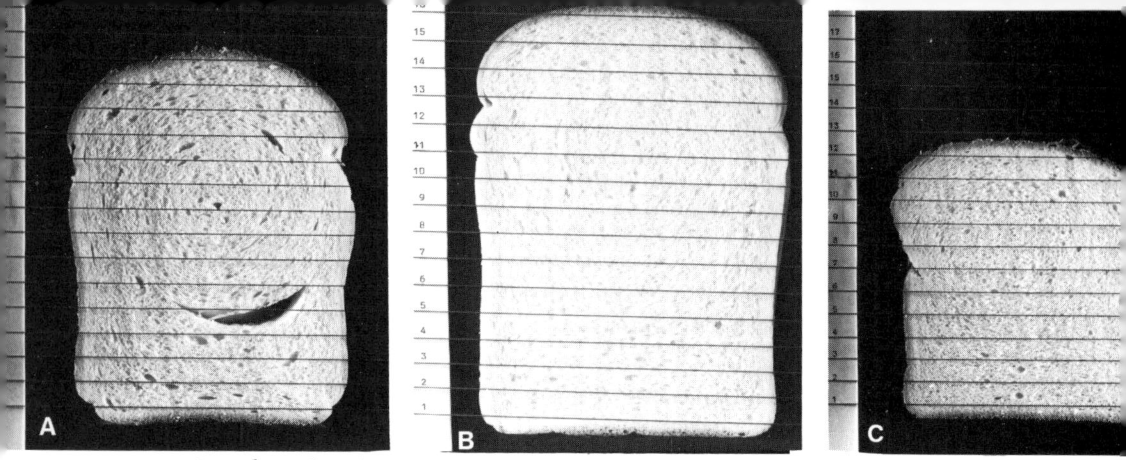

Bread produced by the CBP method with varying amounts of water.
(a) contains too little. (b) is the optimum loaf. (c) contains too much.

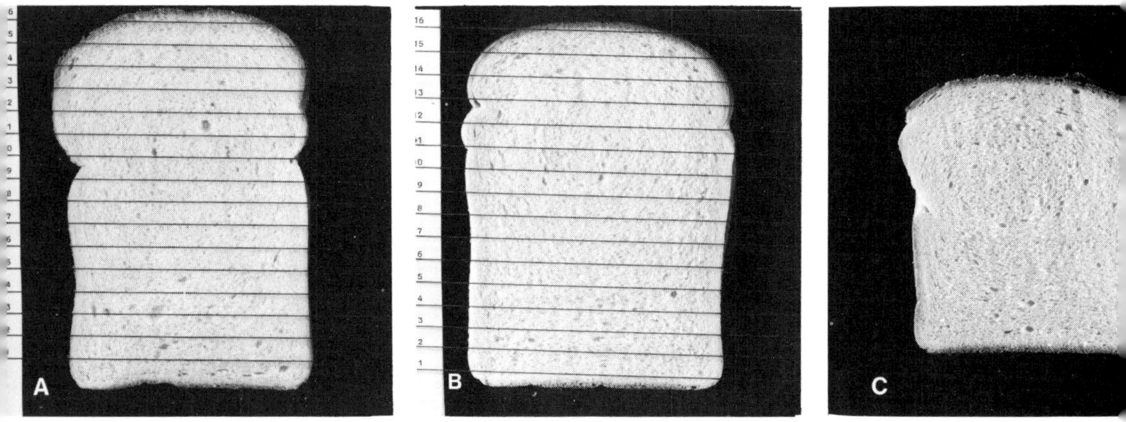

Bread produced by the CBP method with varying amounts of salt.
(a) contains too little. (b) is the optimum loaf. (c) contains too much.

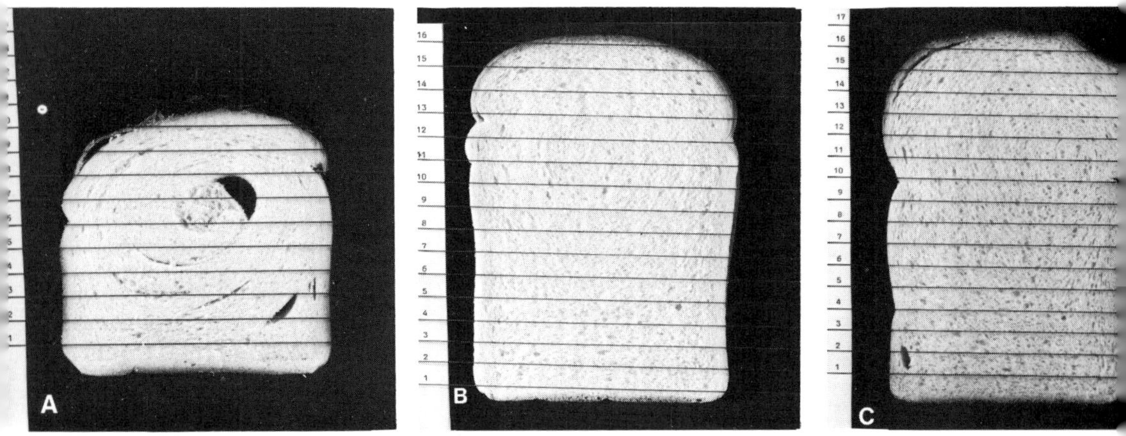

Bread produced by the CBP method with varying amounts of yeast.
(a) contains too little. (b) is the optimum loaf. (c) contains too much.

Turning to the remaining basic raw materials, water, salt and yeast:

Water

The CBP is not tolerant of wide variations in water content in the dough made from a particular flour on a particular plant. Too little water in a dough gives moulder problems. The resultant loaf has a cut slice which exhibits streaks and swirls whilst holes in the bread tend to be prevalent. Bakers, for the best of reasons – economic ones – are not prone to slip into this trap. The converse, too much water, is not usually a severe detriment to bread quality. Before the loaf suffers to excess there are usually processing problems – stick-ups on the plant – which push the baker back into the right range of water absorption. Incorrect water absorptions, when they do occur, are nearly always due to inaccuracies or inadequacies of the plant and will be discussed at the appropriate point.

Salt and yeast

Salt and yeast must be considered together. It is unusual to find an unbalanced recipe, though one can make mistakes in making up batch tanks for continuous mixers. Errors do occur in weighing – double yeasts or salt additions are patently obvious in the finished bread, as are the omissions of either one or the other. Double yeast runs away with the dough – outsize dough pieces at the end of proof and oversized bread result. Lack of yeast simply results in a dead dough – not to be confused with double salt which gives some gas production and a very distinctive taste. A dough without salt might be confused with one containing excessive yeast, but the totally insipid taste is uniquely characteristic.

It is much easier to mismeasure either one or the other of these ingredients, in particular to include one more or less packet of yeast into the mix. It is essential to have a sensible routine, rigidly adhered to, so that the possibilities of such mistakes are absolutely minimised.

Dough additives

The success of bread production by the Chorleywood process is so critically dependent on the nature of the small ingredients that incorrect

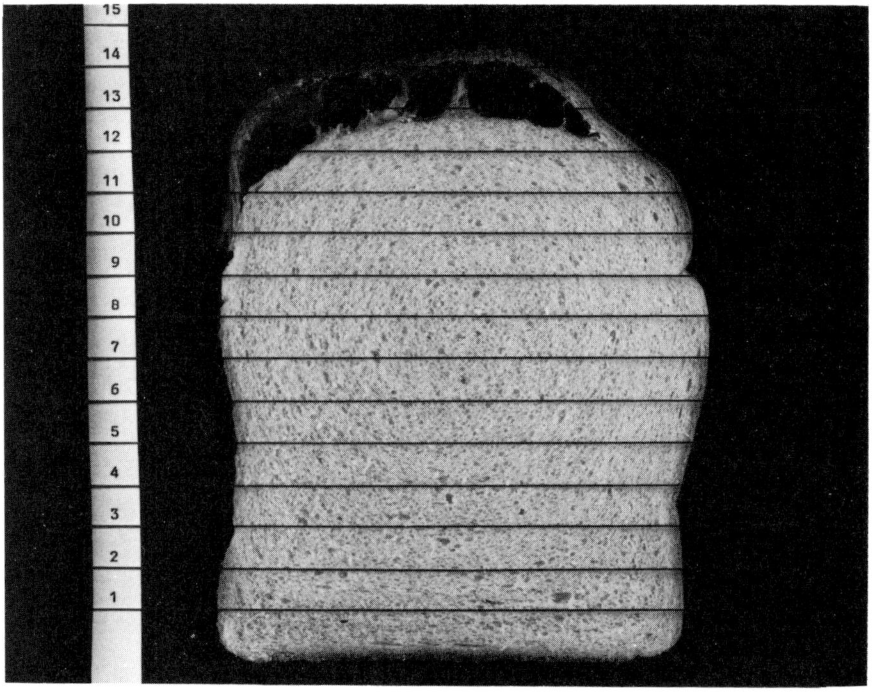

This loaf was produced by the standard CBP method and contained all the necessary ingredients apart from the fat.

or inadequate improvers can be directly responsible for quite severe faults.

The principal defects are due to either fat faults or oxidant faults. The classical fat fault is due to there being an insufficient amount of the correct type of fat in the dough. The loaf has a very characteristic appearance, there is a very poor volume, no oven spring, and the cut surface has a very poor colour and a dense crumb texture with very poor softness and crumb quality. There is a very marked change in loaf quality over a very narrow range of fat addition. The critical range can vary from flour to flour, so it is essential to ensure that there is an adequate 'safety margin'. This is built in to correctly developed dough additives – if additional fat is required to maintain bread quality, the improver should be regarded as inadequate and should be changed.

The great majority of improver oxidant systems contain both

potassium bromate and ascorbic acid. A straight oxidant deficiency is manifested as a general loss in bread quality, particularly a loss of oven spring and loaf volume. The effects are generally similar to a fat fault, but in this case there is no extremely narrow critical range comparative to that of fat.

If oxidant shortage is suspected an analysis of the improver for oxidants is not difficult and a total oxidant level of less than 45 ppm on flour weight – at the level of improver being used – might well begin to exhibit such defects.

There is one further oxidant problem – it is possible to overtreat CBP bread doughs. Ascorbic acid has little or no adverse effect on loaf quality even at very high levels – 200 ppm on flour weight gives perfectly normal bread. Potassium bromate must be used with more caution. Here excessive levels give rise to a characteristic defect – the loaf volume becomes very large with a wild oven break. The cut surface shows an open texture often with large holes along moulding lines and the crumb has a poor colour and a characteristic damp sticky feel. Higher than normal levels of potassium bromate have been used to increase loaf volume, but this may result in an unstable dough. Any adverse processing step – a slightly longer than normal divider hopper dwell time or first proof – can lead to symptoms of over-oxidation.

Finally, the manufacturer of dough additives designs his product to be used at a recommended level. The baker, being human, has a habit of reducing this level and relying on the safety margin so thoughtfully provided for him. It is therefore not surprising that he is occasionally caught out.

Loaf A contained all the necessary ingredients apart from the oxidant.
Loaf B is the optimum.
Loaf C contains a large excess of potassium bromate.

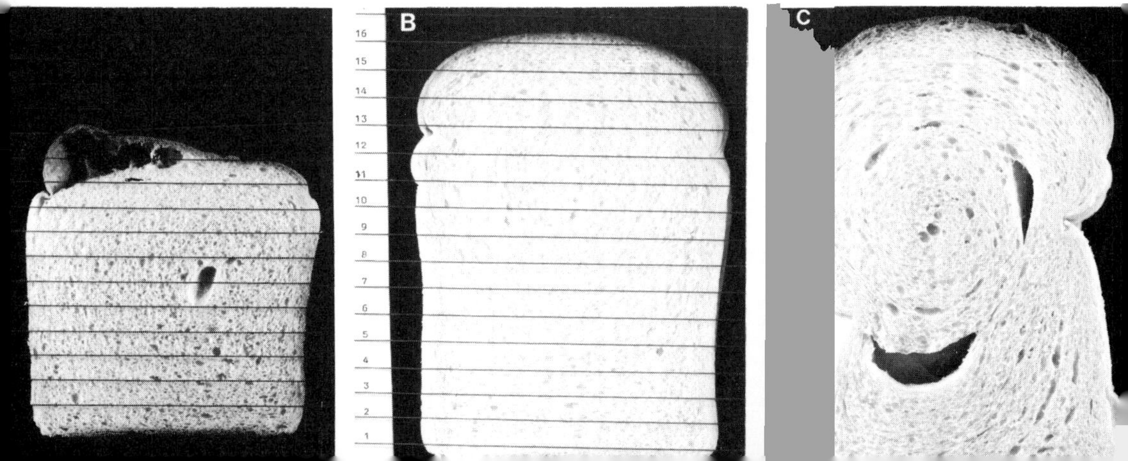

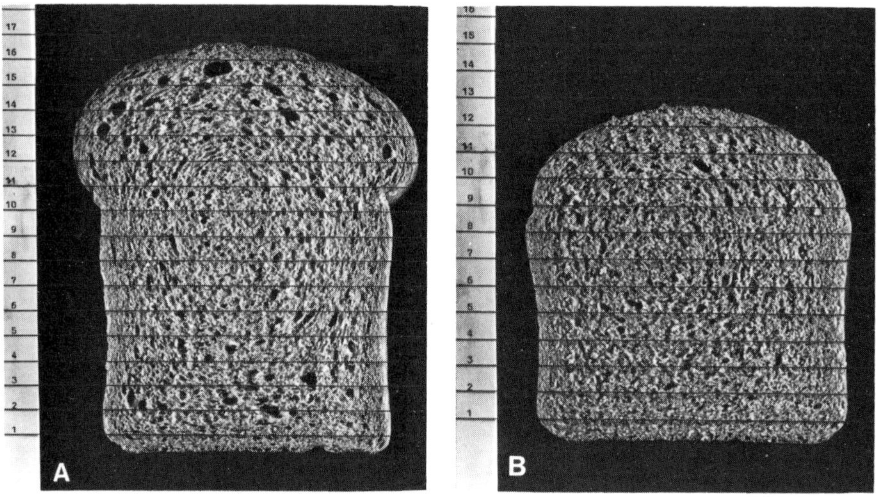

Loaf A was made from freshly milled flour, loaf B from the same flour, six weeks old.

Raw materials in speciality bread

Brown bread and wheatmeal bread production

Brown bread and wheatmeal bread occasionally appear deficient in oven spring, and hence finished loaf volume, due to the age of the wheatmeal flour used. This could be classed as a raw material fault, though usually it is due to prolonged storage in the bakery because of inadequate stock rotation rather than deliveries of 'old' wheatmeal flours from the mill. The causes of the fault are obscure but the effect is a very real one. It is not good practice to allow wheatmeal flour to lie in the bakery for more than one week before it is used.

Milk bread and skimmed milk bread

Skimmed milk powder when used in milk bread or skimmed milk bread – as legally defined by the British Bread and Flour Regulations – is required to be added at a level of 17 lb per 280 lb of flour. If the milk powder which is added is not high heat treated milk powder, then the soluble protein fraction may adversely affect the final loaf, in particular volume and crumb texture suffer.

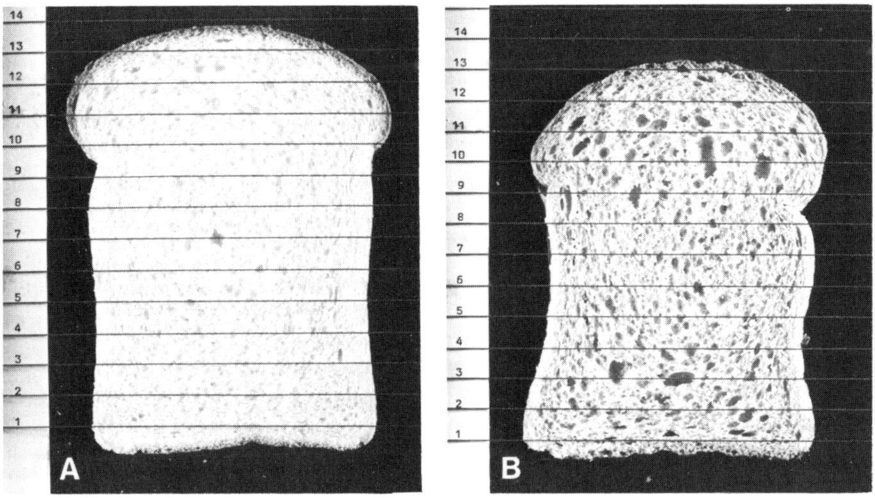

Loaf A is a milk loaf containing high heat processed skimmed milk powder. Loaf B contains a low heat processed skimmed milk powder.

High-volume bread

Dry gluten is considered a necessary ingredient in some high-volume goods and is used as a protein supplement in gluten and high-protein bread. The nature of the gluten and also the drying conditions to which it has been subjected can have a considerable effect on its baking properties and hence on the quality of baked goods in which it is included. The critical factor appears to be the rate of hydration of the gluten, and this is clearly more critical in the CBP with the comparatively short dough development stage compared with the much longer bulk fermentation periods of conventional processes. In the case of high-volume bread, it is best to keep the gluten to a minimum and to rely on dough conditioners containing the newer emulsifier systems to improve proof and baking tolerance.

For gluten and high-protein breads, again a specialised dough conditioner is a great help, but it is wise to establish a consistent reliable source of dried gluten.

If gluten must be used which appears inadequate (the loaf will lack proof and baking tolerance) the problem can be reduced by prehydrating the gluten for twenty to thirty minutes. It must be remembered that the weight of water added to the dough will require appropriate adjustment.

There are many more raw material defects which occasionally occur that could be examined. The baker is fortunate that by and large the raw materials he receives are correctly and consistently prepared and are appropriate to his requirements. If this were not so his task would be virtually impossible.

It is now necessary to examine in some detail dough processing in the bakery. This is an area which is, or should be, directly controlled by the baker himself.

10. Process troubleshooting in the Chorleywood Bread Process

Parameter to be examined

Scales and water meters

The accurate weighing of flour and the delivery of the correct weight of flour to the Tweedy mixing chamber may present many minor difficulties. Scales must be checked at least once every two weeks. The accuracy of the scales is vitally important. A regular service contract is available from the major manufacturers of scales, which is a very useful process control aid. Water meters also require checking at regular intervals.

Symptoms of incorrect levels of flour or water being delivered to the mixer are:– a) tight doughs b) slack doughs and c) irregular and uncontrolled yields.

Vacuum – optimum level 17 to 20 in.

Rules

It is very important to ensure vacuum pipes, filters, etc., are clear of flour and that the vacuum is pulling the correct level. Sometimes the gauge does not show what is actually being pulled. Also ensure that the pump is in operation before the machine starts the mixing cycle to remove some of the air from the flour. At the dough stage too low a vacuum will give a more open texture or feel, particularly at the end of the dough.

Symptoms of incorrect vacuum in baked bread

Too high a vcuum gives a close cheesey texture which could lead to blistering on the surface of the loaf and eventually a collapse of the internal structure.

Too low a vacuum gives the finished bread a more open texture (cell size) – this becomes more apparent near the end of a dough.

Work level – optimum between 4½ and 5 watt hours per pound of dough. Lower limit 4½ watt hours per pound.

Rules

Ensure that the watt counter is balanced correctly. The 'no load', as it is referred to, ought to be looked at at least every two weeks. Obvious symptoms of an imbalance are dough temperatures that are too high or too low. As a rough guide, on a sack basis 9 watts on the counter give 1°F rise on the dough temperature.

Finished bread

Too low a work level gives close texture and a rather dead-looking crumb internally, streaks become prevalent and externally the bread is lower in volume. Generally speaking, very little bread made on CBP is over-developed. The symptoms are easily recognisable at the dough stage by the dough being sticky and of a higher temperature than normal. The bread would tend to have a higher volume and weaker, soggy crumb.

Loaf A was produced by the standard CBP procedure but too low a vacuum was applied to the mixer.

Loaf B is a standard 17:hg.

Loaf C was mixed under very high vacuum (26 in. hg.).

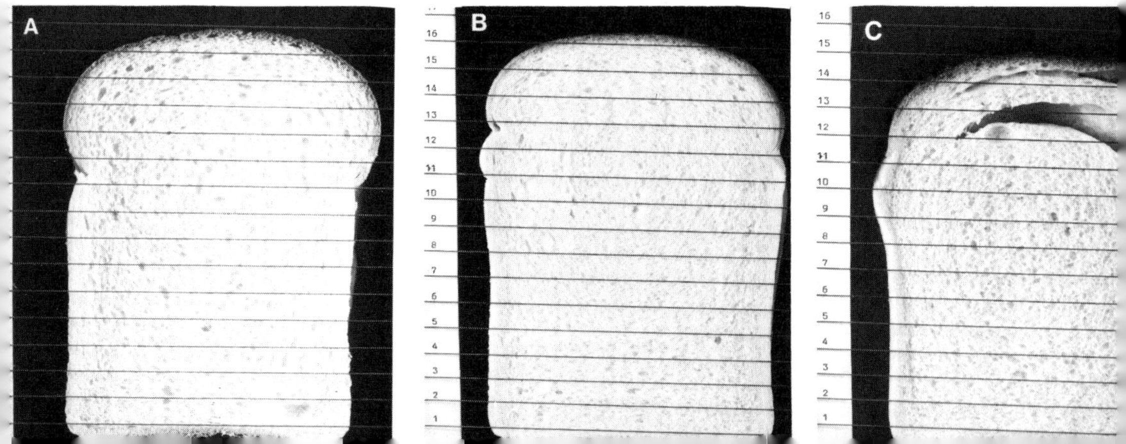

Mixing time

Obviously this is normally dictated by the work level being used, but variations in the mixing times do occur from machine to machine.

Rules

Mixing time should never be less than 2 minutes. It is most important to ensure that the clearance distance on the impact plates is correct and that the bearing housing is free from dirt, etc. Normally it is difficult to damage the plate, but lifters being broken off or bent can make a considerable difference to mixing times. This in all probability could lead to longer cycle times and in some cases the inability of the particular machine to feed the plant at the correct rate. The configuration of the plates have been arrived at through a great deal of experiment and experience. If these are incorrect, then uneven dough temperature may result throughout the dough mass. This will lead to excessive streaks and swirls and other internal texture problems in the bread.

Dough temperature

Optimum 84°F–88°F
Low 82°F High 90°F and above

Rules

Check the temperature of as many doughs as possible, particularly at the beginning of the run.

Loaf A is standard CBP with a work level of 3½ wh./lb.
Loaf B is the optimum.
Loaf C is standard CBP with a work level of 10 wh/lb.

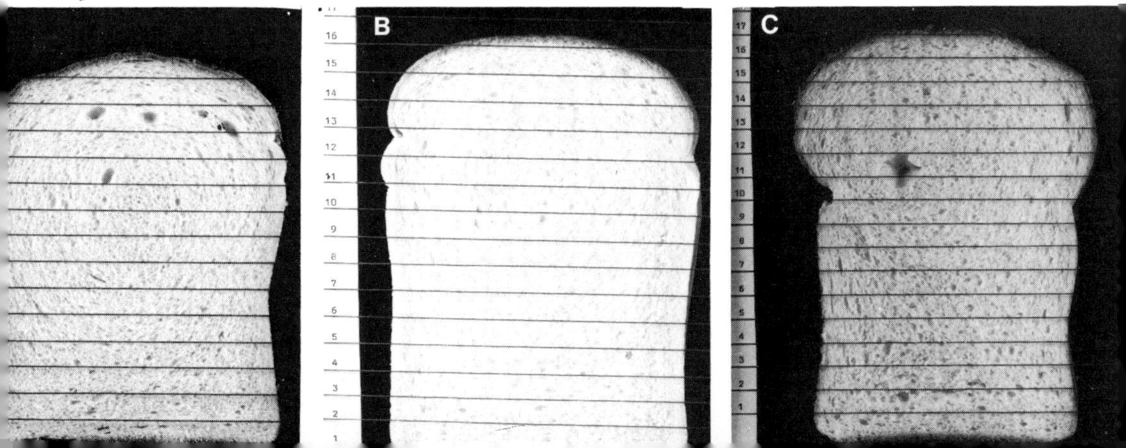

On start-up when all the make up plant is cold it is advisable to add an extra 8 oz. of yeast per sack to the first six doughs.

Discrepancy in the dough temperature shows itself during final proof. The lower the temperature the slower the final proof of the dough piece. The higher the temperature the faster the final proof.

Finished bread

Cold doughs

Externally cold doughs tend to have flying tops and are low in volume. Internally, close texture is apparent. Streaks are often apparent where the top of the loaf has left the body of the loaf. The crumb of the bread tends to have a rubbery feel.

Warm doughs

Externally the bread is of high volume, and if open-topped tends to have a mushroom-shaped top. Internally, the texture becomes open, particularly at the top of the loaf. This leads to holes and a weak crumb which is difficult to slice and butter.

Dough ejection

When the machine has completed mixing the dough may be ejected by the use of an 'inch' button. Obviously it is most important to ensure that all of the dough is ejected from the mixer. It is most unwise to leave dough from the previous mixing in for the next cycle. A so called

Loaf A is standard CBP with a dough temperature of 80°F.

Loaf B is the optimum.

Loaf C had a dough temperature of 95°F.

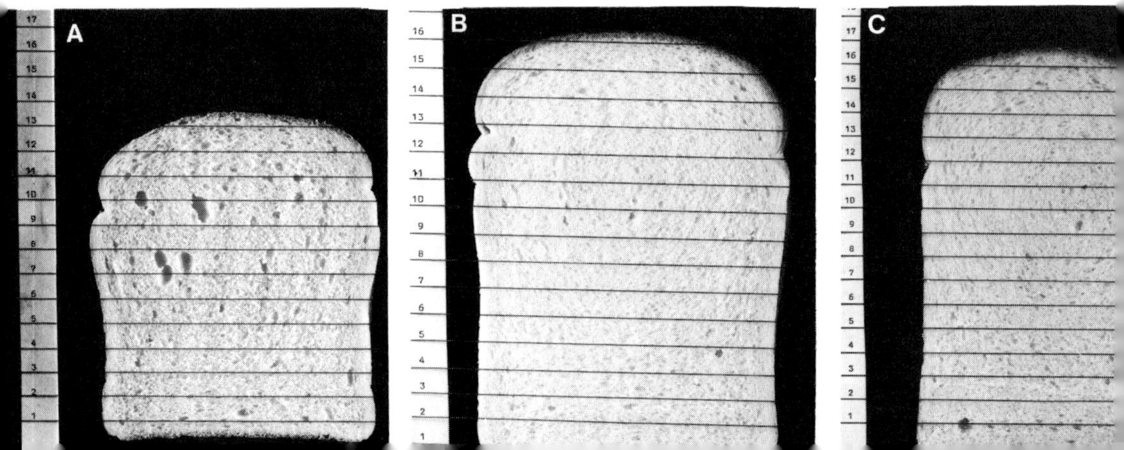

ejection plate' or 'reverse scroll plate' has been designed to help the complete emptying of the tub. This is not always successful and the system described in the chapter on automatic ingredient feed is a better solution to the problem.

Dough returns

This subject is similar to the above in that the bread produced has similar symptoms. When the auto-plant or moulder has mechanical problems it almost becomes habit to put returned dough back in the mixer no matter how much. This practice should be avoided if possible; certainly the quantity of old dough should be restricted to 15 lb maximum in any sack mixing at any time. No other change to work level, etc., is necessary.

Bread returns

A common practice in a number of bakeries, when conventional processing was involved, was that of soaking old bread crumb and then incorporating it into the dough. This practice was as unwise then as it is now. The return of old bread to new dough is one way in which the level of rope bacteria in the bread can be built up till it reaches a level at which the effects of the organism can be detected in the bread during its normal shelf life. It must be avoided at all costs.

Finished bread

Incomplete ejection and return dough into the mixer can lead to open texture, streaks and swirls if not controlled.

Dividing

Rules

(1) The minimum quantity possible for the minimum time is a good rule for the quantity of dough in the divider.

(2) Never return old or rejected dough into the divider. The timing and size of dough to the divider is all important. Doughs should never be made earlier than necessary, although it is important to feed the

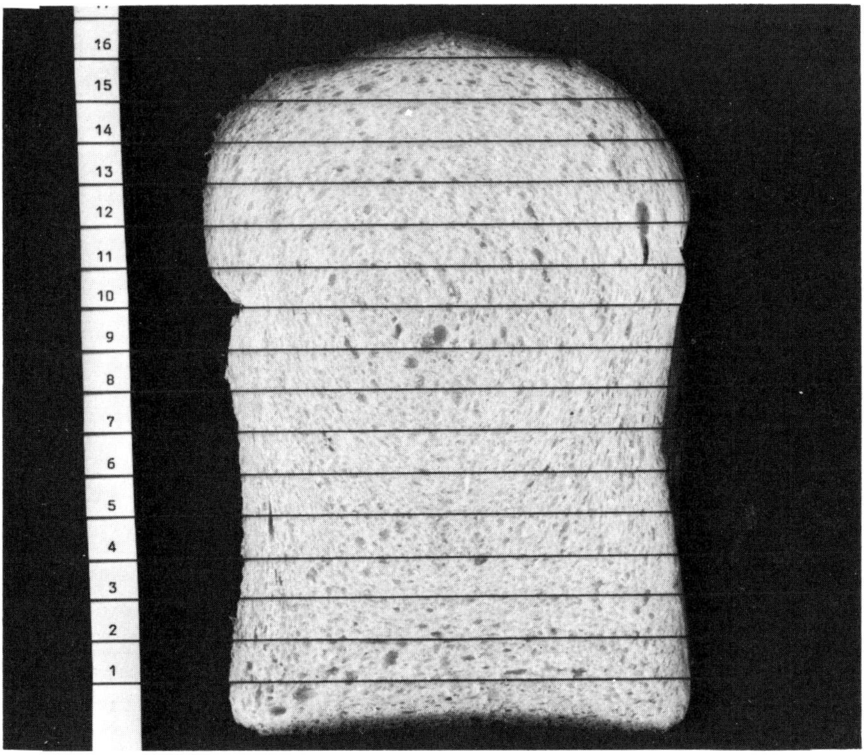

A standard CBP loaf with a divider dwell time of twenty minutes.

divider with sufficient dough to give continuous operation commensurate with accurate weights.

(3) A dough should never be in the divider for longer than eight minutes.

Finished bread

If these rules are not adhered to the resultant bread will have a gradual opening of the texture, eventually leading to streaks and over-oxidation. Streaks and swirls are particularly apparent in one-piece bread. Another problem which may occur at this stage is that the execessive oil in the divider shows itself in the form of holes which have a sheen on their surface. Externally, greyish white streaks appear on the top crust.

Conical moulding

Rules

(1) Use the correct collar for the weight of dough piece being handled.

(2) Do not use too much air.

(3) Do not use dusting flour.

Very few faults emanate from this piece of equipment. If the rules above are disobeyed then the finished bread could possibly have holes due to skinning or a badly shaped piece being presented to the final moulder. Normally it is unlikely that conical moulders create these faults. It is much more likely to be final moulding.

First prover

Rules

(1) Change the pockets weekly.

(2) Keep the doors closed.

(3) Avoid skinning – earlier temperature and humidity control of these cabinets has been advocated; if these controls can be put into the cabinet *effectively*, then it is important to do so. Generally, insufficient control of the humidity leads either to skinning of dough pieces at the one extreme or sticking in the pockets at the other. Therefore this control is not frequently used in practice. Skinning in the first prover is a most common fault. This leads to hard cores of dough in the moulded dough piece, which all too often only become apparent in the finished bread. Streaks and bad texture become prominent particularly if dusting flour or excess air has been used on the transfer from conveyor to pockets.

Final moulding

Rules

(1) Adhere rigidly to the various settings for the moulder once they have been set.

(2) Avoid 'knob twiddlers' at all costs. Manufacturers and produc-

tion supervisors are gradually being made aware, through bitter experience, that the settings of both rollers and pressure board should be left only to those who understand the machine; otherwise this particular piece of equipment can cause untold worries and problems. If moulding faults do occur and the settings appear correct, it is as well to check that:

(a) The roller gaps are even over the length between each of them.

(b) No movement is apparent in the bearings of the rollers.

(c) The Armorcote or PTFE coating is not worn or does not have grooves in it.

(d) The scrapers on the rollers are correctly adjusted to avoid the above.

(e) Excess air is not being put into the rollers.

(f) There is no incorrect tracking or slip in the main belt which delivers the dough piece from the rollers under the pressure board into the pan.

(g) The curling chains are correctly positioned.

(h) The pressure board is evenly sprung and gives a gentle even pressure throughout.

(i) The splitting knives for four-piece bread are evenly set and cutting almost through the dough piece.

(j) The automatic panner is dropping the pieces correctly. (This equipment can be very difficult to set up and is temperamental even to small changes in dough consistency.) Many bakeries who have automatic panners obtain between 85–95 per cent efficiency in panning properly, but design changes are being made continually by manufacturers and the very latest models are 99 per cent efficient.

Loaf A is a standard CBP with no first proof.

Loaf B is the optimum.

Loaf C is a standard CBP with a first-proof time of twenty minutes.

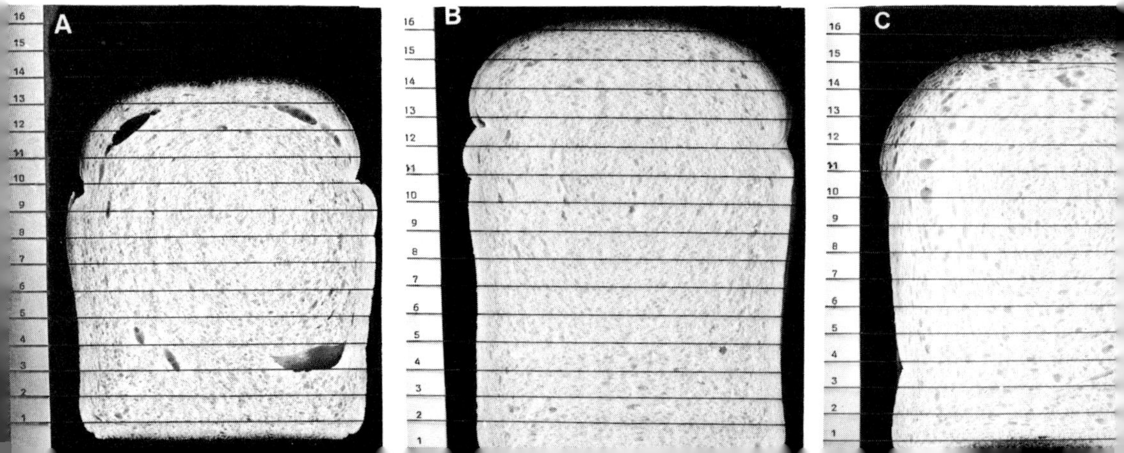

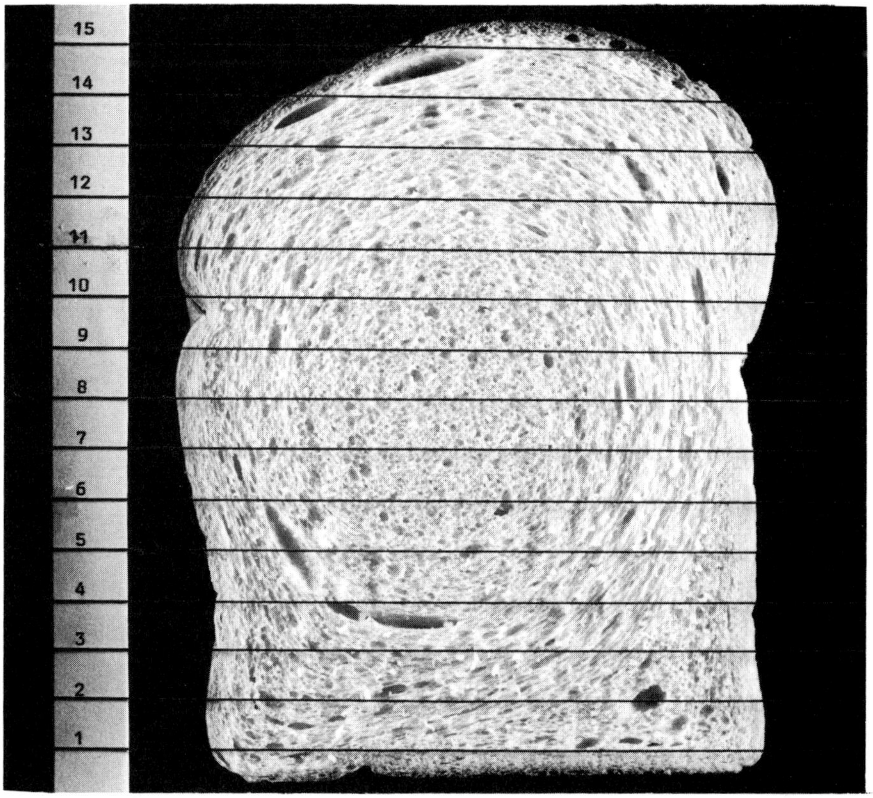

A loosely moulded CBP loaf.

Finished bread

Generally bad texture can be caused by any or a combination of two or more of the above being incorrect. Two of the most common faults in CBP can be exaggerated by maladjustment of the final moulder.

Greasing of pans

In general, tins are greased automatically with proprietary equipment and emulsions.

Rules

Ensure that any greasing emulsion used is completely homogenous. If the emulsion separates, this can cause blow holes to appear in the bottom of the bread, particularly four piece. The reason for this is that free moisture creates steam between the surface of the pan and the loaf. This expands during baking and causes the hole. A few bakeries still grease by hand or grease the dough piece. The only problems that occur with either system is when the emulsion oil or grease is used to excess. This causes greyish streaks to appear on the top crust of the bread.

Tins

Rules

(1) Do not use bent or dented pans.

(2) Ensure any silicone treatment which is used is both even and regular.

(3) Use the correct size of pan, bearing in mind the extra volume given by CBP.

(4) Do not use hot tins.

Obviously the shape of the pan can enhance or detract from the appearance of the loaf. Silicone treatment of pans is popular. This does not allow bread to be baked without the greasing of the pan but less emulsion is required. If silicones are used and the coating wears off, bad release of the bread from the pans takes place. Holes under the bottom surface of the loaf tend to appear as the coating becomes worn or is uneven. Another interesting point related to this type of fault is that it may be alleviated by drilling three holes in the bottom of the pan. This relieves the pressure built up by the steam, which is given off by the faulty emulsion. The temperature of pans which are to receive the dough piece should be kept at 90°F–120°F.

Final proof – *Optimum conditions* 100–110°F.: 75–85% R/H.

Rules

(1) Ensure the temperature and humidity controls are accurate.

(2) Ensure the valves which create the humidity are not blocked with dirt, etc.

(3) Internal loaf temperature at the end of proof should not exceed 95°F.

Apart from overproof and underproof, the majority of faults created in bread are caused by inaccurate or inactive instruments. Occasionally, hot spots in the prover are caused by faulty fan heating elements.

Overproof

Proof height can be difficult to judge because of the variation in pan size, etc. Overproof in the unbaked dough piece usually shows itself by dough pieces blistering on the surface and thus eventually leading to collapse, particularly in transfer from prover to oven.

Finished bread

Externally open-topped bread tends to have a mushroom top. Sandwich bread forces the lid off the top of the tin – this causes misshapen bread also. Open loose texture leading to holes (particularly in farm-house tins where there is little support for the sides of the loaf) and the eventual collapse of the internal structure is the result of overproof.

Underproof

The doughpiece is much lower in the pan.

Finished bread

Gross underproof gives low volume and excessive flying tops. Slight underproof gives flying tops externally which internally leads to bad texture, particularly where the top of the loaf breaks away from its base. A close soggy crumb is also apparent.

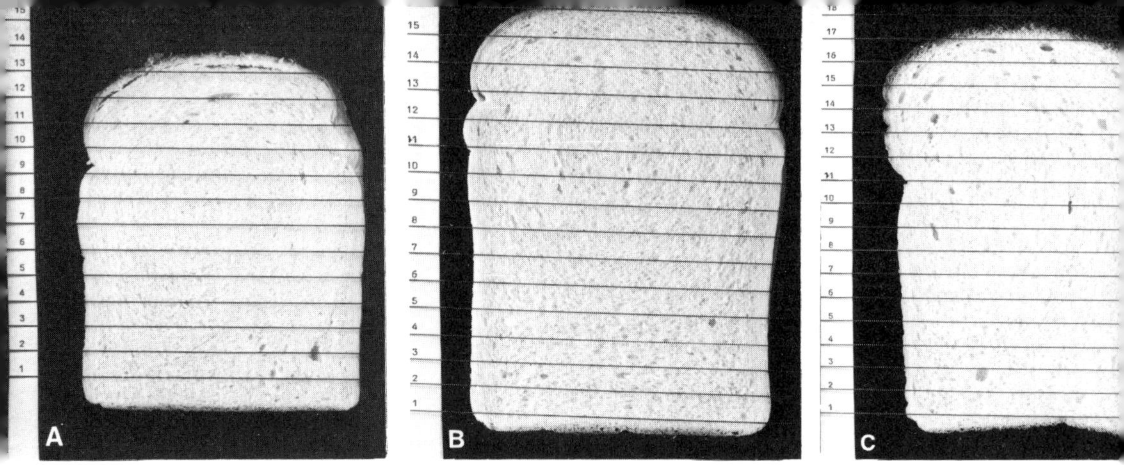

Loaf A is a standard CBP, underproved.
Loaf B is the optimum.
Loaf C is overproved.

Transfer from prover to oven

Rules

Do not bang the tins otherwise collapse occurs. This leads to bad shapes and poor texture.

Oven

Rules

Bake properly and thoroughly. Every process carried out prior to this can be undone by poorly baking the bread. The faults of underbaking and overbaking bread are obvious.

Underbaking

Pale exterior with soggy interior, sometimes with higher volume.

Overbaking

Dark exterior – grey, dry interior.

Other more subtle faults may be caused by incorrect positioning of steam jets or steam at too high or too low pressure. The baffles in the oven may be incorrectly positioned or the turbulance fans may be malfunctioning. The faults which the baker may be able to overcome are usually either too much steam, or, too much or too little heat in

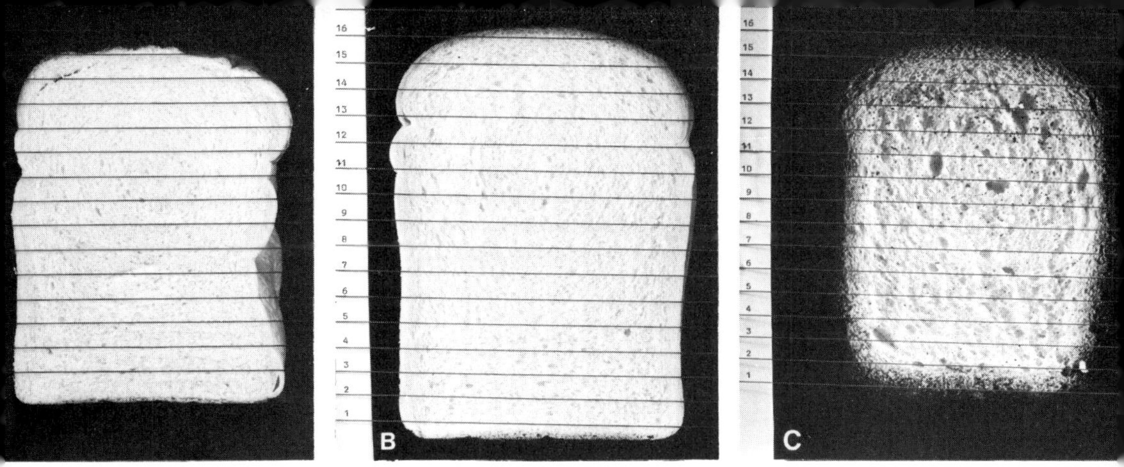

Loaf A is underbaked by seven minutes.

Loaf B is the optimum.

Loaf C is overbaked by ten minutes.

the various sections of the oven. The other faults which occur, such as underbaked patches in the loaf, etc., are best ironed out by the bakery engineer and oven builder.

Cooling

Rules

(1) Cool thoroughly and hygienically before slicing.
(2) Clean out the cooler regularly.
(3) The optimum loaf centre temperature for slicing is 75–80°F.

Very few faults are caused by the cooler, although it is absolutely essential to check temperature and humidity controls from time to time.

Faults which may occur from incorrect settings are leathery crust and rapid staling. The most common fault is usually fluctuating weight of the cooled product. If the cooler is not cleaned properly and regularly, mould growth may become apparent more quickly than normal.

Slicing

Rules

(1) Slice at the correct temperature.
(2) Ensure the blades are sharpened regularly.
(3) Tension the blades correctly to avoid worn comb plates.
(4) Slice at the correct speed.

Most of the faults associated with slicing can be avoided if the rules are adhered to, but other slicer faults can occur either because of flour with too high alpha-amylase activity (see ingredient section) or because of holes in bread. Any slight hole in the bread tends to be dragged into an even bigger fault by the slicer blades, particularly if they are in poor condition.

Wrapping

Rules

(1) Seal the wrapper properly.
(2) The more paper the sloppier the wrap, the greater the apparent softness of the loaf and the less economic the operation becomes.
(3) Use the correct type of paper, properly labelled and of the correct quality.

The finished volume of the bread can become a problem. If the bread is too high it has to be sliced and wrapped on its side. This practice is bad. It leads to a poor, unsightly outside appearance and makes the loaf difficult for the housewife to handle.

Despatch

Rules

(1) Ensure that the bread is the correct legally acceptable weight.
(2) Ensure the conditions in despatch do not lead to rapid staling of bread – ideally 70°F.
(3) Ensure that no return bread is in the slicing, wrapping or despatch area, as mould growth often emanates from here.

Note:

Scales

Obviously it is essential to ensure that the scales, water meter, etc., are weighing accurately.

Many problems that the baker has can be put down to incorrect flour or water being put into the mixer. Ensure that both scales and water meter are serviced regularly and periodically checked for accuracy.

11. Common faults encountered in the Chorleywood Bread Process which have multiple causes

Holes in four-piece bread

A widespread and aggravating fault is that of holes in bread, in particular holes at the bottom of four-piece bread and at the top of single-piece bread.

Let us consider the four-piece bread problem. The fault is demonstrated in the form of a hole situated about half an inch above the bottom crust of the loaf. It usually runs through one of the four pieces, but is more often found in one of the two centre pieces. In extreme

Holes in four-piece bread.

cases they appear to link, giving a long hole through the bottom centre of the loaf.

The character of the hole is distinctive, and is illustrated on page 191.

A probable explanation is that the sheeted dough piece, after wrapping under the pressure board, does not knit in the prover into a uniform mass, but retains a 'Swiss roll' structure with a weakness at the edge of each layer. In some cases a cut across one of the four pieces from the moulder may reveal small holes between layers already incorporated into the structure.

When a poorly proved four-piece dough is thrown into a hot tin, the first of a series of strains is introduced, which will cause the layers to part and form the fault. The uncut dough at the end of each piece is stretched and twisted, causing internal strain. As the dough piece grows in proof, the heat may cause the outer layer of each piece to skin or harden and stick to the tin, whilst the rest grows rapidly in the hot proof conditions.

All these factors make it possible for the dough piece to pull apart at a weak point. The condition is made worse by the rapid and uneven vertical growth due to the tall, steep-sided tins and unequal weights of the dough pieces.

Overcoming the fault

(1) Avoid tight doughs.

(2) Avoid excessive pressure on the moulder sheeting rolls and pressure board.

(3) Ensure an even four-piecing and that each dough piece is cut as nearly as possible into separate pieces, so as to reduce strain.

(4) Cool all tins as far as possible.

(5) Use low-sided tins, to assist natural growth in the tin.

(6) Reduce the work level slightly.

(7) In the last resort a change to single-piece bread production may be considered.

The complete solution seems to be dependent upon correct proof and baking conditions. A long, cool proof is definitely beneficial, any 'hot spots' in the prover are likely to add to the problem. Control of the baking temperature should be exercised to ensure an even bake at the correct temperature. Careful experimentation and adjustment of final proof and oven conditions usually suffice to eradicate the trouble in a bakery.

Holes in single-piece bread

Hand bagging refers to holes at the top of single-piece bread, especially farmhouse bread baked in very low-sided tins.

It must be stressed that the system being examined here is the no-time system employing a high dough temperature and a high yeast level. This combination can lead to overproving, which is the main cause of the fault.

The recommended remedial treatment would be as follows:

(1) Do not overprove. Note – with production changing from 2 lb bread to farmhouse or similar types made in low-sided tins the final prover is rarely altered. However, rather less proof is required for these varieties, so a reduction in yeast level should be investigated.

(2) Avoid banging the tins during the change from the final prover to oven. An automatic transfer system which gives the fully proved dough pieces a severe shaking or knocking can greatly contribute to this fault.

(3) Moulding is, as ever, important. The optimum moulding settings must be determined for each variety of bread produced and must be adhered to precisely.

(4) The practice of putting the 'old dough' back into the mixer should be avoided since it appears to contribute to this fault, possibly by causing irregular proof conditions.

Reel or rack ovens

A further specific problem is concerned with 'Reel Ovens'. Here, it is possible to be troubled with flying tops, with no-time dough system in this type of oven. The cause appears to be a lack of heat capacity in this type of oven. In other words, the bread when placed in the oven at the usual 450°F temperature rapidly absorbs heat causing a large drop in oven temperature in the early stages of baking. This results in the crust of the loaf baking normally, but the centre of the loaf continuing to grow, resulting in the crust bursting open into a flying top.

In order to eliminate or minimise this fault, steps have to be taken which will inevitably lead to a reduction in quality of the final bread and these are:

(1) The initial oven temperature may be raised to 500°F so that the drop in temperature which occurs results in a final oven temperature suitable for baking bread.

(2) Steps can be taken to reduce oven spring by a reduction in the yeast level, or a reduction in dough temperature, or a reduction in work input at the mixer together with a full final proof. All these points are normally regarded as being undesirable and deleterious to the quality of the final loaf. Steam would also appear to be helpful in overcoming these problems, provided oven temperature can be maintained.

Rope and mould in bread

To complete this section it is necessary to comment on a potential problem common to all bakeries, that of rope and mould in bread. It must be stressed that, as with all other common baking faults, prevention is better than cure. A properly run bakery where due attention is paid to hygiene and a sensible system of cleaning and inspection is in force will minimise, if it does not eliminate, bacteriological problems. Nonetheless it is a fact that even in well run bakeries it is possible for outbreaks of bread spoilage by either rope or mould to occur. The bakery staff must therefore be able to deal quickly and efficiently with such outbreaks, which can rapidly damage a bakery's reputation.

In order to understand the nature of the problems which rope and mould cause in bread, it is necessary to know something about them. They are both living organisms which come under the general classification of micro-organisms, and they are both carried into bread by their spores. Spores are about the size of the finest grain of flour and are harmless until they meet conditions favourable to their development. Unfortunately, spores can multiply very rapidly and form colonies which contain many millions of descendants and in the case of moulds produce millions of new spores. Spores are a form of organism which, like seeds, are capable of surviving when conditions do not allow growth.

The main requirements for growth are:

(1) Moisture.
(2) Food.
(3) Suitable temperature.

Without any one of these factors spores will not germinate, but once conditions are right, a short acclimatisation period is followed by one of slow growth until a maximum multiplication rate is reached. This rate depends on the exact balance of the three requisites and is maintained until such time as the supply of any one of them, usually nutrients, becomes exhausted at the site of growth. During this growth the organisms pass out their waste products and digestive juices into the bread. The graph below illustrates the general shape of the growth curve. The time base varies with conditions but it is seldom that physical spoilage becomes apparent in less than two days even under ideal conditions.

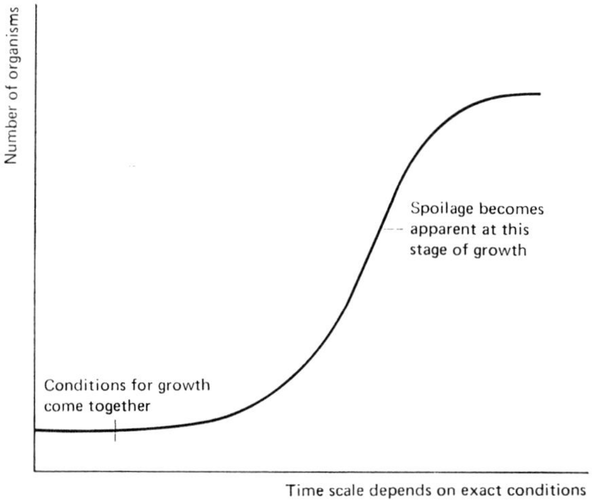

Let us first of all consider the rope organism. This condition is caused by a bacterium with the latin name *Baccillus mesentericus.* It is typical of most of its group in that it forms spores which are resistant to heat. This factor is important in bread because these spores can survive the baking process to become troublesome in the loaf. The organism is harmless to man and but for another characteristic it would probably go unnoticed in bread along with many other spore-forming bacteria which are present. Its particular form of villainy is that, in

The effects of a very high level of infection with Bacillus mesentericus *after an incubation period of three days.*

growing, it produces an enzyme called amylase which dissolves the starch to form sticky materials called dextrins. These dextrins are the cause of the typical 'ropes' which form when bread, showing advanced action of *B. mesentericus*, is pulled apart. A characteristic fruity smell is also produced which is the first sign that large numbers of bacteria are growing in the bread.

Spores of *B. mesentericus* are present in almost all bakery raw materials to some extent. The usual cause of an outbreak of rope in finished bread is that one or more of the raw materials contains a high level of contamination. Rope spores are very common and widely distributed in soil and because of their resistance to attack it is probable that every loaf baked contains some of the spores. They then survive the baking process and start to grow when the temperature has returned to the normal ambient one. About 100°F represents the temperature at which most rapid growth occurs. Fortunately modern hygiene in the manufacture of all ingredients has resulted in spore counts being on average a small fraction of those which prevailed twenty-five years ago so that rope outbreaks from this source are quite rare these days. The longer shelf life of modern wrapped bread gives a greater chance to the few which are present. Another source of infection is caused by the multiplication of the bacteria in the bakery in a position where they are transferred to the dough by physical contact between the dough and the localised growth. Such growth can result from flour dust sticking to a wet surface and building up into a thick moist layer.

Turning now to moulds, it can be shown that many different kinds grow on bread producing many different colours, namely black, white, green, pink and brown. Each different species of mould has its own characteristic colour and mode of growth. The reason why any particular mould grows on the surface of bread is because a spore of that particular species has landed more or less by accident on the exposed surface of the loaf. All mould spores are killed by the conditions inside the oven. Mould spores will not penetrate the wrapper of the loaf (unless it is torn) so that the only time where mould contamination can occur is after baking and before wrapping. All air, unless specially purified, contains a number of mould spores. Their numbers can be increased dramatically by the presence of an active growth in the vicinity of the bakery. It has been estimated that spores from a growth can diffuse around most of a building in less than fifteen minutes. The nearer the infection to the cooler and slicer the more serious is the effect. Once on the surface of the loaf the mould has the food and temperature for growth but the crust is too dry at this stage to allow growth. Only when the bread is wrapped is the moisture drawn from the interior of the bread to the crust and prevented from evaporating. This moisture provides the remaining condition for growth and a colony will appear after two or more days depending on how the loaf is stored. Moulds generally grow best at about 80°F. If bread is not wrapped then moisture moving to the surface evaporates, so no mould growth occurs.

Prevention in the bakery

From the above descriptions it is apparent that it is practically impossible to obtain bread from a plant bakery which does not contain some rope and mould spores. The question then arises why is there not more incidence of these problems than exists at the moment. The answer is that in order to present a problem the spores must grow and produce large numbers. Preventive measures aim at having very few organisms present to start with and then retarding their growth in some manner. With rope the manufacturers of ingredients have achieved the first condition but with mould it is only too easy to find in or around the bakery growth which will be propagated on the bread. This can occur anywhere but the following are some of the more common places which have been noticed.

(1) On the inside walls of the prover. The high humidity and warm temperature provide good conditions and the best way of preventing growth is by making sure that surfaces are clean and so provide no nutrients.

(2) Inside the cooler. This is a serious place to have growth and regular inspection and cleaning is sound practice.

(3) The slicer. Contamination from this source is shown by mould growing on the surface of the slices.

(4) Returned bread. This should always be discharged from vans away from the bakery and disposed of daily.

If growth is found in a bakery the best way of removing it is to wash the surface with a detergent which will remove the growth and the dirt on which it is growing. Finally it is given a treatment with a disinfectant to kill any remaining spores.

Mould is best prevented from growing by avoiding the three conditions for growth occurring together. Condensation on walls and machinery can accumulate flour dust and can give growth conditions. This can be prevented by either insulation or ventilation. Mould resistant paints may be used to reduce the chance of growth or a disinfectant rinse will leave a coating layer of effective material. It is always necessary to follow the manufacturers' recommendations and first of all remove all dirt. Mould resistant paint will not kill mould which is growing in the cracks of old plaster or paint.

No surface treatment remains effective if the surface layer is covered with a layer of dust which insulates the mould spores from the effect of the treatment. When cleansing a wall prior to a disinfectant rinse or when mixing detergent and disinfectant to do both jobs at once it is essential that the disinfectant and detergent are compatible or the effect of both can be neutralised.

Disinfectants fall into four general categories:

(1) Those based on chlorine are cheapest, the most common one being hypochlorite. These disinfectants need care in use as they are very corrosive and can harm skin and bleach fabric. They are quickly inactivated by dirt.

(2) Iodophors are efficient but expensive and not used in bakeries to any great extent.

(3) 'Cationic' disinfectants. These are reasonably economical in price and efficient. They are easier to use because of their low toxicity and corrosive powers.

(4) Ampholytic disinfectants are more efficient than cationic ones but are more expensive.

A list is appended to this article giving some of the manufacturers of disinfectant and detergent materials. They can give advice on any particular problem in a bakery. None of the materials at present available will kill rope spores effectively and the best which can be hoped for is that growth is retarded.

Prevention in the dough

Even with the complete absence of sources of spores inside the bakery there will always be a number of mould and rope spores which find access to bread. Once inside the wrapper the conditions are good for growth. The only methods of control are control of temperature and adding some antimicrobial agent to the dough. Temperature control inside the bakery is of limited value as low temperatures encourage staling, and it is of course impossible outside the bakery. There are several substances which are added to dough in order to reduce the rate of growth of micro-organisms.

These slow growth by altering the acidity of the loaf or by interfering with the living processes of the micro-organisms. In products like pickles all growth is stopped by the acidity. As the degree of acidity is reduced, micro-organisms are capable of increasing rates of growth until the optimum is reached when no acidity is present. Because of this fact many people have the belief that materials like vinegar, acid calcium phosphate (ACP), lactic acid and other similar acidulants will slow the growth of micro-organisms in bread. It is true that the addition of these materials affects the acid level in bread but the effect of this is mainly on the bread flavour. In order to slow mould growth to a worthwhile extent by adding acid the effect would be catastrophic to the flavour, yeast, and gluten in the dough.

The only permitted preservative for use in bread is propionic acid which is generally added in the form of calcium propionate (Mycoban). The practical limit to the use of this material is about 9 oz* per sack above which the flavour of the bread is affected. Normally Mycoban is used at 6 oz per sack. At this level a worthwhile extension of shelf life is obtained with a slight reduction in yeast activity. In conventional doughs the gassing is restored by the addition of between 6 to 12 oz extra yeast per sack. Chorleywood doughs do not normally need extra yeast but in certain cases 4 to 6 oz extra may be required. The use of Mycoban is practically essential in the summer months when high overnight temperatures keep the bread near the optimum temperature for microbial growth.

One minor problem with this product is that it is dusty when being handled. To overcome this Arkady have produced a special Dynarex for the summer months which includes the correct level of mycoban.

Manufacturers of detergents and disinfectants suitable for use in bakeries

Glovers (Chemicals) Ltd,
Wortley Low Mills,
Leeds LS12 4RF. Tel. 0532 637847

Diversey Ltd,
Cockfosters Road,
Barnett,
Herts. Tel. 01 449 5566

Hough, Hoseason & Co. Ltd,
Chapel Street,
Levenshulme,
Manchester M19 3PT. Tel. 061 224 3271

British Hydrological Corporation,
Colloidal Works,
Deer Park Road,
London S.W.19. Tel. 01 542 1021

It is not intended to imply that the products of manufacturers on this list are superior to the products of manufacturers not included here. This list is by no means exhaustive and customers are recommended to evaluate the claims made for individual products before considering their use.

* The maximum permitted level of calcium propionate in the United Kingdom is 3000 p.p.m. as propionic acid on flour weight, i.e. approximately 1lb per sack (280 lb) flour.

PART V

Future developments

12. Future developments in the Chorleywood Bread Process

It is a difficult task to attempt to predict those developments which might be expected to most radically affect the future commercial application of the Chorleywood Bread Process.

Many possibilities occur. There are large numbers of minor modifications and refinements which could benefit one or another section of the baking industry.

The three particular developments which are to be considered have been chosen because they might be expected to be of interest to all sections of the industry and each might radically change one or another facet of the baking industry in the United Kingdom.

Section 1. The EEC and the United Kingdom baking industry

In the framework of the EEC legislation wheat flour and bread are considered under two separate Articles. Flour is under Article 45 as agricultural produce whilst bread falls under Article 100 as a processed foodstuff.

The draft regulation on flour – if it is not amended – could possibly mean that a severe limitation would be imposed on the treatments and additions which would be permitted at the mill; flour treatment by chlorine dioxide, benzoyl chloride and potassium bromate could all be banned, though this is still a matter of interpretation of existing proposed legislation and subject to further negotiations by the UK Government.

The position regarding bread is more complex but in some ways more optimistic. The proposals at present being considered are described as 'optional harmonisation'. Roughly this means that there will be two sets of regulations in the UK to produce two distinct types of bread:

(1) EUR bread which must be produced using only strictly defined ingredients. This bread would be standard throughout Europe; it could for example be exported. The permitted ingredients for this type of bread, its scaling weight and even the labelling requirements are still under discussion.

(2) The second type of bread – described as regional bread – will be produced according to the modified UK 1963 Bread and Flour Regulations, i.e. the baker will be able to make use of the additives he uses at present and those which will be permitted once the amendments to the existing regulations become law.

It is certain that almost all bakers in the UK will choose to make 'regional bread'.

Initially the spider's web of legislation emanating from the Commission in Brussels appeared to be the most menacing feature in the EEC from the viewpoint of the British baking industry. As the various trade associations have become better organised and informed, working together in the Bakery Industry Consultative Council and within their respective European associations as well as co-operating with the Ministry of Agriculture officials, the prospect is much less alarming.

It has become clear that the UK will not readily 'sell the pass' on matters vital to the interest of the baking industry. The necessity to continue to ensure that the viewpoint of the industry is heard in Europe remains. However, it has become evident that the process of proposed legislation will take a matter of years rather than months.

A much more immediate and serious problem which is already having considerable effect on the industry is due, in part, to the economic structure of the EEC regarding cereal pricing.

Briefly the system is that, within the EEC, a minimum price for wheat is set at which the EEC grown wheat is sold into intervention. This effectively sets the minimum price at which wheat grown in the EEC sells to the miller. Under normal economic conditions this price is higher than that which the wheat would fetch on the open market. To protect the EEC wheat grower any wheat imported into the EEC is subjected to an import levy equal to the difference in price between the price of the cheapest wheat sold on the world market and the EEC intervention price. Thus under normal world market conditions there will be imposed on imported wheats this additional cost even though the wheat itself is initially more expensive than an EEC wheat.

The result is strong economic pressure to use the maximum percentage of EEC wheat. This can best be achieved by simple blends of EEC (French or English) wheats with relatively lower percentages of good quality Canadian and American wheats.

The economic restrictions generally placed on the industry, the very considerable increases in world wheat prices, and the working of common agricultural policy, all push the miller towards the situation in which he will feel it necessary to produce breadmaking flours with higher levels of European wheats than have previously been thought to be desirable if the traditional standards of bread quality in the United Kingdom are to be maintained. This presents two major possible problems:

First, the average level of protein for a Chorleywood Bread Process flour has been in the past about 11·5%; this could drop to 10·5% or lower if unfavourable economic conditions prevail. As has been stated, there is little the baker can do to make up for this loss in protein – it may be some comfort that if he had still to rely on bulk fermentation processes his task would be far more difficult. It may well be that the concept of 'protein quality' which has been thought to be of little importance whilst an adequate amount of protein was present will have to be re-examined. It may need the co-operation of the plant breeder, the farmer, the miller and the baker to establish which of the European wheats available are most suitable for breadmaking. Once the best European wheat varieties can regularly be purchased by the miller – as named varieties – and the importance of recognising protein quality as well as quantity is fully understood, then it should be possible to produce from these lower protein flours better and more consistent bread. In addition, it will give a more uniform base for the improver manufacturer to work from in order to further enhance bread quality with the sophisticated blends of emulsifiers and oxidants which are now available to the baker.

The first practical result from the baker's viewpoint will be a loss in yield. As the average protein content of CBP flours drops from 11·5% to approximately 11·0%, water absorption falls by at least 5 lbs per sack, so that the average water absorption for standard white bread in 1974 is between 167 and 173 lb per sack and may well fall even lower. The miller can offset this lack of yield to some extent by increasing the level of damaged starch in the flour but the point must be re-emphasised that this may well be at the expense of bread quality. If the balance between protein starch damage and water quantity is not maintained liquor logging may occur resulting in a soggy, coarse textured crumb.

To combat any general loss in bread quality one processing change which will help is to reduce the work level from 5 watt hours per pound to 4·5 watt hours per pound. This can also result in a drop in dough temperature from the mixer to about 84°F. This lower dough temperature may well become more popular.

These steps should increase the dough stability particularly at the area of greatest risk, the transfer from prover to oven.

The emulsifier based improvers, previously used mostly in high-volume goods (Spiral, Crystal, Dynacrust, etc.), are also helpful in increasing dough stability.

Secondly, there is the problem of excessive cereal alpha-amylase. The alpha – and beta-amylases are enzymes naturally present in wheat flour. Their role in the wheat berry growth cycle is to break down the starch in the berry into maltose which provides energy for the growing plant. Under normal harvesting conditions the level of these enzymes in a final flour can be continued within the range desired for bread production – if necessary by blending wheats of differing enzyme activities. However if the wheat becomes wet for any length of time before milling then the process of germination can commence. Amongst the earliest of these is the build-up of the cereal amylase levels to enable the germ to make use of its food store of starch once it begins to germinate. There is always considered to be an excess of beta-amylase which breaks off individual sugar units from straight chain starch molecules. It is the level of alpha-amylase – the enzyme which breaks branched starch chains – at the point of branching, which is critical. The significance of this enzyme's action is that it is active at the acidity range (pH) of dough – its optimum temperature range being 140°–150°F whilst beta-amylase is most active at a lower temperature 118°–123°F, and yeast is no longer active above a temperature of 104°F.

Wheat starch gelatinises at 122°–131°F; thus, during the early stages of breaking when the starch is most susceptible to the action of enzymes, the alpha-amylase is at its most active, breaking down starch molecules to shorter chain dextrins which are not subsequently removed from the system by the further action of beta-amylase and yeast.

A build-up of these dextrins results in a progressive weakening and increasing stickiness in the crumb which usually manifests itself as a problem at the slicer. It is difficult to set a maximum safe limit for cereal alpha-amylase levels in bread flours but plant experiences suggest that 5 Farrand Units of cereal alpha-amylase (approx. 250 second Hagberg falling time on a 7 gram flour sample) is about the highest one can go without risk. As the level rises to 7 Farrand Units (approx. 200 seconds) slicer problems begin to occur and above 10–11 units (approx. 150 seconds), although the bread might still appear not too poor in quality, it would be virtually impossible to put it through automatic slicing equipment.

The eventual use of high levels of English or European wheats in breadmaking grists is an economic inevitability and in years when there are wet harvest conditions the presence of what are now considered high levels of cereal alpha-amylase in breadmaking flours will have to be accepted.

Present bakery technology and technique will not cope with large excesses in cereal alpha-amylase, but if the baker is presented with a flour in the 6–8 Farrand Units of cereal amylase range, then he should be able to process it quite successfully by paying sufficient attention to the following practical details in his bakery.

The baker in the United Kingdom has been fortunate. For many years excess cereal alpha-amylase has been a very rare occurrence.

This however has had one unfortunate effect, in that a number of old wives' tales now exist which confuse the problem and delay effective action being taken. Two particularly widely believed legends are:

(a) That acid (acid Calcium Phosphate or cream powder) added at levels of between 1–2 lb per sack appreciably reduces cereal alpha-amylase activity. Even at 5 lb sack the changes in pH are far too small to have any appreciable effect.

(b) That Potassium Bromate increases the stickiness of the crumb in bread and thus adds to the problem when high alpha-amylase flour is used. There is no evidence to support this theory and the oxidant requirement of the CBP remains the same irrespective of cereal alpha-amylase levels.

The problem manifests itself at the slicer so the baker's main method of combating the problem is to have the loaf in the optimum physical condition for slicing and to ensure that the slicing machine is at its maximum efficiency.

Therefore the bread should be baked thoroughly so that the crust gives the loaf some stability as it is sliced. It should be cooled correctly – i.e. the centre of the loaf should be no higher than 75°F.

A small addition of fat (1–2 lb. per sack) is also thought to aid slicing – though this may be just another baker's folk myth.

The slicer blades must be cleaned, sharpened and changed regularly, and when suspect bread is being sliced it must be closely watched for signs of build-up of sticky crumb.

The normal slicer blade for white bread has blades 12 thousandths of an inch in thickness, though blades at up to 18 thousandths of an inch thick can sometimes be found. A thinner profile blade 10 thousandths of an inch thick and commonly referred to as a 'cake slicer blade' which causes less drag on the crumb, is also beneficial, especially as this type of blade is designed to have 60% more cutting edge.

It should be noted that the thinner blades cannot be resharpened as frequently and therefore there may be some economic disadvantages in switching from traditional ones.

Finally, when high alpha-amylase flours are being used it is even more important to avoid holes being present in the baked loaf. A sticky slicer blade and possibly a weak crumb structure can drag an existing small hole into a major one.

Section 2. The Effect of the Amendments to the 1963 Bread and Flour Regulations

As has been stated the British baker is likely to continue producing bread using as his legal framework the 1963 Bread and Flour Regulations. The present proposed amendments are therefore of vital interest to the UK baking industry.

In particular two new functional additives are bound to have considerable effects on the industry in general and the CBP in particular:

L-Cysteine Hydrochloride and Azocarbonamide

It is necessary to stress that these two ingredients, although they have been considered together by the Food Additives and Containments Committee, are not interdependent in functional effect. Each has its separate function and each should be discussed separately.

L-Cysteine Hydrochloride Monohydrate

It is one of the twenty-two naturally occurring alpha amino acids. This class of compounds are the sub units which link together into long chains to form the proteins. L-Cysteine HC1 H_3O is unique amongst alpha amino acids in its ability to link one protein chain to another.

In the wheat protein water complex of gluten it is these cross links which give the structure stability and elastic properties. If free L-Cysteine Hydrochloride Monohydrate is added to a gluten it may rapidly react at the cross links to free the protein chains one from another. In a breadmaking process it is then possible during the relatively gentle conventional mixing action to re-arrange the separated chains into the optimum configuration.

By also including a slower acting oxidant in the system the re-arranged gluten structure can be re-stabilised during proof and baking. Thus the combined effects of a correctly balanced system of L-Cysteine Hydrochloride Monohydrate and oxidant can parallel the beneficial effects of bulk fermentation or mechanical dough development.

The British Arkady Company has been aware of the potential of L-Cysteine Hydrochloride Monohydrate in the British baking industry for a number of years.

In 1965 sufficient work had been carried out in the companies test bakery and laboratory to make the first approach to the Food Standards Committee for the inclusion of L-Cysteine Hydrochloride Monohydrate in the permitted list of ingredients for bread. At that time the Committee decided that its consideration should await a general revision of the 1963 Bread and Flour Regulations. The Company accepted this decision, but it was thought that as it was a naturally occurring amino acid it would be perfectly safe in use at the levels required for bread dough processing, therefore a product should be developed to take advantage of its particular functional effects. This product could then be put on the shelf until such time as the 1963 Regulations were revised in the hope that such a revision would, in fact, permit the use of L-Cysteine Hydrochloride Monohydrate in bread up to a reasonable maximum level.

It was also noted that the baking industry in Eire, which was at the time by no means fully converted to the Chorleywood Bread Process, even in plant bakeries, could benefit from an L-Cysteine containing bread improver.

The food legislation in Eire was such that L-Cysteine on the toxicological evidence available, was accepted as being safe to use at the levels needed for breadmaking processes. A product was designed incorporating all the necessary ingredients for a 'complete improver' which could be added to a dough of flour, salt, yeast and water only, to produce a loaf of good commercial quality from a no-time dough mixed in a conventional mixer. The product was named Eire FAD.

It contained a carefully balanced system of L-Cysteine whose action is described as a reducing action, and the two oxidants currently permitted in both the UK and Eire, potassium bromate and ascorbic acid. The blend was so designed that the fast-acting L-Cysteine relaxed the gluten in the dough during the mixing process so that the dough structure could be modified by the relatively gentle action of a conventional mixer in a way similar, but not identical to, that which took place during mechanical dough development in a Chorleywood Bread Process mixer. The oxidant system, which acts more slowly, was needed to re-build and stabilise this modified dough structure during final proof and in the early stages of baking. As with Chorleywood Bread Process additives the types and amount of fat present was found to be of importance so that the optimum blend of fats had to be derived. Enzyme-active soya flour was also included, the doughs were to be mixed atmospherically making good use of natural bleaching effect of soya and the traditional Arkady 'yeast foods' ammonium chloride and calcium sulphate were also found to be of value.

The complete improver 'Eire FAD' found an immediate and expanding market in bakeries of a wide range of sizes in Eire. Its commercial success led to a fuller understanding of the finer points of the use of L-Cysteine based products in commercial bakery practice and an increasing expertise has been built up by Arkady technical staff. A second product was specifically designed for export and is currently in use in Dutch bakeries, where further problems of food legislation had to be considered.

All this background work and feed back of information has been used in the formulation of a new addition to the Arkady range of bread improvers, FAD.

FAD, as soon as L-Cysteine is permitted in the UK,* will be offered as the standard product for both the UK and Eire markets, and will pro-

*L-Cysteine was permitted for use in bread in the UK in November, 1972.

vide a valuable tool in a number of different situations in the baking industry. It is probable that the smaller bakery units, especially those who have not invested in Chorleywood Bread Process mixing machinery, will be among the first who will wish to take advantage of a product of the FAD type. Firstly, we will therefore describe in detail how FAD may be used in a no-time conventional process to produce bread of a quality at least equal to that which may be produced by a bulk fermentation process whilst retaining some of the advantages of the Chorleywood Bread Process.

Recent developments have shown that it is also possible to produce small ferments and morning goods of very high quality on a no-time system based on a product containing cysteine. In the same way that FAD may be compared to Dynarex a second new product Crystal has been designed to equate with Spiral, and its application will also be discussed.

FAD for the family baker

FAD is recommended for use at 3 lb per 280 lb of flour which is equivalent to 2½ oz per 14 lb flour.

The application of the product is fairly straightforward. The family baker is only required to follow one or two simple rules to obtain the optimum result. If he is currently producing a one- or two-hour dough by a conventional process it will be necessary to eliminate all the bulk fermentation period and instead increase the mixing time (in any mixer) by 20–25%. An increase in yeast quantity is required and—most important—an increase in water quantity of approximately half a gallon per sack is essential. The working-off procedure, dividing, handing up, moulding, final proof and bake, all remain the same as for the normal conventional method.

A typical recipe for 14 and 28 oz pan bread would be:

	lb	oz	lb	oz	
Flour	140	—	14	—	
Salt	2	12	—	4½	
Yeast*	3	—	—	5	
FAD	1	8	—	2½	
Water*	83	—	8	—	or 6½ pints

* Variable depending on bakery conditions.

Lard or other ingredients may be added if desired.

Mixing method

Mix for twenty-five minutes in a normal dough mixing machine or give an extra five minutes' mixing in a Universal type mixer. Dough temperature 83°F. Divide immediately then preferably give ten minutes first proof before final moulding. Final proof should be between fifty and sixty minutes at a temperature of about 105°F and 80% relative humidity. The baking time and oven conditions should be the same as for a conventional system.

Over the past six to seven years experience has shown that when a family baker uses this process to replace a conventional no-time dough system much improved results may be obtained. (No extra water or yeast is required changing from a no-time to a FAD process.) The loaf is whiter and softer with a finer, silkier, crumb and better keeping quality.

If the baker is switching from a bulk fermentation process, then one would usually expect improvements in loaf quality, and major advantanges in increased yield and better consistency. Fermentation losses are reduced, and an extra 5 lb of water per 280 lb flour may be included in the dough simply because the softening off which would occur during bulk fermentation is eliminated. Consistency is improved, the uncertainties and errors attendant with bulk fermentation are removed and divider accuracy is better with the 'dead' dough of constant density.

To enable the family baker to produce the full range of morning goods and crusty bread on this revolutionary process the British Arkady Company have developed another specialised product named Crystal; this product is the latest in a long line of additives which will help him to obtain the very best results. Crystal is closely related to two products. Spiral and Super Vencrust which were written about in *The Arkady Review*, Volume 48, No. 1, 1971. Apart from containing a very finely balanced system of oxidants and L-Cysteine, it also incorporates a specialised emulsifying system which has been developed over the past eighteen months.

Crystal is recommended for use at a level between 3 and 5 lb per 280 lb of flour ($2\frac{1}{2}$ to 4 oz per 14 lb) dependent on the type of morning goods being produced. The same basic rules which apply to FAD apply to Crystal, i.e.,

(1) It is only for use on a no-time process.

(2) The mixing time for Crystal dough has to be increased by 20%–25%.

(3) The level of both yeast and water requires increasing if converting from a normal bulk fermented process.

(4) Dough temperature ought to be increased to 82°F–83°F.

Recipes

Vienna goods or crusty breads

	lb	oz	lb	oz
Flour	17	8	14	—
Salt	—	5	—	4
Yeast*	—	12	—	9½
CRYSTAL	—	5	—	4
Water*	1 gall.		8	—

Mix for approximately 4 minutes slow speed. 10–12 minutes approximately second speed in a Universal type mixer. Dough temperature 82°F. Leave in bulk for 5 minutes and then work off normally.

*Variable depending on bakery conditions.

Morning rolls

	lb	oz	lb	oz
Flour	17	8	14	—
Salt	—	5	—	4
Yeast	—	10	—	8
CRYSTAL	—	5	—	4
Water	1 gall.		8	—

Mix for approximately 4 minutes slow speed. 10–12 minutes approximately on second speed in a Universal type mixer. Dough temperature 82°F. Work off the dough immediately. Prove and bake as for conventional rolls.

Yorkshire teacakes

	lb	oz	lb	oz
Flour	17	8	14	—
Salt	—	5	—	4
Yeast*	—	10	—	8
CRYSTAL	—	5	—	4
Fat	—	12	—	9½
Sugar	—	4	—	3
Water*	1 gall.		8	—

Mix for approximately 4 minutes slow speed. 8–10 minutes approximately second speed in a Universal type mixer. Dough temperature 82°F. Preferably give 10 minutes first proof before pinning out. Work off the dough immediately. Prove and bake normally.

*Variable depending on bakery conditions.

Cookies and rich ferments

	lb	oz	lb	oz
Flour	17	12	14	—
Salt	—	4	—	3
Yeast	—	12	—	9½
CRYSTAL	—	3	—	2½
Fat	2	—	1	10
Sugar	2	—	1	10
Water	1 gall.		7	12

Mix for 4 minutes slow speed. 8–10 minutes approximately second speed in a Universal type mixer. Dough temperature 82°F. Work off the dough immediately after mixing. Prove and bake normally.

The use of Crystal in all the above mentioned products will enable the baker to produce the best possible morning goods on a no-time dough process.

From an economical point of view the elimination of bulk fermentation and consequent increase in water quantity are very interesting, but another distinct advantage we have found is that scaling weights may be reduced by at least 10% and one can still achieve the same volume as a conventional product.

The tolerance of these doughs is very good indeed, but if at all possible, they should be worked off within 20 minutes of finishing the mixing process.

Generally speaking dough made with both FAD and Crystal will machine better than other types of dough and smoother handling procedures will result.

This new system will inevitably be compared to the Chorleywood Bread Process. Certainly some of the advantages of this process are similar to the high-speed mixing system, but we believe that L-Cysteine as an integral part of a very carefully designed additive will stand up in its own right as a new process and very useful aid for the family baker.

L-Cysteine based products for the plant baker

We are of the opinion that both FAD and Crystal will also be of considerable benefit to the larger bakeries.

FAD offers three separate applications for the fully automatic plant bakery.

(1) *For a plant which is currently employing conventional mixers using a no-time or a bulk fermentation process.* Quite a large sackage of bread flour is still processed in the UK by these two systems. We feel that the bread being manufactured from a two to three hour dough can be equalled in quality by the use of a no-time system with the help of FAD. The same basic rules which have been discussed for the production of the family baker's bread also apply.

(a) A no-time dough system must be used. This requires an increase in yeast quantity and an increase of 5 lb of water per 280 lb of flour. An extension of the dough mixing time is also most important.

The following formula is suggested for the production of 28 oz and 14 oz bread.

		lb	oz
	Flour	280	—
	Salt	5	8
(a)	Yeast	6	—
	FAD	3	—
(b)	Fat	1	—
(a)	Water	168	—

(a) Variable according to bakery conditions.

(b) The addition of fat is optional. The total fat requirements of the dough are present in FAD but some bakers are of the opinion that fat improves the slicing properties of the finished loaf.

Dough Temperature 82–84°F.

Mixing time RVK 25–30 min.
Artofex 25 min.
Conventional BP High Speed mixer 2 min. slow speed 4–5 min. fast speed.

Generally speaking the more efficient the mixing process the better the finished bread quality.

The dough should be divided immediately and processed in the normal manner, working off within 20 minutes of the completion of mixing. A shorter first-proof time of 10 minutes is desirable if the prover can be adjusted.

Final proof and baking is the same as for conventional processes but the moulder has to be adjusted to take the denser dough pieces.

We have found that this process offers some of the advantages of CBP without the need for specialised equipment.

It is however our firm opinion that from both a technological and economic point of view CBP is the superior process.

Nevertheless FAD may mean that the days of conventionally fermented plant produced doughs are numbered.

It is worth noting that, based on experience in Eire, it is probable that good quality batch bread may be produced in Northern Ireland and Scotland by the FAD process.

This is particularly interesting because as yet, for various reasons, only a very small percentage of batch bread is produced by CBP in Scotland.

(2) *Plant using either conventional or CBP mixers requiring a 'stand-by' process in case of breakdown.* Mechanical problems with plant and equipment are not uncommon but thankfully seem to become rarer as both knowledge of design and maintenance is improved. If it should be necessary bread of a high standard of quality can be made from a conventional mixer in about 1½ hours production time. Those few extra quarterns needed on Saturday or when the so-and-so machine breaks down are no longer a problem when FAD can be used.

(3) *Use of FAD in CBP batch and continuous mixers.* This is probably the least expected use for FAD but possibly the most important.

FAD will produce better bread incorporated into a CBP system than any additive previously developed by the British Arkady Company Limited.

Two distinct advantages can be seen immediately and only minor modifications are required in dough formulation and processing.

FAD helps to relax the CBP dough throughout the make-up process and in our experience this will give bread which has a much more even crumb texture – the cut surface being comparatively free from streaks and swirls. This shows up particularly well in single-piece bread where flaws of this nature show up more readily. The manufacture of four-piece bread is also improved, there being less tendency to the formation of the triangular hole at the base of the loaf and a decrease in the other faults associated with cross panning.

The other major advantage to be gained by using FAD in CBP 14 oz and 28 oz bread production is that this additive allows the baker to reduce significantly the work input to the dough from the normal optimum level of 5 watt hours per pound without the drop in quality which would otherwise occur.

It is common practice during the summer months for bakers to reduce work levels in order to keep dough temperatures down to the optimum range of 85°F–87°F.

The three main reasons for excessive dough temperatures in summer are.

(i) high ambient bakery temperatures.
(ii) high flour temperatures – either because of a high flour temperature as delivered from the mill or because of a high temperature in the bakery flour silo or heat gain during flour transfer from the silo to the mixer.
(iii) Difficulty in obtaining sufficient cold water at the correct temperature (38°F–44°F) due to
    (a) too small a chilling unit.
    (b) poor maintenance and lagging of pipes from the unit to the mixer.
    (c) chilling units placed considerable distances from the mixer.
    (d) a high mains water temperature.

Using FAD it is possible to cut the work level to 4 watt hours per pound of dough and produce bread equal in quality to that made from a normal CBP system at a work level of 5 watt hours per pound.

This means that the baker can *either* maintain the desired finished dough temperature with a flour 10°F warmer than normal *or else* with a water temperature 10°F warmer than would be the case if the full work level was imparted to the dough.

In practical terms the dough temperature rise in the mixer is reduced from 25°F to 20°F and the watt counter on a one sack mixer (280 lb of flour capacity) will be reduced from an average 235 to 187.

We recommend that in order to achieve the best from the new product the following recipe should be used.

Pan bread

	lb	oz
Flour	280	—
Salt	5	8
Yeast*	5	8
FAD	3	—
Water*	174	—

*Yeast and water vary according to bakery conditions.

Dough temperature 86°F. Work level 210 for 280 lb flour.

The dough should be divided within 8 minutes – given 6–8 minutes first proof and moulded. Final proof and baking times will vary according to the type of plant available. The work level is slightly reduced, this is desirable to give a good control of the final moulding and therefore finished bread texture.

Some difference in the extensibility of the dough will be noticed but the water absorption remains the same as that of a normal CBP dough containing Dynarex.

Crystal for the larger baker. Crystal may be used to improve both conventionally mixed and CBP morning goods.

Excellent morning goods can be produced using the same formulae and mixing procedures with conventional mixers as were given in the section of the article dealing with family bakers. They compare favourably with the normal one hour fermentation process with all the advantages of a no-time system.

It is most important that the size of the dough should be related to the rate at which it can be worked off. For larger doughs (140 lb of flour) it is necessary to ensure that the dough is worked off within 25 minutes of completing mixing.

The rules to follow using Crystal in an ADD process are that it is a no-time process and requires:

(i) more water in the dough ($2\frac{1}{2}$ lb per 140 lb flour).
(ii) more yeast.
(iii) extended mixing times – in the region of 25 minutes in an R V K or Artofex machine.
(iv) dough temperatures of 82°F–84°F.

The larger baker who is already producing morning goods by CBP can gain unique advantages from the use of Crystal. It will produce high volume and enriched breads of a more even texture and will considerably reduce the problem of holes and swirls in high specific volume breads.

The following formula is suggested for the production of a 14 oz loaf in a 28 oz tin or a large 14 oz pan – a type of loaf frequently sold in bags.

	lb	oz
Flour	140	—
Salt	2	12
Yeast*	4	—
Cascade	2	—
CRYSTAL	2	—
Shortening	1	—
Water*	86	—

*Will vary according to bakery conditions.

Work level $4\frac{1}{2}$ watt hours per pound of dough, i.e. 106 on the watt counter. Dough temperature 86°F. Work off in the normal manner, but it is important to take the Crystal dough just a little lower in proof than a less sophisticated additive such as Dynarex.

Crystal may be used in every type of bread in which there is emphasis on volume but it will also produce excellent morning goods.

One of its main advantages is shown in the production of pinned out morning goods such as morning rolls, Yorkshire teacakes, current teacakes, baps, etc.

The problem of holes under the top crust in this type of article was discussed in *The Arkady Review* of December 1969, but it still plagues plant bakers, mainly because doughs have to be handled which have less than the optimum water quantity and the first provers on roll plants are just too short.

Crystal, by allowing the dough to relax and flow out, helps to counteract these two disadvantages.

Generally, using CBP, it has been found better to work at lower work levels in morning goods than with bread, this applies particularly to the very rich type of article. Crystal should be worked at a slightly lower input than standard morning goods.

The following recipes have been used successfully although they may require some adjustments for local taste and differing equipment.

Morning rolls

	lb	oz
Flour	140	—
Salt	2	8
Yeast	5	—
CRYSTAL	2	8
Water	84	—

Mix the dough atmospherically to 4 watt hours per pound. Dough temperature 85°F. Follow normal plant procedure.

Note: Malt flour may be added at 8 oz per 140 lb of flour if very strong flours (all Canadian, etc.) are in use.

Yorkshire teacakes – bridge rolls, etc.

	lb	oz
Flour	140	—
Salt	2	8
Yeast	5	—
CRYSTAL	2	—
Fat	6	—
Cascade	2	—
Sugar	2	—
Water	85	—

Work level $4\frac{1}{2}$ watt hours per pound. Mix atmospherically. Dough temperature 86°F. Give at least 12 minutes first proof before pinning out. Prove and bake normally.

Vienna and small crusty bread

	lb	oz
Flour	140	—
Salt	2	12
Yeast	6	—
CRYSTAL	2	8
Water	86	—

Work level 4½ watt hours per pound. Mix atmospherically. Dough temperature 86°F. Leave in bulk for 10 minutes. Process normally.

Cookies and Swiss fingers

	lb	oz
Flour	140	—
Salt	2	8
Yeast	8	—
CRYSTAL	1	8
Fat	14	—
Sugar	14	—
Water	80	—

Work level 3¾ watt hours per pound. Mix atmospherically. Dough temperature 86°F. Follow normal procedure.

Fruit may be added to the dough in a conventional mixer or by means of the specially modified impact plate.

No doubt the functional benefits of L-Cysteine Hydrochloride Monohydrate will be further investigated and exploited by bakery technologists as experience with this newly permitted material grows. We feel that FAD and Crystal are ready now to play a useful and increasing role in the British baking industry. They represent the results of seven years practical bakery experience and applied research; we trust that the baking industry will find them of value.

Azodicarbonamide

This is a fast acting oxidant with a rate of reaction in the same region as that of potassium iodate. In fact it was first used in the United States (as a fast acting oxidant in continuous bread processing systems), when potassium iodate became suspect as a possible health hazard.

It has also found use in the USA as a treatment at the flour mill either, together with, or in place of, potassium bromate.

The rapid reaction rate of this compound (usually referred to as ADA) is the reason why it has a distinct technical advantage and also makes it difficult for it to be used in commercial practice.

The disadvantage is that the rapid rate of reaction makes its level of use in a particular process critical. It is very easy to produce over or under oxidised doughs and quite sophisticated oxidant blends are required to build in sufficient tolerance to use the material successfully.

The advantage is, that, if the correct oxidant blend is used – incorporating ADA – then it is possible to devise both batch and continuous CBP systems in which the first-proof stage – with all its attendant problems – is eliminated, and moulding can almost immediately follow dividing of the dough.

Section 3. The further automation of the breadmaking process

The third and final consideration is mainly of concern to the large plant baker. If full advantage is to be made of the CBP, then it must be as far as possible automated and made to operate continuously. It is not difficult to have a continuous production process incorporating a batch mixing stage, providing the batch processing cycle time is short enough.

Automation of high-speed batch mixer for the production of bread dough

The standard electro-pneumatically controlled mixing sequence of high-speed batch mixers has been described in an earlier chapter; therefore this section will deal primarily with:

(1) The automatic feeding of flour, water, fat and minor ingredients to the mixing chamber.

(2) The synchronisation of dough production with make-up plant and the additional requirements needed to give a completely automatic dough producing system, incorporating automatic sequencing of all mixing operations, i.e. calling for ingredients, mixing within stipulated limits, discharging dough from the mixing chamber and transporting it to the divider hopper at the appropriate time.

Automatic ingredient feeding

Bulk flour handling and storage. (See illustration page 224.) The Tweedy bulk flour storage and handling system, which has been used for several years in plant bakeries, is an excellent example of how flour can be stored and automatically fed to batch mixers.

This forms the basis of automatic feeding of any number of flours, alone or collectively, to any number of mixers.

Flour is delivered in bulk, which results in worth-while savings when compared to sack handling methods. Silos are situated outside the bakery giving easy access to road tankers. Silos take up very little area and in the Tweedy system the skilful use of insulating material eliminates the need for expensive weather-housing and they also have a very low cost per ton stored when compared to conventional storage. Explosion relief facilities and access to the roof-chamber and base are also special features of this system.

A master control panel, usually in the form of a schematic diagram of the actual plant, enables the operator to have flour blown from a selected silo and discharged into the mixer weigh-hopper.

The diagram on page 225 shows the complete flour handling system.

To fill the silo, flour is blown from a tanker and conveyed to the top of the silo.

When a mixer in its automatic sequence calls for flour, air is blown past the cone outlet at the base of the selected silo, and flour is released into this air stream with help from the fluidisation system. This also prevents 'bridging', or build-up, in the base cone of the silo and ensures a smooth and rapid discharge rate.

The flour now passes through cyclone separators and sifters before being diverted into the mixer hopper.

Flour feed to the Tweedy 300 mixer hopper is regulated so that it fills at the rate of 300 lb in $2\frac{1}{2}$ minutes.

The type and quantity of flour for each batch is controlled as follows:

(a) When the two flours are used, as in a brown-bread dough, their types are selected at the mixer-control.

For example in a brown-bread dough 210 lb of brown flour and 70 lb of white flour may be required.

The quantity of brown flour is set at 210 lb on the flour weigh dial (see diagram page 225) and the total weight of brown plus white flour is set at 280 lb.

Tweedy bulk flour silos

WATER WEIGHER

Item No.	*Key*
(1)	Low Pressure Input
(2)	Manifold (nine outputs)
(3)	Weighing Indicator
(4)	Intermediate Air Switch
(5)	Intermediate Air Switch
(6)	Final Air Switch
(7	Setting Indicator
(8)	Rear Mounted Zero Air Switch
(9)	Overload Air Switch
(10)	Diaphram Valve Giving Final Switch
(11)	Diaphragm Valve Giving Intermediate Signal
(12)	Diaphragm Valve Giving Intermediate Signal
(13)	Diaphragm Valve Giving Zero Signal
(14)	Diaphragm Valve Giving Overload Signal

FLOUR WEIGHER

(15)	Weighing Indicator
(16)	Intermediate Air Switch
(17)	Final Air Switch
(18)	Setting Indicator
(19)	Rear Mounted Zero Air Switch
(20)	Overload Air Switch
(21)	Diaphragm Valve Giving Final Signal
(22)	Diaphragm Valve Giving Intermediate Signal
(23)	Diaphragm Valve Giving Zero Signal
(24)	Diaphragm Valve Giving Overload Signal

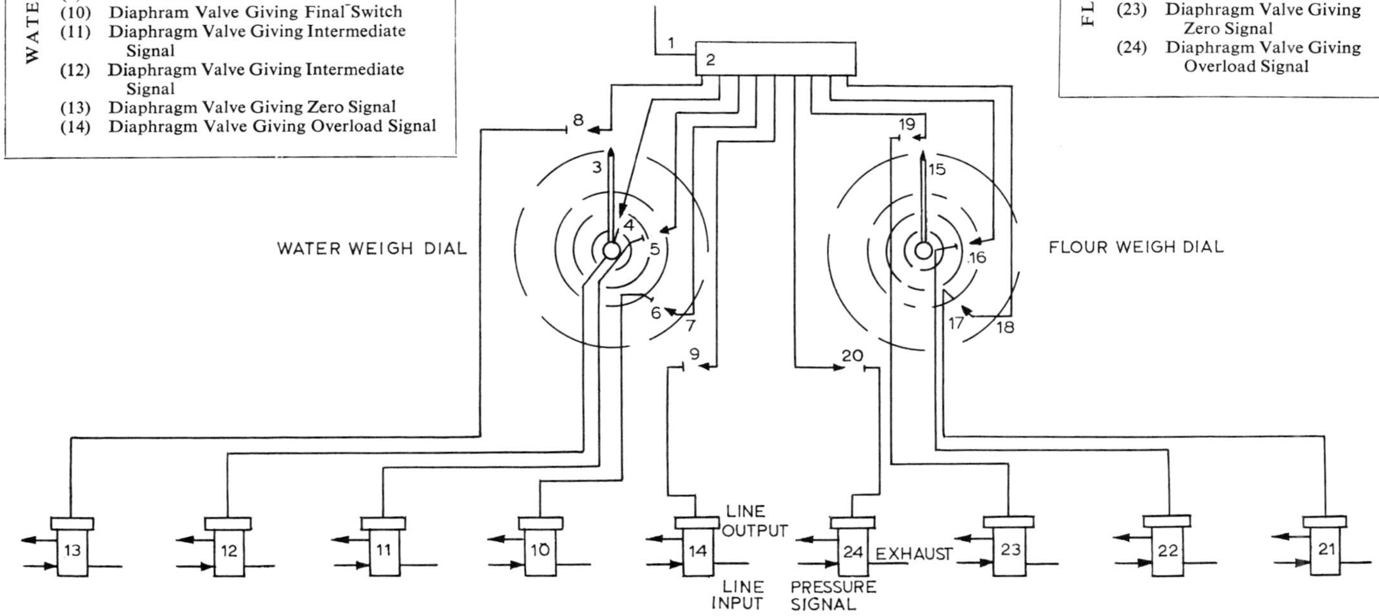

When the zero signal from diaphragm valve (23) indicates that the weigher is ready to receive flour, brown flour is diverted from the bulk-flour system to the mixer-hopper. The brown flour continues to load the mixer-hopper until weighing indicator (15) passes intermediate air-switch (16). Now the brown flour supply will stop with a signal from diaphram valve (22).

The mixer control now diverts white flour to the mixer hopper. The weighing-indicator (15) moves on until final air-switch (17) is passed and a signal from diaphram valve (21) causes the flow of white flour to cease.

Both flours are now ready to be fed into the mixing-chamber during the next mixing cycle.

When the flours have left the mixer-hopper, the weighing-indicator (15) returns to zero air-switch (19) and the whole sequence can now be repeated.

(b) In normal production where only one flour is required the mixer-control selects only the white flour and the intermediate part of the weighing sequence is by-passed.

Water. For obvious reasons water is the easiest of dough ingredients to handle mechanically.

On semi-automatic machines, it is metered from the water chilling unit into a water batch tank situated above the mixing chamber ready to be gravity fed into the mixer when needed.

This method does not readily lend itself to the automatic feeding of minor ingredients in solution, since a digital meter is needed for each solution used and the specific gravity of the solution would have to be calculated for various temperatures so that appropriate calibration would be possible. This would be costly to build and complex to operate.

On automatic machines a different method is used. Instead of metering the water it is actually weighed. The operation for delivering a certain quantity of water is similar to that for flour. The required water quantity is set by the final cut-off switch (6) on the water weigh dial and when the machine calls for water during its cycle, a valve in the supply line from the chilling unit is opened and water flows into the weigh tank (sited above the mixing chamber) until the weigh dial pointer reaches the cut-off switch (6). At this point the water supply ceases and the water is held in the weigh tank ready for the next mixing cycle when it is gravity fed into the mixing chamber.

This lends itself very easily to the automatic weighing quantities of brews or slurries. For example, when a twin tank brew method, as described a little later in the chapter, is used, the liquid weighing system functions as follows (see diagram on page 225). This shows the arrangement of the pneumatic switches for both the water- and flour-weigh dials):

(1) The balance of the water, which is not in either the yeast brew or the minor ingredients suspension.

(2) A yeast brew in tank X.

(3) A suspension carrying Dynarex, etc., in tank Y.

The required quantity of each material is determined and the water-weigh dial intermediate cut-off switches (4 and 5 in diagram on page 225) are set up at corresponding quantities.

When the mixer sequence calls for these ingredients, water first flows into the weigh tank. The weighing indicator (3) moves until air switch (4) is reached, and at this point the diaphragm valve (12) signals to the water inlet valve to close and it shuts off the flow of water into the tank. At the same time the discharge pump of tank X is energised and the yeast suspension flows into the water-weigh tank until the weighing indicator (3) reaches air switch (5). A signal from diaphragm switch (11) now stops the discharge pump of tank X. The small ingredients and salt suspension begin to flow from tank Y into the water-weigh tank, and the weighing indicator (3) moves on until air switch (6) is reached. The signal from the diaphragm switch (10) stops the pump and also the flow of the suspension.

The three liquid ingredients are now ready to be gravity fed into the mixer during the mixing cycle.

When the ingredients have left the water-weigh tank the weighing indicator (3) returns to zero air switch (8) and this signals to the main mixer control that the water-weigh tank is ready for the next mixing sequence.

On the Tweedy 6600 a gantry is built into the top frame of the mixer to facilitate cleaning of the water-weigh tank following periods of production employing brews and suspensions.

The following are groups of ingredients that need to be fed to the mixer:

Minor ingredients. These include: salt, yeast, Dynarex (or other improver), malt flour, sugars, soya flour, milk powder, mould inhibitors and fat.

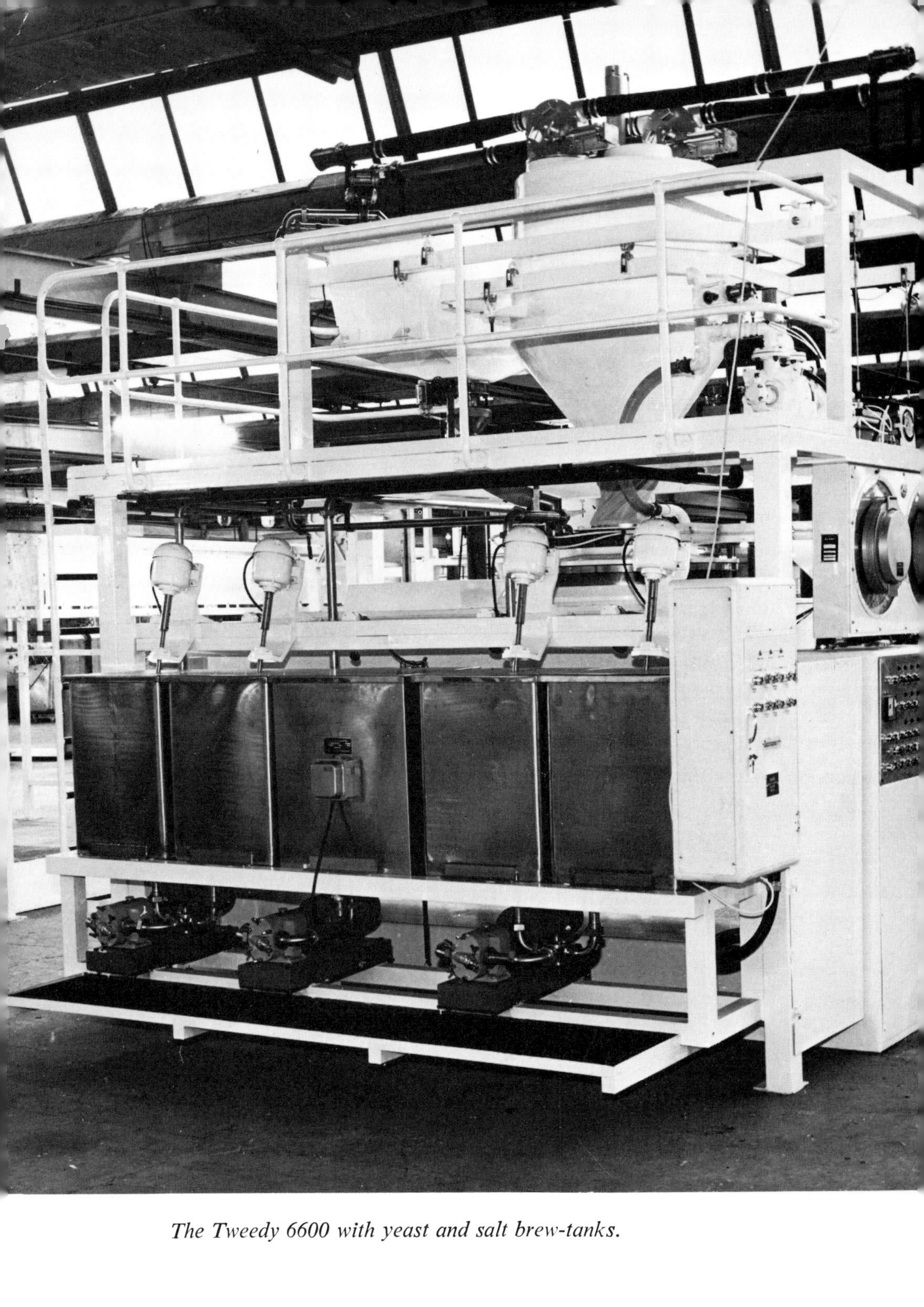

The Tweedy 6600 with yeast and salt brew-tanks.

All the other ingredients in the list apart from the fat will either dissolve or remain in even suspension when agitated by a high-speed stirrer.

Fats. Semi-liquid fats cannot be pre-mixed with the water and must be added directly to the mixing chamber. Specially emulsified fats, or fats contained in bread improvers such as Arkady's Dynarex and Spiral, blend quite easily into water and remain evenly dispersed by a little agitation.

The easiest method of adding fat automatically to the mixing chamber is to melt it in a heated tank at about 130°F. It can then be pumped through an insulated line and out into the mixing chamber through a non-return valve. The pump and valve are timed to the mixing cycle and are energised for a predetermined length of time to allow sufficient fat to pass into the mixing chamber. The amount of fat added is controlled by a timer which starts when the valve is energised and closes by breaking the circuit as it reaches zero.

The timer can be calibrated in pounds of fat, e.g. for each interval of one second the valve passes one pound of liquid fat.

Yeast. There can be many combinations or groups of ingredients present in the solution to either stimulate or control yeast activity. Consideration must be made to the yeast before placing it in solution with other dough ingredients. If the yeast's gassing power is stimulated or damaged in any way, the quality of the bread will be inconsistent, and variation of loaf volume will result.

In general terms the following items should be considered before making a brew for automatic feeding. Once this is done, the type of brew which best suit a particular production unit can be chosen.

Osmotic pressure in brews containing yeast. Since the yeast cell is surrounded by a semi-permeable membrane, its metabolism is dependent on and effected by osmosis. If the yeast is placed in a highly concentrated salt solution, then osmotic pressure will cause the water inside the yeast cell to pass into the concentrated solution and damage the yeast cell.

Common salt, having the highest osmotic effect of the minor dough ingredients, causes the greatest change in osmotic pressure. It has been established that a salt solution in excess of 18% causes severe damage to the yeast cell. Salt solutions around 15% are quite safe for the yeast cell for fairly long periods at temperatures of approximately 45°F.

Sugars have only one tenth the effect of salt on osmotic pressure, but because simple sugars stimulate yeast action they should be used at fairly low levels to avoid changes in bread quality over a time period.

PH. of brews containing yeast. Mould inhibitors such as propionic acid or its salts should be used with care and will reduce yeast gassing property when used in a concentrated brew.

Temperature of brews. The temperature of the brew is important. It should be kept, if possible, at 45°F. Firstly, this temperature appears to promote the smallest changes in the yeast's gassing power and concentrated brews kept at this temperature have been used for up to sixteen hours without experiencing changes in bread quality during that time.

Secondly, the brew temperature should, if possible, be nearly in line with the dough water temperature, especially where a large portion of the dough water is used in the brew, otherwise it is difficult to achieve correct dough temperatures in a high-speed mixer with a minimum chilled water temperature of 40°F.

It must also be remembered that when a brew is being pumped out of a tank the diminishing mass will be increasingly influenced by the surrounding ambient temperature. If measures are not taken to maintain an even brew temperature, then dough temperature fluctuations will be encountered and this may lead to a variation in bread quality.

Other ingredients. The other minor ingredients in the list are virtually inert when in a yeast solution and have very little effect on the yeast.

It should be remembered, however, that sufficient water must be added with these ingredients to produce a suspension that can be pumped. In most cases the correct liquidity can be obtained if the dry ingredients are mixed with three times their own weight in water.

Ingredient feed schemes

Here are two possible minor ingredient feed systems in use in plant bakeries which have been designed by Tweedy of Burnley Limited.

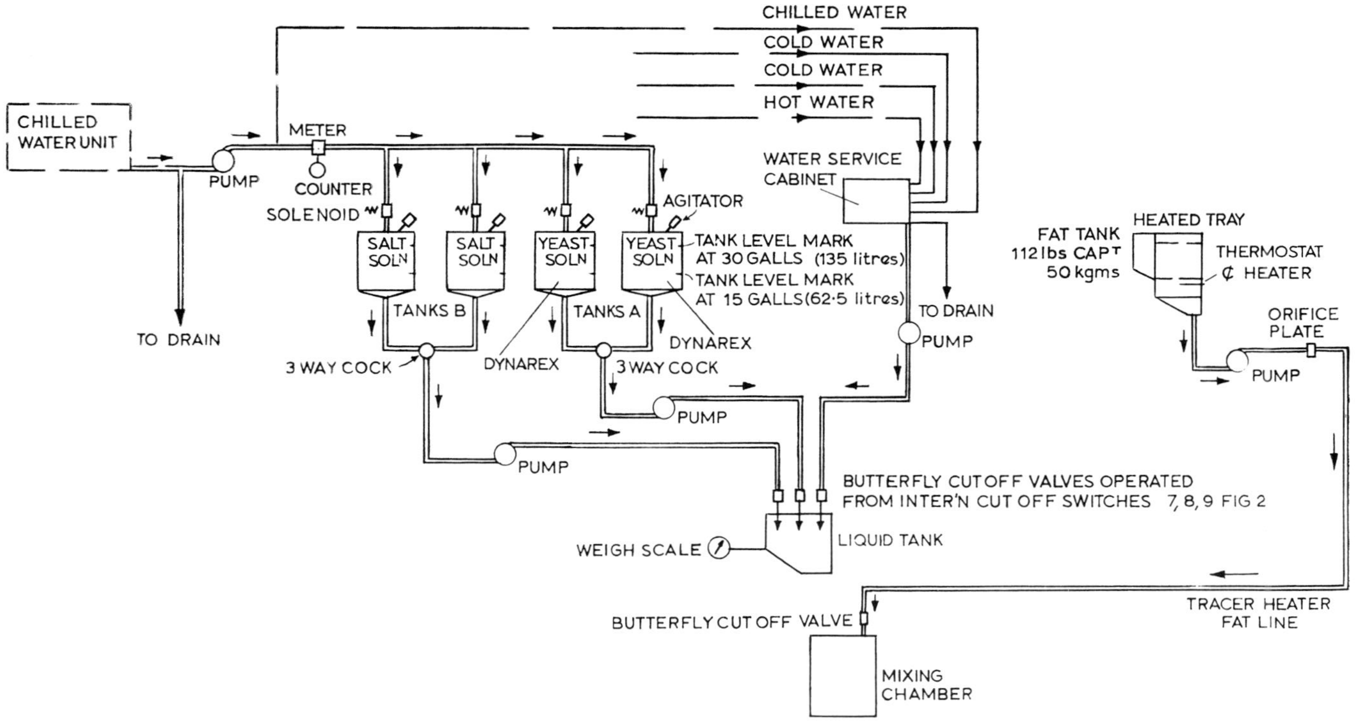

Scheme A, showing layout of minor ingredient feed system for long running times.

The ingredient balances shown are for white pan bread doughs.

Both schemes help to reduce the manpower requirements for individual mixers.

Their advantages are:

An increase in the accuracy of dispensing ingredients thereby improving quality control and generally aiding better stock control and rotation.

They lend themselves to bulk handling of small ingredients and improved standards of hygiene in the mixing area. The systems are almost self-cleaning and in most cases only require flushing with fresh water after use.

Scheme A, page 231. The first system consists of four 50 gallon stainless steel tanks (see scheme A). These tanks are used in sets of two and the capacity of each set of tanks lasts approximately one hour.

In each set of two tanks the ingredients are dispersed as follows:

Set 1

Tank A		*Tank B*	
Water	400 lb	Water	400 lb
Yeast	50 lb	Salt	60 lb
Dynarex	30 lb	Dosoy	20 lb
		Mycoban	4 lb

For each dough, 48 lb is pumped from tank A and 48½ lb from tank B.

The water is dispensed to each tank by a joint pipe from the chilled water unit. The supply is then diverted to each tank as required. Any other ingredients are added to the selected tank by hand.

The contents of each tank are discharged to the water-weigh tank by constant displacement pumps.

The balance of the dough water is pumped into the water-weigh tank as normal, then the required amounts of yeast suspension and brine solution are automatically weighed on top of the water by the second and third settings on the water-weigh dial as previously described.

When the solution in each set of tanks reaches the low-level mark on the tank wall, the operative changes to the second set of tanks by opening corresponding valves in the flowlines from each of the com-

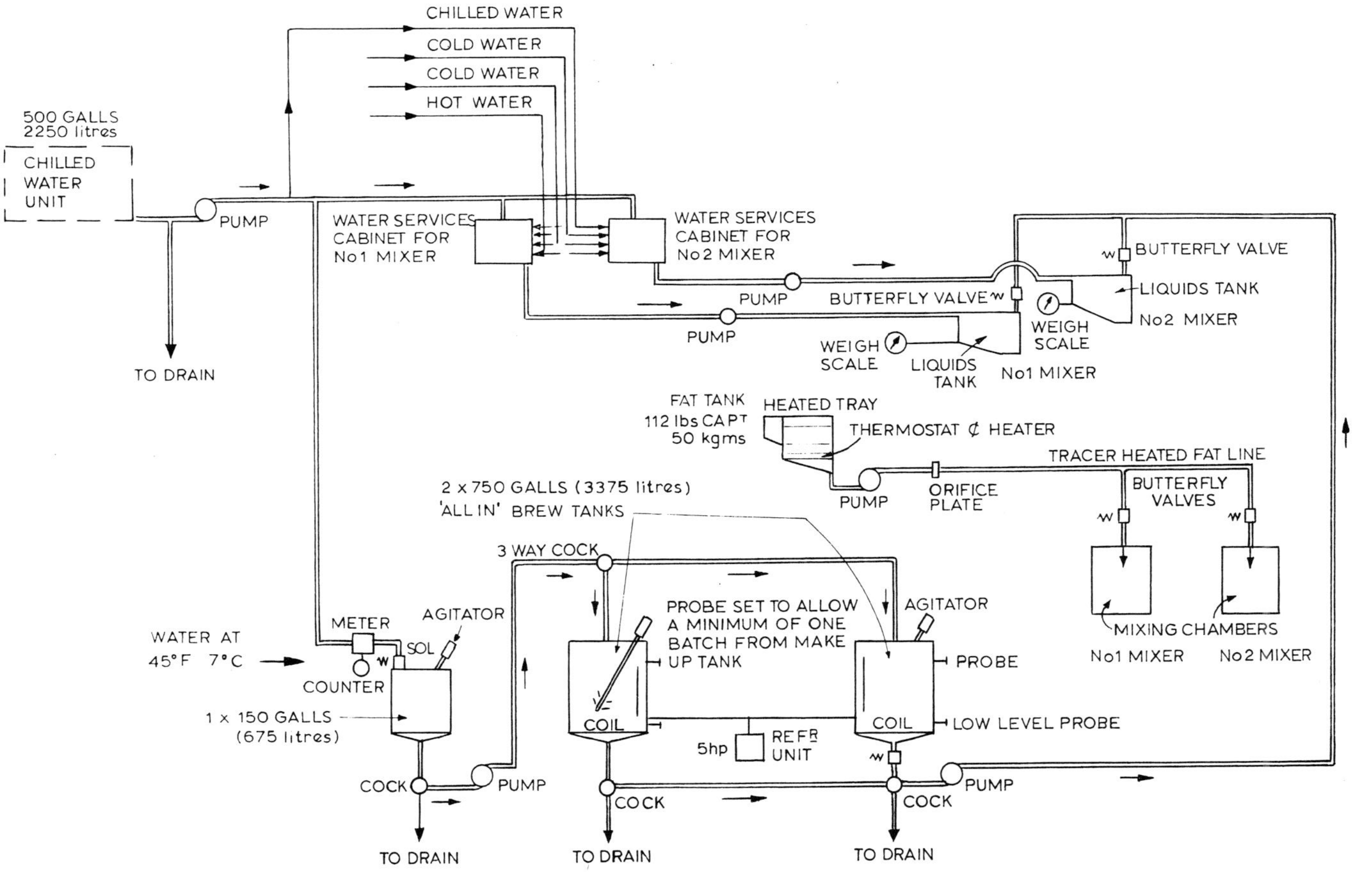

Scheme B, showing layout of minor ingredient feed system using separate tanks for salt and yeast solutions.

plimentary tanks. Once the second set of tanks is in use the first set can be replenished and the operation repeated.

This system is relatively cheap to install and since two solutions are used simultaneously and for fairly short periods, the system lends itself quite well to roll and bun production where the yeast can be kept independent of the salt and high levels of enriching agents used in these recipes.

Scheme B. The second system (see Scheme B, page 233), designed for longer running periods of one type of product, requires far less attention and is in some ways simpler in its conception.

It consists of stainless-steel tanks with provisions for cooling jackets. Their capacity can range from 100 to 1000 gallons, depending on size of production and length of shift.

The basic idea is to make up one brew containing the yeast and all other minor ingredients in a concentrated solution that does not promote yeast damage. This one brew is made up only once per shift in each tank.

As one tank empties, the mixer control panel automatically switches to the second tank and a low-level probe indicates that the tank needs replenishing by showing a light on the control panel. The tanks are replenished from a premium tank.

The concentration of the solution depends on the bakery's own recipe. The more salt used, etc., the more the water quantity has to be increased.

Here are two recipes with different proportions of minor ingredients, giving some idea of how water quantity varies.

No. 1
Use 44 lb per sack dough

Water	300 lb
Yeast	50 lb
Salt	50 lb
Dynarex	30 lb

No. 2
Use 65 lb per sack dough

Water	550 lb
Yeast	50 lb
Salt	60 lb
Dynarex	30 lb
Dosoy	20 lb
Malt Flour	6 lb

Obviously No. 1 brew is more concentrated and would make the best use of the tank's capacity but it could not carry the extra salt and extra ingredients of No. 2 brew without damaging the yeast.

Both these brews at temperatures between 50 and 65°F would produce consistent bread quality for eight hours. At temperatures between 40 and 45°F the brews produce consistent bread quality for up to sixteen hours.

The brew from the tank is pumped by a constant displacement pump into the water weigh tank on top of the balance of dough water by again using a dual marker weigh dial.

Here is an example of how ingredients are brought together ready for mixing in a one sack dough for simple white bread.

(1) Flour 280 lb to flour weigh hopper from bulk handling system.
(2) Water 140 lb (balance) from water chilling unit to water weigh tank.
(3) Salt 5 lb, Yeast 5 lb, Dynarex 3 lb, Water 30 lb } from brew tank to water weigh tank.
(4) Fat 2 lb delivered to mixing chamber from liquid fat tank if required.

The synchronisation of dough production with make-up plant in an automated system.

Let us now follow the sequence of events of a fully automatic Tweedy 6600 mixer producing dough and see how all the various points mentioned are utilised.

The cycle at the beginning of a shift is started by pressing the cycle start button. The panel is then switched to automatic and from this point on the mixer itself will control the flow of dough to the plant as it is required.

Each subsequent mixing cycle is started by a dough-piece counter with contacts attached to a divider cam or first-prover transfer mechanism. The number set on the counter is such that there is sufficient dough left in the divider hopper when the number is reached so that another dough can be mixed and tipped just before the divider hopper empties. For example, if each batch of dough renders 470 lb, to be divided into 2 lb pieces at the rate of 50 pieces per minute, each dough will take some 4 minutes 42 seconds to divide. The counter, if counting single units, will be set at 50 for the first batch and at 25 for all subsequent batches. At the completion of this count the mixing cycle will start. The counter will reset to zero and begin counting again while a batch counter, preset to the total number of mixes required by the production staff, will decrease by one. When the batch counter reaches zero the machine will cease production until the batch counter is reset.

When the sequence is initiated by the dough piece counter the Tweedy HI-TIP (where used) would be in an elevated position, having just tipped the previous dough. It moves downwards and receives a spray of emulsion from a nozzle situated on the elevator frame. This spray is delivered by the HI-TIP bowl activating a pressure switch in its downward travel and at the same time the Tweedy mixing chamber, which is at full tilt position having discharged the previous dough, moves to half-tilt position.

At the half-tilt position the mixing chamber waits for a predetermined length of time to receive the liquid fat pumped in from the fat holding tank. The mixing chamber returns to vertical position and receives the flour from the flour weigh hopper and the water, plus yeast and the other minor ingredients brew, all held in the water-weigh tank.

The vacuum pump evacuates the air from the mixing chamber and the main motor starts.

At a predetermined watt-hour count (standard count reduced by 10 watt-hour (X10)) an auxiliary timer cuts in, the vacuum is released, the lid lifts and the HI-TIP bowl is sent forward to receive the dough. The mixer tilts whilst it is still at full speed and this ejects the dough into the HI-TIP bowl which elevates and tips the dough into the divider hopper. The main motor stops 20 seconds after reaching the desired watt-hour count. During the mixing cycle, as soon as the weigh tanks are emptied they are automatically replenished. Flour is blown into the weigh hopper and water is pumped into the water-weigh tank until the first contact point is reached on the water-weigh dial. At this point the brew is pumped in until the dial pointer reaches the second contact. If the two tank system is employed, the yeast suspension would then be pumped into the weigh tank until the third contact point was reached.

The whole sequence is now ready to be repeated when it is signalled from the dough-piece counter.

The mixer will continue to produce dough at the rate the plant requires it, providing ingredient supplies are kept up. Low-level warning devices in the form of lights or klaxons can be incorporated on the brew and fat tanks.

The mixer sequence will stop if either the flour, water, brew or fat supplies do not function. More sophisticated techniques of mixing control are also possible. One is a punch-card operation which can be used to select ingredients electronically from automatic feeding supplies and collate recipe information and quantity of goods required, so that the mixer can be programmed once a day and will produce white dough, brown-bread dough, speciality bread dough, roll doughs, etc., in the right quantity and at the right time to fit in with tin changes, etc.

Systems can also be built that will warn the rest of the plant when a certain type of dough is about to be processed. They can change divider weights, divert dough pieces to alternate moulders, adjust proving/baking conditions and times and tie in coolers and prepare wrappers.

In Conclusion

The three topics which have been reviewed were selected as areas where present practice and potential future developments already merge. Looking at the wider picture, the United Kingdom baking industry appears once again fairly stable; technically the Chorleywood revolution is almost complete. The plant bakery which does not produce a large proportion of its goods by some form of mechanical dough development is the rare exception. A generation of bakers, managers and operatives is growing up who accept the CBP as the standard method of bread production.

Not all craftsmen bakers are fully convinced that they can obtain all the economic benefits of mechanical dough development and still maintain the very highest levels of bread quality. Here the smaller semi-automatic machines have yet to play their full part in the industry.

This apparent slowing in the rate of evolution of baking technology could well be, however, no more than a pause whilst the industry digests the changes which it has brought upon itself.

Those engaged in the production of bread are now more aware of the potential benefits of new processes and techniques. This must result in a greater readiness to accept the challenges, and take the risks involved, in investigating even more revolutionary changes to the breadmaking process.

For example in a mechanical dough development system half the total time taken in producing a loaf of sliced white bread is taken up by cooling the bread after baking. The Tweedy Vacuum Modulated Cooling system, now being commercially developed, can cut this to a matter of minutes. Again the micro-wave baking techniques under investigation at the FMBIRA Chorleywood could finally answer the problems of low protein high alpha-amylase flours which so bedevil the industry at present.

Further in the future, could we not find ways to eliminate the autoplant and produce satisfactory bread by direct panning from a mixer or divider? Is there the possibility of injecting gas into the dough so that final proof could be eliminated?

Meanwhile, mechanical dough development itself is becoming increasingly accepted throughout the world. In more than twenty different countries, at least some of the bread produced commercially is made on this process.

The Chorleywood Bread Process has been successful in producing bread of many different types from a wide range of raw materials and has competed in sophisticated markets such as Holland and Israel, whilst showing itself to be viable in relatively less technically advanced nations such as Brazil. Though one can not imagine any single method of bread production becoming totally dominant internationally the many advantages of mechanical dough development will ensure that it commands an increasing share of world bread production for some time to come.

13. Baking with computers

With the advent of micro-miniaturisation, the micro-chip has been successfully employed in a rapidly increasing number of roles. In fact, the only limitations on the final packaging or marketing size of control or product are that control switches or knobs must be of a sensible size to prevent inadvertent or incorrect selection, and that displayed data and information should remain legible.

This dramatic reduction in size and scale can be more easily grasped when it is appreciated that in order to reproduce the mathematical capability of an average hand-held calculator, the first-generation mainframe computers of the early 1950s would have occupied over 2000 cubic feet of space. The power consumption of an old-style computer in comparison with that of a modern calculator is almost incalculable, and the degree of accuracy and speed of operation has increased, since the 1950s, beyond recognition.

The ability of microprocessors to communicate with each other enables system controls to be devised in such a way as to allow complete integration of the various departmental functions which one would expect to find in any large organisation.

There is always a constant flow of up-dated information, decision-making, stock-control information, consumer demand and market-fluctuation figures and other related activities that take place in any mass-production situation. It then becomes a logical progression to apply such a system using microprocessors to the typical bakery plant, which provides an almost ready-made environment. Such systems are already with us, with the introduction of the new Tweedy 7700.

It is the most recent model in the range of Tweedy High Speed Mixers, and embodies the latest control technology in dough-mixing. At the heart of the control system is a microprocessor which is linked to a system of input and output databanks, which receive a constant stream of information regarding flour and water and other ingredients,

The Tweedy 7700.

as well as other relevant information about energy usage, mix times and other data.

The microprocessor is also capable of linking into existing plant control systems to allow remote print-out facilities, and it will also provide information to allow for optimum proover and oven settings. The programme for each control system varies according to each individual plant requirement and provides a comprehensive list of data: total flour usage, batch quantities, number of batches to go, total ingredients used, etc. These are essentially management tools which allow a much closer and accurate monitoring of stock levels, production control, consumer demand and general performance.

Other facilities include the automatic selection of the flour source according to the recipes programmed into the control system memory, the automatic feeding of ingredients, and their weighing, proportional to the actual weight of the flour charge for that particular mix, and of course the ability to edit the number of mixes being produced, so as to allow for sudden fluctuations in customer demand.

The entire shift productions for either day or night requirements are programmed in at the commencement of each shift. This can be done, either by the operative or by the supervisor, as the level of programming is infinitely variable, depending on the bakery requirements. Once the system is activated after the production schedule has been entered, verified, and accepted into the control system memory, the entire production for that shift is automated, when linked to batch counters, which may be attached either to divider cams, or first proof transfers.

Full manual override is provided, however, and, as the programme is tailor-made for each bakery, different levels of editing during production are provided.

Standard features of the control system include a full-colour visual display unit on the control panel, which presents various items of information, such as Mixer status, production data, and other details concerning the condition of the dough when requested by the operator or supervisor. It will also instruct the operator, step by step, how to take the Mixer through a full cycle when operating it manually.

Another standard feature, which is extremely useful, is the 'self diagnostics' provided on the display screen, in the event of breakdown or malfunction. Should this occur, an audible warning is given, usually by a klaxon or bleeper, and the fault is displayed on the screen, together with instructions on where to locate the fault, and what action to take.

The mechanical content of the 7700 Mixer is largely based upon the sound basic concepts of the 6600 Mixer, but with added refinements. The flour hopper fitted to the weighframe now contains an access door for inspection and cleaning. Belt slip from the motor-drive is now eliminated by the use of a single-toothed drive belt, which after initial setting up and tensioning requires no further adjustment during its working life. Access to the main swingframe, which contains the drive motor and mixing chamber, is also improved by using two smaller access doors on each side, replacing the original single panel. The cantilevered lid has been redesigned so that the lid assembly is now mounted either on the base frame or top superstructure according to specification.

Design objectives

The design of the Tweedy 7700 Control System is a classic example of a manufacturer responding to the changing need of the bakeries as technology progresses; it incorporates an entirely new, up-to-date control system which is capable of being the 'nerve centre' of a plant set up, and provides accurate inplant information at a variety of levels, precise control over flour, water and ingredient quantities and constant monitoring of variable data. The design objectives of the Tweedy 7700 can be summarised as follows:

1. Accuracy of scaling and temperature control etc.
2. Dough consistency
3. Flexibility in recipe applications
4. Twin level of status information
5. Scheduling of production requirements on demand.

Accuracy

The flour and water tanks are mounted on an independently mounted weighframe above the mixing chamber and this frame is suspended within the top superstructure. A single-point four-way suspension system is linked to a scalehead on the superstructure. The scalehead employs a transducer for receiving the mechanical pull from the weighframe as it fills with flour.

Because both flour and water tanks are suspended from the weighframe, which in turn exerts a pull via a single link, the electro-mechanical interface is greatly simplified, and this results in a significant reduction in the margin for error.

The weight requirements for the water to be introduced into the mixing chamber are calculated by the Microprocessor as a percentage of the actual flour residing in the hopper, and therefore the ratio of flour and water remains constant throughout the production run unless it is edited and altered within the recipe programme entered into the microprocessor memory.

Water is supplied in three modes to a storage tank directly above the water weightank, i.e. chilled, hot and blended. Temperature sensors monitor the overall temperature and the control circuitry transmits operating signals to the controlling solenoid valves to open and close the individual supply lines to obtain the overall optimum water temperature blend that is needed to achieve the final dough temperature target programmed into the recipe format.

Consistency

This is a natural adjunct of accuracy. Because the basic ingredients are being accurately metered prior to the mix taking place it is possible to achieve a high rate of consistency. The circuitry is designed to allow restricted access (i.e. to designated key holders) to alter recipe formats within the overall programme. Owing to the self-monitoring function, the VDU display shows the actual temperature required for the dough against the theoretical optimum, and asks the operator to decide by means of physical operation of the appropriate control knob whether to override the monitor and proceed with the mix, or else to make physical adjustments to the water supplies feeding the mixer installation, usually a water services cabinet. This override facility is designed to allow for a designated range of temperature discrepancy which normally would not affect the final dough, but at the same time physically involves the operator in decision-making, thus making personnel aware of any particular circumstance that could affect consistency.

Flexibility

Because the mixer is pre-programmed for daily and nightly production runs, each with their own particular production requirements, selection can be made prior to each shift of the various recipes and quantities required. However, requirements do vary, so a facility is provided for altering batch quantities selected and recipe details even after the mixer has commenced operating, and until the run of that particular recipe has been completed, at which point the original values return. Again, this is achieved by selective keypad control, and is a function normally assigned to designated keyholders.

Information status

Different levels of information can be provided on demand to suit the level of management requesting it. At operator level, the number of decisions to be made are the type readily associated with normal production and are confined to commands and questions requiring yes/no decisions. At senior or supervisor level, access to the memory bank is gained by keyswitch only. This then permits temporary changes to be made to the recipes already programmed. There is also a print-out interface which allows print-outs to be obtained at a remote point, controlled from the mixer control panel. This print-out will provide a hard copy of the production, i.e. recipe details and total flour and water usage.

Scheduling

As mentioned previously, it is necessary to compile daily schedules of requirements for day or night production relating to that particular day of the week. However, for various reasons they may alter even after the schedules have been drawn up and fed into the programme. It is still possible to alter either recipe or quantities whilst the mixer is in operation from the next mix onwards. This is a keyswitch operation, but this alteration can only be made at the start of each mix. Up to ten different recipes per shift can be put into a programme.

Index

Compiled by F. D. Buck

Page references in italic figures indicate an illustration or a diagram